Three Skeptics and the Bible

Three Skeptics and the Bible

La Peyrère, Hobbes, Spinoza, and the Reception of Modern Biblical Criticism

JEFFREY L. MORROW

☙PICKWICK *Publications* • Eugene, Oregon

THREE SKEPTICS AND THE BIBLE
La Peyrère, Hobbes, Spinoza, and the Reception of Modern Biblical Criticism

Copyright © 2016 Jeffrey L. Morrow. All rights reserved. Except for brief quotations in critical publications or reviews, no part of this book may be reproduced in any manner without prior written permission from the publisher. Write: Permissions, Wipf and Stock Publishers, 199 W. 8th Ave., Suite 3, Eugene, OR 97401.

Pickwick Publications
An Imprint of Wipf and Stock Publishers
199 W. 8th Ave., Suite 3
Eugene, OR 97401

www.wipfandstock.com

PAPERBACK ISBN 13: 978-1-4982-3915-8
HARDCOVER ISBN 13: 978-1-4982-3917-2

Cataloguing-in-Publication Data

Morrow, Jeffrey L.

Three skeptics and the Bible : La Peyrère, Hobbes, Spinoza, and the reception of modern biblical criticism / Jeffrey L. Morrow.

xii + 186 p. ; 23 cm. Includes bibliographical references.

ISBN 13: 978-1-4982-3915-8

1. La Peyrère, Isaac de, 1594–1676. 2. Hobbes, Thomas, 1588–1679. 3. Spinoza, Baruch, 1632–1677. 4. Bible Hermeneutics. 5. Skepticism. I. Title.

BS476 M69 2016

Manufactured in the U.S.A. 01/18/2016

This book is dedicated to my loving wife Maria and our five wonderful children, Maia, Eva, Patrick, Robert, and John.

Contents

Acknowledgments | ix

   Introduction | 1
1 The Emergence of Modern Biblical Criticism | 10
2 The Biblical Criticism of Isaac La Peyrère in Context | 54
3 The Biblical Criticism of Thomas Hobbes in Context | 85
4 The Biblical Criticism of Baruch Spinoza in Context | 104
5 Biblical Hermeneutics and the Creation of Religion | 139
   Conclusion | 150

Bibliography | 153

Acknowledgments

THIS BOOK WOULD NOT have been possible without the assistance of a great many individuals and institutions. First, much of the material in this present volume represents greatly expanded and revised versions of articles I published under different formats over the past few years, which are here brought together in a more accessible form. In most cases they are updated and expanded. The first chapter is based on two articles I previously published, concerning the history of modern biblical criticism.

The first article was "The Politics of Biblical Interpretation: A 'Criticism of Criticism,'" *New Blackfriars* 91 (2010) 528–45. The second article was "The Modernist Crisis and the Shifting of Catholic Views on Biblical Inspiration," *Letter & Spirit* 6 (2010) 265–80. I originally presented an early version of the second article at the St. Paul Center for Biblical Studies' Letter & Spirit Summer Institute in 2008. I wish to thank *New Blackfriars* and *Letter & Spirit* for granting me permission to rework material from those pieces. I also include material from an earlier conference presentation, "Revisiting the Seventeenth-Century European 'Wars of Religion,'" *The Ohio Academy of Religion Scholarly Papers* (2005) 66–80.

The second chapter is based on work I did in two of my previous articles dealing with the biblical exegesis of Isaac La Peyrère. The first of these articles was "French Apocalyptic Messianism: Isaac La Peyrère and Political Biblical Criticism in the Seventeenth Century," *Toronto Journal of Theology* 27 (2011) 203–13. That material is incorporated, revised, and expanded, and is here, "Reprinted with permission from University of Toronto Press Incorporated (www.utpjournals.com)." The second article, which was an expansion of that first one, was "Pre-Adamites, Politics and Criticism: Isaac La Peyrère's Contribution to Modern Biblical Studies," *Journal of the Orthodox Center for the Advancement of Biblical Studies* 4 (2011) 1–25. Both of these articles were based on an earlier version that was presented at the American Catholic Historical Association's Spring Meeting at Princeton University in

2010. I wish to thank both the University of Toronto Press and the Orthodox Center for the Advancement of Biblical Studies for granting me permission to reuse my material they originally published. Significant research that went into this chapter was funded by a summer research grant from the Faculty Fund for Vocational Exploration of the Program for Christian Leadership at the University of Dayton in 2009. I owe a word of thanks to them for generously funding of my project.

The third chapter is based on my article, "*Leviathan* and the Swallowing of Scripture: The Politics behind Thomas Hobbes' Early Modern Biblical Criticism," *Christianity & Literature* 61 (2011) 33–54. An earlier draft of this article was presented at the Society of Biblical Literature Annual Meeting in 2007. I owe thanks to *Christianity & Literature* for granting me permission to use material from this article. This work originated as a research paper in a doctoral seminar I took at the University of Dayton, and I am indebted to William Portier, my doctoral advisor and the professor for whom I wrote this paper, for his helpful critique and scholarly advice.

The fourth chapter is based on my article, "Historical Criticism as Secular Allegorism: The Case of Spinoza," *Letter & Spirit* 8 (2013) 189–221. Some of the research that went into this paper was funded by a summer research grant from the University of Dayton's Summer Student Fellowship Grants in 2005. I conducted most of that research while I was a visiting research scholar in the Summer Scholars' Program at Tantur Ecumenical Institute in Jerusalem, 2005.

The fifth chapter is based on my article, "The Bible in Captivity: Hobbes, Spinoza and the Politics of Defining Religion," *Pro Ecclesia* 19 (2010) 285–99. I wish to thank *Pro Ecclesia* for granting me permission to reuse material from that article. An early version of this was presented at the American Academy of Religion Annual Meeting in 2008.

I owe Maria Morrow and Biff Rocha tremendous thanks for critiquing numerous drafts of the chapters contained in this volume. I also owe Scott Hahn and Benjamin Wiker thanks for providing me with drafts of their book before it came into print. I owe thanks to Tantur Ecumenical Institute, where some of the research on Spinoza was conducted while I served as a visiting scholar in their summer scholars program in 2005. The final revisions and editing of this book was completed while I was on sabbatical from Seton Hall University and while I served as a visiting scholar at Princeton Theological Seminary. I owe thanks to Seton Hall University, and especially to my Dean of Seton Hall's Immaculate Conception Seminary School of Theology, Msgr. Joseph Reilly and my Provost, Larry A. Robinson, for granting me the sabbatical leave. I also owe the staff and administration of Princeton Theological Seminary thanks for their generosity, and especially to President

M. Craig Barnes who appointed me a visiting scholar for the academic year 2015–2016. Finally, I am indebted to numerous people for conversations and correspondence at various stages that helped me research, write and revise this book: Susanna Åkerman, Michael Barber, Jana Bennett, John Bergsma, Vincent Branick, Damien Costello, Dennis Doyle, Travis Frampton, Timothy Furry, Fr. Pablo Gadenz, Gregory Glazov, Scott Hahn, Michael Homan, Kelly Johnson, Eric Johnston, Michael Legaspi, Matthew Levering, Ramón Luzárraga, Alasdair MacIntyre, Colleen McDannell, Jay Morrow, Maria Morrow, Brant Pitre, William Portier, Biff Rocha, James Sanders, Joel Schickel, Nicolai Sinai, Victor Velarde-Mayol, Benjamin Wiker, and Edwin Yamauchi. Unless otherwise mentioned, all English translations throughout this volume are my own. All infelicities remain my own.

Introduction

THE COMPLEX HISTORY OF the interpretation of the Bible has often been narrated as a wresting from the magisterial domination of the Catholic Church's authoritative interpretation in order to place Scripture into the realm of scientific objectivity. In this conventional narrative, the supposed objectivity allows for an analysis of Scripture in its historical context in order to propose numerous authors for single books, identifiable editorial processes, and underlying intentions of the community from which these texts come. The easy acceptance of this conventional narrative has led to the hegemony of a particular biblical criticism within the academy. Biblical studies must be carried out using the provided framework in order to be acceptable to the scholars who have long been trained in the method of historical criticism and its related post-critical counterparts (feminist criticism, queer criticism).

In this present book I do not seek to debate the positive or negative significance of historical criticism on the overall field of biblical studies. Along with the founders of the historical critical method, I assume that there is indeed value in examining texts in their historical context. Historical criticism and its corollary criticisms have undoubtedly secured many gains for the field of biblical studies, for example, in detailing the understanding and significance of Jesus' Jewish background. This book does not seek to undermine the contributions of biblical criticism but rather to consider its origins in detail.

Hence the task of this project is to reexamine a conventional narrative through the close study of three figures of the seventeenth century who were instrumental in the beginnings of the historical critical method: Isaac La Peyrère, Thomas Hobbes, and Baruch Spinoza.

The many biblical scholars who have built upon the work of these three claim scientific objectivity in their embrace of the historical critical method. However, this method of criticism, like any form of interpretation, has a history of development best seen in the context of the times and the overarching objectives of its founders. To some in the field of biblical scholarship and theology, this history is quite surprising, especially since the key figures are not known primarily for their work as Scripture scholars but as political figures. And, as this book indicates, political motivations were, in fact, at the heart of their new methods for biblical interpretation. La Peyrère, Hobbes, and Spinoza were highly interested in questioning the integrity of the biblical text so as to undermine its authority and consequently also to undermine the authority of the churches and the synagogue. Having done so, the authors were able to propose a different authority, namely, the modern nation state, which would have ultimate jurisdiction over the people, and would exclude the Church from involvement in secular and publicly religious affairs.

This work is interdisciplinary and hence has significance for several areas of scholarship: history, biblical studies, and theology. From an historical point of view, this project looks to La Peyrère, Hobbes, and Spinoza to examine and describe the beginnings of the historical critical method. As noted above, I take my cue from these authors themselves by seeking to understand their work in the larger context of the historical time period. The conventional historians of these figures are often concerned with political impact and do not often focus their attention on issues of religion or biblical interpretation; hence this examination fills in the gap by elaborating on the figures' influence with regard to Scripture scholarship. For those in the field of biblical studies, this work is significant, not because it challenges the numerous benefits of the historical critical method, but rather because it calls attention to the impossibility of objectivity in this area. This project hence invites a closer analysis of the origins and the potential inherent biases in the methods long regarded in the field as scientific and neutral. Many theologians regard the Bible as crucial to their theological work and look to the field of biblical studies to ascertain the conventional conclusions in this field and build upon them. For these theologians, this project is valuable as a first step toward reclaiming a more theological interpretation of the biblical text that does not necessitate the undermining of ecclesiastical authority or traditional interpretation, but, in contrast, holds the earlier biblical interpretation in high esteem. For all areas of study, this project is one of uncovering bias in order to reinvigorate conversation on this topic and to enrich the academic work in these areas. Hence it has potential to contribute to each of these disciplines by redirecting ongoing conversations as to the importance of historical context when considering method, as well as encouraging a reexamination of other methods of biblical interpretation, those often referred to as "pre-critical."

Most studies of the rise of modern biblical criticism and of the historical critical method begin their narrative in the eighteenth and nineteenth centuries. One of the most recent and important exceptions to this trend examines historical criticism's late medieval origins in the fourteenth century.[1] Only a few scholars have located the origins of modern biblical criticism with textual critical works in the Renaissance.[2] Even fewer have emphasized the pivotal role of the seventeenth century particularly with regard to the newer conceptions of history.[3] In short, very few scholars identify an early date for the origins of modern biblical criticism and the historical critical method.

However, numerous precursors to the modern historical critical study of the Bible may be found throughout history. Medieval Muslim studies of Jewish and Christian Scriptures are especially important, since many of the ideas found in their works were transported into the medieval Jewish and Christian world by such sages as Ibn Ezra and Peter the Venerable.[4] The critique of traditional allegorical interpretations found in Marsilius of Padua and William of Ockham are likewise significant and often overlooked.[5] Travis Frampton has done important work underscoring the significant role Protestant Reformers like Martin Luther and John Calvin played in the history of the development of modern biblical criticism. Frampton's study, however, downplays the significance and denies the pivotal role of the seventeenth century in historical criticism's rise to near hegemonic status in the late nineteenth century.[6]

This book claims the seventeenth century as crucial to the development of historical criticism by focusing upon three figures from the seventeenth century whose works are interrelated: La Peyrère, Hobbes, and Spinoza. These three figures span four religious and denominational boundaries, and they therefore also prove interesting studies: La Peyrère, a French Calvinist who eventually converted to Catholicism; the Anglican Hobbes; and the Jewish Spinoza, who, after being expelled from the synagogue community, found himself lying more in the theological camp of the Dutch Collegiants.

1. Hahn and Wiker, *Politicizing the Bible*.

2. E.g., Kugel, "Bible in the University," 143–65; Goshen-Gottstein, "Textual Criticism," 365–99; and Goshen-Gottstein, "Christianity," 69–88.

3. Although, for exceptions to this trend, see the works e.g., Kugel, *How to Read the Bible*; Dungan, *History of the Synoptic Problem*; Goshen-Gottstein, "Foundations of Biblical Philology," 77–94; and Reventlow, *Bibelautorität*.

4. Lazarus-Yafeh, *Intertwined Worlds*.

5. Hahn and Wiker, *Politicizing the Bible*, 17–59; and Minnis, "Material Swords," 292–308.

6. Frampton, *Spinoza and the Rise of Historical Criticism*.

Despite their diverse theological backgrounds, they had similar goals and employed similar methods.

Of course, it is always difficult to pinpoint the origins of an intellectual trend. My first chapter indicates my reluctance to overextend my claims by downplaying or denying the importance of figures and ages before the seventeenth-century intellectuals I examine in this study. Rather, I wish to emphasize the central place of the seventeenth century for the turn to history, as in the history behind the biblical texts. This turn became significantly more pronounced in figures like La Peyrère, Hobbes, and Spinoza than it had in prior centuries.

Hans Frei's classic study has shown that the eighteenth century is a key period for the birth of modern historical biblical criticism, where the tools forged in the seventeenth were honed and perfected and came to blossom in the nineteenth century.[7] In the present study, I focus upon seventeenth-century biblical criticism so as to situate it in its broader historical and political context. One of the most neglected contexts in historical accounts of modern biblical criticism is the centuries-long church and state conflict.[8]

The age old conflict between the Catholic Church and European state rulers intensified after the Reformation in the early modern period, with the birth of modern centralized European states.[9] The main battleground was threefold. First, episcopal appointment: who had the authority to appoint bishops, the Church, or the local governing authority? Second, ownership of land: was property owned by religious orders or the local Church, or the state? Third, direction of revenue: should taxes be paid to Rome, or only to state rulers? If we examine England, for example, we find that royal income in England more than doubled after the Reformation redirected money previously earmarked for Rome and monastic communities, which were forcibly liquidated by the state. The English Reformation's usurpation of church land was the original meaning of the word "secularize," and this often violent process became normative in many places.[10] Moreover, English politics continued to dominate church state relations well after the Reformation.[11]

---

7. Frei, *Eclipse of Biblical Narrative*. See also Legaspi, *Death of Scripture*; and Sheehan, *Enlightenment Bible*.

8. Hahn and Wiker, *Politicizing the Bible*; and Dungan, *History of the Synoptic Problem*, are two of the few exceptions here.

9. Cavanaugh, *Myth of Religious Violence*; Marx, *Faith in Nation*; and Cavanaugh, "Fire Strong Enough," 397–420.

10. Duffy, *Stripping of the Altars*; and Marx, *Faith in Nation*, 56–67 and 94–107.

11. Marx, *Faith in Nation*, 128–39, 153–61 and 175–84; and Tumbleson, *Catholicism in the English Protestant Imagination*.

Early modern France in the seventeenth century, which emerged victorious from its civil wars, also proves paradigmatic here. France had state appointed bishops, and this is perhaps one of the biggest contributing factors for the country's remaining Catholic following the Reformation.[12] This, moreover, provides the proximate background for La Peyrère who lived in the France of this time. The French Revolution unleashed a new saga in this conflict, with a century wherein the university was reconstituted, and the papacy so politically weak that two popes ended up in French prison, with one actually dying there.[13]

Finally, the nineteenth century brought these conflicts to a pitch with Italian desires for unification and with the German *Kulturkampf*.[14] Throughout all of these conflicts, the papacy and Catholicism in general foremost appeared as obstacles to emerging European state powers, as a transnational authority over and above any state sovereign. As William Cavanaugh has demonstrated, and as we will see in this present volume, the so-called wars of religion had more to do with reconfiguring the power structures in Europe from the carcass of the medieval order. This provides the ultimate context for the story of biblical criticism's birth in modernity.

In this first chapter, "The Emergence of Modern Biblical Criticism," I will provide a concise overview of the history of biblical interpretation, highlighting the place of seventeenth century thinkers like La Peyrère, Hobbes, and Spinoza within the broader context of the rise of modern biblical criticism. The chapter begins with the polemical literature of antiquity, moves through the development of philological and textual studies in antiquity and the medieval period, and continues through the Renaissance, Reformation, early modern and Enlightenment periods. Its purpose is to provide background in order to situate properly the seventeenth century figures on whom this book focuses.

My overarching argument in this chapter is an underlying one for the rest of the book, namely, that one must understand the birth of modern biblical criticism in its historical framework, which is the political context of the church-state debate. It is the background of political authority and the role of the churches, particularly in modern Europe, that provides the ultimate backdrop for the development of modern biblical criticism, which emerged at the same time as early modern European states. In the wake of the carnage of the so-called religious wars of the sixteenth and seventeenth

12. Marx, *Faith in Nation*, 45–56, 86–94, 122–8, 148–53; and Portier, "Church Unity," 27–37.

13. Duffy, *Saints & Sinners*, 230–305; Marx, *Faith in Nation*, 168–75; Tavard, "Blondel's Action," 151–65; and Portier, "Church Unity," 27–37.

14. Gross, *War Against Catholicism*; Lease, "Vatican Foreign Policy," 31–55.

centuries, which were brought to an end by the Treaty of Westphalia in 1648, early modern political theorists like Hobbes and Spinoza, and early modern biblical interpreters like La Peyrère, sought an ostensibly objective method for interpreting Scripture that would bring an end to sectarian violence.[15] The work of these seventeenth century scholars provided a foundation for the development of modern methods, which also claimed neutrality. The modern methods, moreover, progressively brought the study of the Sacred Page into the new state-sponsored secular universities. I conclude this chapter by emphasizing the pivotal role of the seventeenth century for launching the modern biblical critical project.

The figures in this book will be examined chronologically. Hence I turn in the second chapter, "The Biblical Criticism of Isaac La Peyrère in Context," to the earliest of these seventeenth century exegetes, and I place his work within its broader historical and political context. Isaac La Peyrère is a man whose work is typically unknown by Bible scholars; many may never have heard of him at all. La Peyrère played an important role in the European politics of his age, as the secretary and diplomat for two successive Princes of Condé. He is arguably the most important non-royal political figure in France at that time, apart from Cardinals Richelieu and Mazarin.

Richard Popkin and Susanna Åkerman have uncovered a plot among the Prince of Condé, Queen Christina of Sweden, and Oliver Cromwell to overthrow Louis XIV and place the Prince of Condé on the French throne.[16] La Peyrère found himself in the middle of this plot, as an agent for Condé with Christina (patroness to both La Peyrère and Descartes) and with Cromwell, as he worked on his most important works in biblical criticism. La Peyrère's historical and textual critique of the Mosaic authorship of the Pentateuch made explicit arguments that had previously been more implicit in the works of earlier Jewish and Christian interpreters. His work was also significant in its turn to the history behind the text, a move that went beyond the Protestant Reformation exaltation of the literal sense of Scripture.

Most significant, as I will make apparent in successive chapters, is the relationship between La Peyrère's works and those of Hobbes and Spinoza. La Peyrère's influence is evident by those who followed him, especially Richard Simon, who used his work. In particular, La Peyrère is known, like Joseph Scaliger, for using documents from other cultures across the globe for reconstructing biblical history, as well as for contributing to source criticism, something which has earned his status as a pioneer of the historical critical method for interpreting the Bible. This chapter seeks to provide the

---

15. See, e.g., Levenson, *Hebrew Bible*, 117–25.
16. See, e.g., Popkin, "Millenarianism and Nationalism," 78–82.

context for La Peyrère's method, but more importantly, for his conclusions. The chapter argues that these conclusions of La Peyrère's biblical criticism had important theological ramifications that were also political. That is, they undermined the authority of the biblical text itself, hence undermining traditional interpretation that accepted biblical authority, and consequently they undermined the Church that had supported traditional interpretation. From a political standpoint, these conclusions worked to transfer this authority to his French nationalistic messianic vision, and hence undergird his employer the Prince of Condé's political machinations.

In the third chapter, "The Biblical Criticism of Thomas Hobbes in Context," I turn to one of the most important but often overlooked figures in the advent of modern biblical criticism, namely the early modern English political theorist, Thomas Hobbes. In Hobbes's most famous work, *Leviathan*, he set out numerous examples of how he believed the Bible should be interpreted. Most of these interpretations simply supported his political arguments for the sovereignty of state rulers. Significantly, however, as with La Peyrère, Hobbes highlighted the importance of the history behind the texts much more than earlier generations of biblical interpreters had done. Prior to figures like La Peyrère and Hobbes, interpreters usually assumed that what was reported in Scripture was more or less what happened. La Peyrère and Hobbes, however, emphasized in new ways a distinction between the history behind the text and the stories within the texts themselves.

Importantly, at the time of his work, *Leviathan* (1651), he could not write texts on political matters without some attention to the Bible, which was still regarded as an important text. Like Peyrère, whom he might have known personally, Hobbes's biblical interpretation had lasting effects on biblical studies for years to come. Hence it is beneficial to note the historical context and theological and political motivations which inspired his methods and conclusions on the biblical text. In particular, Hobbes is noted for his move to naturalize the many miracles described in the Bible. Hobbes was invested in the state having ultimate authority, and there was hence little room for miracles, the supernatural, or anything that would point to a world beyond that governed by secular authority. Punishments beyond death (i.e., purgatory or hell) and rewards in an afterlife (i.e., heaven) posed a threat to the political sovereignty of the state-ruler. Hobbes composed his *Leviathan* while avoiding the English civil war through self-imposed exile in Paris. He moved in the same intellectual circles as La Peyrère, whose initial unpublished drafts of his work circulated widely. In fact, La Peyrère even received published criticisms long before Hobbes completed *Leviathan*, although La Peyrère's main work was not published until after Hobbes's initial

English edition.[17] More important than La Peyrère's plausible role of influence on Hobbes, however, is the more likely impact of both Hobbes and La Peyrère on Spinoza.

In the fourth chapter, "The Biblical Criticism of Baruch Spinoza in Context," I consider Baruch Spinoza's foundational methodological arguments which furthered the modern biblical critical project. Spinoza has had a lasting impact on the field of biblical studies. In particular, Spinoza's *Tractatus Theologico-Politicus* (1670) lays down an elaborate historical hermeneutic as a blueprint for the development of a scientific biblical criticism, the core assumptions of which are now a commonplace in biblical studies. The context for Spinoza's writing, however, was the political turmoil of the Dutch Republic and especially the Thirty Years' War, which ended just over twenty years prior to the publication of his *Tractatus Theologico-Politicus*. He sought to undermine traditional theological interpretations as found in Catholic, Calvinist, and Jewish traditions, in order to declaw religious institutions of wielding any authority in the secular realm. His method was ultimately at the service of creating a freedom to philosophize.

Spinoza was banned from the Jewish community in Amsterdam, and then he became one of the most important philosophical figures of his time. Jonathan Israel's works have shown Spinoza's pivotal role in the later European Enlightenment.[18] Eventually, Spinoza laid down the foundational guidelines that would be followed by over three centuries of modern biblical critics, in his famous political work, *Tractatus Theologico-Politicus*, which implicitly supported a particular strain of democratic politics. Spinoza knew of both La Peyrère's and Hobbes's works, copies of both are still preserved in his library to this day; and the Latin edition of *Leviathan* was available before Spinoza published his own work. The role of secular history which remained more implicit in La Peyrère and Hobbes, became a focal point in Spinoza's arguments for what a scientific biblical criticism should look like. Furthermore, Spinoza adopted, expanded, and solidified La Peyrère's and Hobbes's historical and textual arguments against the Mosaic authorship of the Pentateuch. This was a source critical conclusion that became the bedrock of many of the eighteenth century's critical projects and a main focus of nineteenth century criticism.[19]

The fifth and final chapter, "Biblical Hermeneutics and the Creation of Religion," considers the rise of historical criticism in the work of La Peyrère,

17. See, e.g., Malcolm, *Aspects of Hobbes*, 383–431; and Pacchi, "Hobbes and Biblical Philology," 231–39.

18. Israel, *Enlightenment Contested*; and ibid., *Radical Enlightenment*.

19. Preus, *Spinoza and the Irrelevance of Biblical Authority*; and Freedman, "Father of Modern Biblical Scholarship," 31–38.

Hobbes, and Spinoza, in light of traditional Jewish and Christian biblical interpretation. It discusses especially the role of Jewish and Christian liturgies in traditional exegesis, and emphasizes the shift that occurred in the work of La Peyrère, but especially of Hobbes, and Spinoza, as the Bible began to be looked to, no longer primarily as a liturgical text, but rather as a book like any other, which needed to be read and examined by the same methods as other ancient texts. This chapter also explores the religious wars of the sixteenth and seventeenth century, with their attendant redefinition of "religion" as a category, as a significant context for understanding the biblical hermeneutics these figures were constructing.

1

The Emergence of Modern Biblical Criticism

MODERN BIBLICAL CRITICISM HAS a long history, with deep roots stretching back prior to the emergence of modernity and the Enlightenment, prior to the Reformation and even the Renaissance, into the medieval period. Recently, Scott Hahn and Benjamin Wiker have made the case that modern biblical criticism begins to develop at least by the dawn of the fourteenth century, if not earlier.[1] Their recognition of the early roots of modern biblical criticism, and particularly historical criticism, is certainly one of the strengths of their volume. A further strength is in how well they communicate the many ways in which biblical exegetes sometimes unwittingly become partisans in a much older political conflict: throne vs. altar. In a moment of brutal honesty, Albert Schweitzer conceded that the historical critical method was at root, "an aide in the struggle for deliverance from dogma."[2] Such methods became state-sponsored tools used in the states's battles with the churches of Europe, and initially the Catholic Church in particular.[3] It should come as no surprise that the very states who supported such academic projects most (Germany, France, England), were also states concerned at various times with episcopal appointments, seizing church land, and exiling religious orders.[4]

1. Hahn and Wiker, *Politicizing the Bible*.

2. Schweitzer, *Von Reimarus zu Wrede*, 4. Schweitzer's comment here is specifically in reference to historical criticism as applied to the quest for the historical Jesus.

3. The Catholic Church remained the primary target in these conflicts, but prior to the Reformation, it was the only show in town, as it were. No other religious leader vied for temporal rule the way that the Catholic pope did in medieval Europe.

4. Duffy, *Saints & Sinners*, 230–305; Gross, *War Against Catholicism*, 240–91; Duffy,

In this present chapter, I focus on the historical connection between politics and the biblical criticism which laid the groundwork for later historical biblical criticism. I begin tracing the roots of modern biblical criticism from medieval Muslim politics and polemics into the political world of medieval Christian theology. Next, I continue this trajectory into the Renaissance and Reformation, showing how the post-Reformation "wars of religion" shaped the foundations of early modern biblical criticism. Then I examine Enlightenment and nineteenth-century historical criticism, highlighting nationalistic motivations in such criticism. Finally, I provide an overview of the historical church and state conflict which provides an unrecognized context for understanding the history of modern biblical criticism. This chapter is not intended to be an exhaustive account, but merely an introductory summary of this too often neglected historical genealogy of modern historical biblical criticism.[5]

MEDIEVAL POLITICAL PRECURSORS TO EARLY MODERN HISTORICAL CRITICS

Within both Jewish and Christian communities, certain hermeneutical assumptions and logical interpretive conclusions developed as the Scriptures were being canonized and rules for interpretation were being set forth. James Kugel maintains that there were at least four basic assumptions implied in the exegesis of early Jewish and Christian interpreters. He explains:

> [1] They assumed that the Bible was a fundamentally cryptic text: that is, when it said A, often it might really mean B.... [2] Interpreters also assumed that the Bible was a book of lessons directed to readers in their own day. It might seem to talk about the past, but it is not fundamentally history. It is instruction, telling us what to do.... Ancient interpreters assumed this not only about narratives like the Abraham story but about every part of the Bible.... [3] Interpreters also assumed that the Bible contained no contradictions or mistakes. It is perfectly harmonious, despite its being an anthology.... In short, the Bible, they felt, is an utterly consistent, seamless, perfect book.... [4]

Stripping of the Altars, 383–85, 397, and 402–3; and Costigan, "State Appointment," 82–96.

5. I encourage readers who would like to delve deeper into this history to consult Hahn's and Wiker's massive volume, *Politicizing the Bible*, as well as the extensive sources I mention in Morrow, "Enlightenment University," 899–909, particularly 899–900n6, 900n7, 900–901n9, 903n13, 904–5n18, 906–7n22, and 908n23.

Lastly, they believed that the entire Bible is essentially a divinely given text, a book in which God speaks directly or through His prophets.[6]

Such views of Scripture came under attack even before the Christian period, and particularly on the issue of the divine origin of the Pentateuch. Early heretics attempted to curtail any Jewish claims to the divine authority of the Torah by attacking the history of its origins. The pre-Christian proto-Gnostic group known as the Nasarenes attempted to do this by denying the Torah's Mosaic authorship, which was assumed for the Pentateuch for much of Jewish and Christian history.[7] Later, in the Christian period, the third century Roman Neo-Platonist philosopher Porphyry also questioned the Mosaic authorship of the Pentateuch, as well as other traditional attributions of authorship and origin, in his polemical works against Christianity.[8] These polemicists attempted to attack the history of Jewish and Christian claims concerning Scripture in order to denigrate their claims of the divine inspiration of Scripture.

One important, but often neglected, development that helped pave the way for the modern work of historical biblical criticism was the medieval Muslim appropriation of Gnostic, Roman, and Christian polemical literature attacking the Jewish Torah.[9] Ibn Ḥazm (994–1064) is one of the earliest and most famous examples. He became one of the most important medieval thinkers to use philological analyses and historical arguments to deconstruct traditional Jewish and Christian views of Scripture, particularly regarding historical claims, and to attempt to curb all forms of spiritual interpretation.[10] In his work, "Discerning between Religions, Ideologies, and

---

6. Kugel, *How to Read the Bible*, 14–16. See also O'Loughlin, "*Res, Tempus, Locus*," 95–111; ibid., "Biblical Contradictions," 103–26; ibid., "Controversy over Methuselah's Death," 182–225; ibid., "Julian of Toledo's *Antikeimenon*," 80–98; and Tabet Balady, "La hermenéutica bíblica," 181–93. In the context of how these ideas develop in the medieval period, Thomas O'Loughlin explains that, "If a book is 'in the canon,' then any suggestion that the book's contents lack inerrancy must be countered. In effect, this means that there must be no contradiction within the entire body of works on the list, and further implies that every sentence must be demonstrably consistent with every other sentence, which then entails that each sentence can be read consistently alongside any other sentence and whatever meaning is derived must be considered a valid extrapolation." See O'Loughlin, "Inventing the Apocrypha," 54.

7. Yamauchi, *Gnostic Ethics*, 60.

8. Malcolm, *Aspects of Hobbes*, 400; Kofsky, *Eusebius*, 30; Droge, *Homer or Moses*, 178; and Wilken, *Christians as the Romans Saw Them*, 137 and 143.

9. Lazarus-Yafeh, *Intertwined Worlds*, xi, 18, 28, 30, 42n62, 45, 50, 59, and 63.

10. Al-Azmeh, *Times of History*, 114; Pulcini, *Exegesis as Polemical Discourse*, 57–96; Adang, *Muslim writers on Judaism*; Martinez Gros, "Ibn Hazm contre les

Sects," Ibn Ḥazm employed a host of arguments deconstructing the Jewish Torah as well as the New Testament.[11]

Ibn Ḥazm witnessed firsthand the brutalities of politics within the caliphate structure in Muslim Spain, as his family went from a position of favorable political status with the ruling powers, to political exiles while he was a child. As an adult, Ibn Ḥazm proved to be an accomplished Muslim jurist, as well as a philosopher, philologist, and even poet. Politics would reenter his life in a dramatic way when he found himself bypassed for an elite office in the caliphate that he believed should have been rightfully given to him. To add insult to injury, it was not simply to another skilled Muslim jurist that the office was handed, but rather it was given to the Jewish anti-Muslim polemicist, Shmuel Ibn Nagrela, known in the world of Judaism as Shmuel Ha Naggid (993–1056). This is the context for understanding Ibn Ḥazm's polemical literature.[12]

Ibn Ḥazm's polemical literature, which targeted competing Muslim philosophical and legal schools as well as those of other religious traditions like Christianity, included over one hundred pages of scathing polemics attacking Judaism. In retaliation to Ibn Nagrela, Ibn Ḥazm heaped opprobrium on his opponent, and particularly upon Judaism, and the Torah. In fact, Ibn Ḥazm even wrote a tract specifically aimed at Ibn Nagrela, which he entitled, "Refutation of Ibn al-Nagrela the Jew, may God curse him."[13] In his criticisms, Ibn Ḥazm not only anticipated, on the one hand, modern biblical historical and philological analyses, but, on the other, later anti-Semitic

---

Juifs," 123–34; Adang, *Islam frente a Judaísmo*; Lazarus-Yafeh, "Taḥrīf," 81–88; Adang, "Schriftvervalsing," 197–8; Powers, "Reading/Misreading," 109–21; Arnaldez, *Grammaire et théologie*, 49n1, 72–73, 309, and 319; Algermissen, "Die Pentateuchzitate"; and Goldziher, *Die Ẓâhiriten*, 123–4 and 132. Ibn Hazm's work proved very influential, and it is likely that Ibn Ezra and Maimonides were responding to him, and Spinoza may even have relied upon his arguments in his own work on modern biblical criticism, *Tractatus theologico-Politicus*, as we shall see in chapter four of the present volume. See also Ljamai, *Ibn Hazm et la polémique*, 145–96; Lazarus-Yafeh, "Some Neglected Aspects," 61–84; Guerrero, "Filósofos hispano-musulmanes," 125–32; Lazarus-Yafeh, *Intertwined Worlds*, 73 and 140; Freedman, "Father of Modern Biblical Scholarship," 31–38; Abu Laila, "Ibn Ḥazm's Influence," 103–15; and Arnaldez, "Spinoza et la pensée arabe," 151–74.

11. English translation in Lazarus-Yafeh, "Some Neglected Aspects," 61.

12. On Ibn Ḥazm's conflict with Judaism and with Ibn Nagrela, see Ljamai, *Ibn Ḥazm et la polémique*, 30, 32–33, 40, and 40n193; Pulcini, *Exegesis as Polemical Discourse*, 2–7, 129–31, and 145; Adang, *Islam frente a Judaísmo*; Adang, "Ibn Ḥazm de Córdoba," 15–23; Martinez Gros, "Ibn Hazm contre les Juifs," 123–34; and Rifʿat, "Ibn Ḥazm on Jews."

13. The translation is from Adang, *Muslim writers on Judaism*, 67. For consistency, I changed Adang's transliteration of Ibn Nagrela's name.

diatribes. Indeed, it appears that Ibn Ḥazm may have coined anti-Semitic phrases involving adjectives like "dirty" and "repugnant" used as expletives modifying the designation "Jews." R. David Freedman comments that, " . . . Ibn Ḥazm wrote with such fierce invective that he can scarcely say the word 'Jew' without a prefixed epithet like 'stinking,' 'foul,' 'vile,' 'villainous,' and that good old stand-by 'dirty.'"[14]

One of the foundations of his vitriolic barrage was the Mosaic authorship of the Pentateuch. Although this is a commonplace in contemporary scholarship, we must bear in mind that Ibn Ḥazm was one of the first serious intellectuals to make such a claim; he predates Ibn Ezra (1092-1167) by several decades.[15] Although his arguments clearly anticipated what modern scholars now take for granted, and they were sophisticated, based on rigorously philological analysis (most likely of Arabic translations of the texts), Ibn Ḥazm attacked the idea that Moses wrote the Pentateuch with the purpose of weakening Jewish claims to maintaining any divine revelation.[16] His method of critique sought particularly for apparent contradictions, theological concepts which were untenable for traditional Muslims, and other such infelicities. As Camilla Adang writes, "In this manner Ibn Ḥazm systematically analyzed the entire Tanakh in search of insupportable propositions."[17]

Another key criticism Ibn Ḥazm leveled against Judaism (and Christianity) was to attack allegorical interpretation. Ibn Ḥazm was completely opposed to allegorical interpretations, including of the Qur'an and Hadith.[18] Ibn Ḥazm's arguments critiquing the Hebrew Bible, as well as his other ideas concerning other religious traditions, were adopted by other medieval Muslims, most notably Averroës (Ibn Rushd), and these arguments even entered into Jewish and Christian discourse in the medieval period.[19]

---

14. Freedman, "Father of Modern Biblical Scholarship," 33. Asín Palacios writes that, "The author of the books of the Pentateuch is, in the mind of Ibn Ḥazm, such an imbecile, that 'the ox is more discreet, and the donkey more skillful than he,' and the Jews are 'the race most dirty, disgusting [asquerosa] and repugnant in the land'" (*Abenházam de Córdoba*, 193).

15. Lazarus-Yafeh maintains that it is likely Ibn Ezra was in fact one of the main medieval figures who transmitted Ibn Ḥazm's thought to the Jewish and Christian European world (*Intertwined Worlds*, 73 and 140).

16. Freedman, "Father of Modern Biblical Scholarship," 31-38; and Powers, "Reading/Misreading," 109-21.

17. Adang, "Schriftvervalsing," 199.

18. Arnaldez, *Grammaire et théologie*, e.g., 49n1, 72-73, 309, and 319; and Goldziher, *Die Ẓâhiriten*, 123-24 and 132.

19. This is even the case despite Ibn Rushd's acceptance of allegory. Ljamai, *Ibn Ḥazm et la polémique*, 145-96; Lazarus-Yafeh, "Some Neglected Aspects," 61-84; and

Averroës, over whom Ibn Ḥazm exerted a very strong influence, was even more important in the history of modern biblical criticism in that he placed philosophy and reason as judge over faith and theology. More precisely, Averroës maintained a hierarchy of knowers and of knowledge. Averroës was an important and influential commentator on the work of the Greek philosopher Aristotle. He noticed, as had others, that the teachings of the Qur'an were not always consistent with Aristotle's thought. Thus, Averroës reasoned that truth is known differently depending on the different abilities of the one knowing the truth. Philosophers stand at the pinnacle of his hierarchy. What this Averroist notion entailed was the "superiority of the truths of natural reason to those of revelation," and this led to what has been called the double truth approach of the "Latin Averroist" tradition.[20] This Latin Averroism found an important home at the University of Padua, from whence it spread throughout Europe, becoming especially popular in university systems.

Marsilius of Padua (ca. 1275–ca. 1342) and William of Ockham (ca. 1288–ca. 1348) continued this trajectory, relying in part on the tradition of Averroës mediated in the Latin west. Marsilius of Padua had imbibed Averroist philosophy under the influence of Latin Averroists at the University of Padua. Ockham made similar exegetical moves to Marsilius, particularly in their dual attempts to curtail allegorical interpretation; for Marsilius and Ockham, there could be no spiritual interpretation. Nominalist biblical interpretation then spread throughout Europe from the University of

---

Lazarus-Yafeh, *Intertwined Worlds*, xi, 10, 44–46, 63–64, 68–69, 71–74, 136, and 140–41. On Ibn Ḥazm's influence on the Christian world in general, see Abu Laila, "Ibn Ḥazm's Influence," 103–15. Peter Abelard was likely influenced by such Muslim thought, perhaps only as mediated through Peter the Venerable who was intimately familiar with currents in the medieval Muslim world, and in fact was responsible for the first Latin "interpretation" (translation) of the Qur'an as well as a refutation of Islam. See, e.g., Lazarus-Yafeh, *Intertwined Worlds*, 71–72; Pelikan, *Growth of Medieval Theology*, 243; Arnaldez, *Grammaire et théologie*, 319; and Asín Palacios, *Abenházam de Córdoba II*, 74 and 74n105. The connection with Abelard here is significant, since Abelard seemed to share important philosophical points in common with Averroës, particularly the role of reason as judge of faith. Non-Christian philosophers played an important role in Abelard's thought, and he was especially indebted to Epicurus. See, e.g., de Mowbray, "Philosophy as Handmaid," 15–16; Marenbon, *Philosophy of Peter Abelard*, especially 340–49; and Pelikan, *Growth of Medieval Theology*, 223–25, where Pelikan points out how Abelard's inquiry into authorship and authenticity of texts (which anticipated later text and source criticism) were tools Abelard employed to prune biblical interpretation from patristic interpretation. On p. 76 of his second volume, Asín Palacios makes an interesting comparison between Ibn Ḥazm's voluntarism and that of Scotus and Ockham, which Asín Palacios sees as similar.

20. Hahn and Wiker, *Politicizing the Bible*, 23.

Paris to the Universities of Heidelberg, Vienna, Cologne, and elsewhere.[21] Ockham's students sometimes brought with them a disdain for allegorical biblical interpretation, much like Ibn Ḥazm's, and laid a heavy emphasis on the *sensus literalis*. In a subsection entitled, "Modern Politics as Biblical Hermeneutics," John Milbank offers a lucid account of how the attacks on allegorical biblical interpretation, like Ockham's, served early modern politics.[22] Milbank explains:

> The traditional "fourfold," "spiritual" or "allegorical" interpretation assumed and demanded a literal, historical meaning: every Biblical *signum* referred to a *res*. However, it conceived the *res*, as a divine, "natural" sign, to have a plenitude of meaning which allowed the allegorical edifice to be erected. The literal, historical "violence" of the *res* in the old covenant effaced itself, not just vertically towards "eternal" meanings, but horizontally in the direction of the new reality of Christ-*ecclesia* with its charity, mercy and peace. This allowed the fullness of divine authority to devolve on Christ and then on the tropological interpretations of present Christians in the community of the Church.[23]

Marsilius's and Ockham's critiques of allegorical interpretation and the spiritual sense of Scripture served court politics. Both Marsilius and Ockham resided at the same time under the protection of Ludwig of Bavaria who was in conflict with Pope John XXII. The conflict primarily had to do with control over Italian territories and thus with the temporal authority of the papacy. Marsilius supplied Ludwig with a theoretical justification for his desire for temporal sovereignty.[24] Marsilius's arguments involved both a theo-

21. Ibid., 47–59; Barron, "Biblical Interpretation," 180; Rahe, *Against Throne and Altar*, 152–3; Kärkkäinen and Lagerlund, "Philosophical Psychology," 36–39; Milbank, *Theology and Social Theory*, 17–20; Manekin, "Hebrew Philosophy," 294; Minnis, "Material Swords," 292–308; Antonietta, "Averroes y su influencia," 151–74; Rosenthal, "Heinrich von Oyta," 178–79, 182, and 183n5; Troilo, "L'averroismo," 44–77; Troilo, *Averroismo*.

22. Milbank, *Theology and Social Theory*, 17–20.

23. Ibid., 20.

24. Hahn and Wiker, *Politicizing the Bible*, 17–22, 24–29, 35–44, and 54–56; Miethke, "Der Kampf Ludwigs des Bayern," 39–74; Nehlsen, "Die Rolle Ludwigs," 285–328; Kraus, "Das Bild," 5–70; Thomas, *Ludwig der Bayern*; and Offler, "Empire and Papacy," 21–47. This immediate context is the proximate context for the history of medieval debates concerning papal infallibility. See, e.g., Shogimen, "Relationship Between Theology and Canon Law," 417–31; Heft, *John XXII*; Tierney, "Ockham's Infallibility," 295–300; Ryan, "Evasion and Ambiguity," 285–94; Tierney, "John Peter Olivi," 315–28; Tierney, "Sovereignty and Infallibility," 787–93; Heft, "John XXII and Papal Infallibility," 759–80; Turley, "John Baconthorpe," 744–58; Tierney, "Papal Infallibility," 275–77; Heft, "Historical Origins," 208–11; Tierney, "Ockham's Ambiguous

logical and a political critique of the papacy's claims to temporal authority. In effect, Marsilius desired to place state rulers over the Church within their realms, so that a council of state-appointed bishops could trump a pope.[25]

Ockham's intent seems to have been to defend Franciscan poverty. Ockham was attempting to distinguish realms and defend his idea of Christian perfection which he thought John XXII was challenging. It might seem ironic that Ockham's admonition for the Pope (and clerics) to embrace poverty was an implicit, even if unintentional, call for wealth to be taken out of the hands of the church and placed in the hands of state rulers like Ludwig of Bavaria. Consciously or not, Ockham's challenge to the papacy supplied Marsilius with further means of defending his theo-political ends. In Marsilius's and Ockham's attack on the spiritual sense of Scripture, which they saw as supporting the papacy, in favor of simply a literal-historical approach, we can detect another politically motivated attempt at biblical criticism which supported state politics; in this case, the politics of their protector, Ludwig of Bavaria, who opposed the pope.[26]

The broader historical and political context here is illuminating.[27] An important component in the main context here is the Franciscan poverty debate, i.e. the debate over ownership and use among clergy, like the Franciscans, who took a vow of poverty, but needed to use books, and thus libraries, etc., for various aspects of their religious life, including study for preaching. Pope John XXII entered the theological fray by denying the distinction between use and ownership. Under his predecessors Gregory IX, Nicholas III, and Clement V, such a distinction was permitted, and, under Nicholas, the idea was that the papacy owned the material possessions which Franciscans merely used. The conflict raged within the Franciscans between the Conventuals and the Spirituals. The Conventuals prudentially attempted to apply Franciscan norms to their current obligations, whereas the Spirituals were bent on reforming their order in the face of what they took to be abuses of de facto wealth and luxury among their brother Fran-

---

Infallibility," 102–5; Ryan, "Ockham's Dilemma," 37–50; Tierney, *Origins of Papal Infallibility*; Tierney, "Origins of Papal Infallibility," 841–64; and Ratzinger, "Der Einfluss des Bettelordensstreites," 697–724.

25. Hahn and Wiker, *Politicizing the Bible*, 26, 33–34, and 37–39.

26. Ibid., 35–36 and 54–56; and Minnis, "Material Swords," 292–308.

27. In what follows below, I draw heavily from the magisterial account Hahn and Wiker have provided in their recent work, *Politicizing the Bible*, in their volume's second chapter, "The First Cracks of Secularism: Marsilius of Padua and William of Ockham," 17–59. Hahn and Wiker are among the very few scholars who recognize the important contribution of both Marsilius and Ockham to later developments that paved the way for modern historical biblical criticism. I also rely upon and Minnis, "Material Swords," 292–308.

ciscans who had taken vows of poverty. John XXII demurred against the idea that the papacy owned these possessions, declaring that the Franciscans owned what they used. Moreover, upset with what he took to be the Spirituals's abuses against their vows of obedience, he called them to obey.

At the same time, John XXII was also at odds with Ludwig of Bavaria. Various factions within German realms supported different individuals who were vying for leadership within those realms. Some supported Ludwig, whereas others supported and Frederick I. These political factions thus were in conflict over who would rule as German emperor, a dispute which appeared hopelessly irreconcilable. In light of this impasse, John XXII requested both Ludwig and Frederick to abdicate rule, and he, the pope, would take over in the interregnum. When John XXII reopened the poverty debate his predecessor Pope Nicholas had closed, Ludwig quickly condemned John as a heretic, using the Franciscan conflict with the pope as a political means of attacking the papacy.

Complicating matters further was the actual wealth and luxury of the papal court in Avignon, which made it likely that the papal court could not help but feel the sting of the Spiritual Franciscan critique. Although the Conventuals, and in particular Michael of Cesena, the Franciscan's Minister General, would probably have applauded Pope John's call to the Spirituals for obedience, they were outraged by Pope John's reopening what they thought had been a closed debate, a debate they had won under his predecessor. Marsilius and Ockham found themselves right in the middle of these controversies, as they both came to reside under Ludwig's protection from John XXII.

It is with Marsilius that medieval Muslim Averroist philosophy became important, and eventually exerted a significant influence on later biblical criticism. Marsilius likely imbibed this philosophy while studying at the University of Padua, but almost certainly later as rector at the University of Paris, which was also a major Averroist center in the west. The politics of Marsilius's famous work, *Defensor Pacis* (completed in 1324) were grounded in the notion that reason is to be separated from faith. His primary concern is to secure civil peace, which indeed become the main goal, the highest good, for Marsilius. Marsilius used Scripture whenever he was able to twist its interpretation to serve merely secular ends. In the end, the secular state Marsilius envisioned was to be in control of biblical interpretation. Moreover, for Marsilius, the state should have control of the church offices, so that the state can control ecclesiastical decisions. Additionally, Marsilius asserted a sort-of early conception of *sola Scriptura* where the Bible supplanted church authority and tradition, but it was a Bible authoritatively interpreted, not by the individual, but the state ruler and state appointed exegetes. In his view, the Old Testament no longer played a role for Christians, nor should recourse be made to a spiritual sense of Scripture, but to a literal sense alone. These latter rejections were based on Marsilius's understanding of how pro–papal exegetes used the Old Testament as well as allegorical interpretation to support the authority of the papacy. Marsilius never intended for the *Defensor Pacis* to remain a merely theoretical work, but rather it contained a practical means of subordinating the papacy to the state. Thus, Marsilius jumped on the contemporary Franciscan anti–John XXII bandwagon and made a case for an absolute poverty of clergy grounded in Marsilius's exegesis, in an attempt to remove any form of temporal authority from the papacy with the goal of allowing civil rulers to wield absolute temporal control.

Ockham would eventually join Marsilius, both literally under Ludwig's protection, and ideologically, but with a different and more spiritual purpose. Ockham got into trouble with John XXII, and fled Avignon, along with Michael of Cesena, to the protection of Ludwig, from which Ockham attacked the papacy of John XXII and succeeding popes. In contrast to Marsilius, however, Ockham never completely subjected the Church to the state. Instead, he emphasized the separation of powers (sacred from secular). Because Ockham saw an extraordinary need for church reform, he argued for the ability and necessity of secular rulers ruling over sinful prelates. Tied to this concept was Ockham's emphasis on the role of biblical *periti* (experts) or specialists who should be in charge of biblical interpretation. This would play itself out later in the history of biblical criticism, especially in and after the Enlightenment. For Ockham, the specialist or expert is has authority over a council, over the pope, and even over Catholic tradition, when it comes to biblical interpretation. Finally, Like Marsilius, Ockham would place emphasis on the literal sense, but his understanding of the literal sense differed from more traditional notions (as, e.g., found in Aquinas); for Marsilius and Ockham the literal sense was a reading of Scripture wherein the words of Scripture signified particular realities, as the authors intended, in the way any other human work signified realities.[28]

28. On Aquinas's biblical interpretation, and especially his understanding of the literal sense, see, e.g., Aquinas, *Summa Theologiae* I.1.10; Aquinas, *Quaestiones disputatae de potentia*, 4.1; Aquinas, *In psalmos Davidis expositio*, prooemium; Levering, *Participatory Biblical Exegesis*, 10–11; Boyle, "Authorial Intention," 3–8; Yocum, "Aquinas' Literal Exposition," 21–42; Wawrykow, "Aquinas on Isaiah," 43–71; Baglow, "Rediscovering St. Thomas Aquinas," 137–46; Baglow, "Sacred Scripture," 1–25; Baglow, "*Modus et Forma*," especially 5–51; Hahn, "Search the Scriptures," 12–15; Torrell, *Initiation à saint Thomas d'Aquin*, 41–45 and 84–85; Torrell, "Quand Saint Thomas," 179–208; Waldstein, "On Scripture," 73–94; and Kennedy, "Thomas Aquinas." Latin texts from Aquinas are taken from the Corpus Thomisticum.

REFORMATION POLITICS AND EARLY MODERN RELIGIOUS WARS

This conflict between state rulers and the Church, with a particular focus on the papacy, would only increase as the centuries went by. Between Ockham and the Reformation a whole host of critical tools were developed. In many ways the Renaissance period saw the development of new scholarly tools in philology and textual criticism that would place Scripture study, with a renewed emphasis on the *sensus literalis* on a firm footing. Lorenzo Valla (1406-1457) proved pivotal in his devastating critique of the authenticity of the *Donation of Constantine*, which, alongside the allegorical interpretation of the "two swords" (Luke 22:36), had been used to buffer temporal papal authority. Even before Valla, however, new pre-Reformation shifts were taking place in England with the work of John Wycliffe (ca. 1330-1384).[29]

Wycliffe's metaphysical realism grounded his entire theo-political, and thus, exegetical project. Wycliffe was upset about the popularity of nominalist philosophy, but he was also disconcerted about ecclesiastical corruption. Although Wycliffe never learned Greek or Hebrew, philosophically he thought such study was extremely important for proper biblical interpretation. In a very Marsilian and Ockhamite fashion, Wycliffe passionately argued that the state had an obligation to control the civil realm and should thus take control of the Church's temporal goods. In effect, Wycliffe argued for the Church's disendowment by the state. As with Luther's later teaching on two kingdoms, Wycliffe made a distinction between two types of dominion, "civil" and "evangelical." Based on his discussion in a series of writings—e.g., *De Dominio Divino*, *De Civili Dominio*, and *De Officio Regis*—Wycliffe argued forcefully that a civil ruler must remove any Church holdings when clerics misuse such holdings, or when the holdings are "inordinate," thus assisting clergy in their transformation to being more like the poor Christ himself.

In their chapter devoted to Wycliffe, Hahn and Wiker explain the important background context of English messianic nationalism which illuminates Wycliffe's milieu, and will shed further light to the background of the English Reformation. As we shall see, something similar occurred with French messianic nationalism when we turn in our second chapter to our

---

29. In what follows, I again draw heavily from Hahn and Wiker, *Politicizing the Bible*, in their volume's third chapter, "John Wycliffe," 61–115; and also Reventlow, *Bibelautorität*, 55–67. The sections in these two volumes are the only scholarly treatments, of which I am aware, that adequately situate Wycliffe within this important context in the history of biblical criticism. His significance becomes quite apparent later in Hahn and Wiker's volume when they arrive at the English Reformation, and below we will discuss this significance as well.

discussion of Isaac La Peyrère. Wycliffe must be situated within this broader context of rising English nationalism which moves the earlier Marsilian focus from imperial political power to Wycliffe's concern for English national rule. For understanding Wycliffe's biblical exegesis, it is important to look at his work, *De Veritate Sacrae Scripturae*. Here Wycliffe depicts Jesus as the true Word of God, in contrast to the Scriptural texts which are not the Word of God, but merely are informed by Christ the Word. Wycliffe made it abundantly clear that he saw his metaphysical realism, his philosophy, as a necessary prerequisite for proper exegesis. It is from his philosophical position, informed by his socio-political context, that Wycliffe buttresses his arguments for the state's forceful disendowment of the Church with passages from Scripture. Within this context, Wycliffe savagely critiqued religious orders, and particularly monasteries, which tied up so much land, and represented, for Wycliffe, the Church's corruption. "Court theologians," such as Wycliffe would become, were necessary, so he argued, to aid the state in its job of putting Church authorities in their proper place.

Eventually, Wycliffe's views spread and paved the way for the Protestant Reformation and what would come in later biblical scholarship. Wycliffe's ideas survived, particularly in Bohemia among those Bohemians who came to England during the Bohemian Queen Ann's marriage to England's King Richard II. In Bohemia, Wycliffite theology and exegesis exerted a tremendous influence on John Hus, and his Hussite followers. Both movements, the English Lollards (followers of Wycliffe) and Bohemian Hussites, sparked violent revolution and were thus put down as threats to their respective states. Nominalists, whose philosophy was directly opposed to that espoused by Wycliffe and Hus, were instrumental in attacking Hussites. Hahn and Wiker eruditely make the case that, "Although Wycliffe was a declared enemy of Ockham, insofar as he set forth an almost Marsilian argument he had the unintended effect (as did Ockham) of reinforcing the secularizing, politicizing thrust of Marsilius's thought."[30]

An even more neglected figure than Wycliffe in the rise of modern biblical criticism during this time period is Niccolò Machiavelli (1469–1527). What occurred in the Renaissance was also the replacement of traditional authority with the authority of specialists. The Renaissance turn to textual criticism followed the logic of Abelard's approach to the Church fathers, but involved more careful textual analysis, and was an important step in attempting to establish a standard text for Scripture. Such scholarship also initiated a trend, already present in Ockham, of elevating the scholar over the

---

30. Hahn and Wiker, *Politicizing the Bible*, 113.

Magisterium.[31] Machiavelli's political thought is an area that is well known by scholars. The role played by his interpretation of Moses for furthering his political ideas, and the extent of his influence on biblical interpretation, e.g. on Hobbes's and Spinoza's biblical criticism is less recognized. Machiavelli is especially significant for his early turn to the history behind the texts, which would become the central move Hobbes and Spinoza made in the seventeenth century.[32]

Machiavelli's social and historical context in Florence of the latter-half of the fifteenth century is essential to understanding his oeuvre, and thus his contribution to the later development of historical criticism. The universally recognized instances of the corruption of the papacy and of some members of the clergy constitute the necessary background to this social and historical context. Machiavelli universalized the hypocritical lives of his contemporary Renaissance popes, assuming the same of all religious leaders, and then he read such religious hypocrisy back into the lives of biblical figures like Moses. Unlike what was to come later with figures like Spinoza, Machiavelli did not think such hypocrisy was always bad; in fact he encouraged it. Machiavelli presented the reader with Pope Alexander VI as a paradigmatic prince, for example. It was after being tortured during his imprisonment that Machiavelli would pen his most famous work, *The Prince*. Significantly, by this point, Machiavelli already had a wealth of personal political experience: he served as a secretary in Florence; as a formal representative of Florence he had numerous dealings with Cesare Borgia, Alexander VI's son; he sought to create an effective army for Florence; and, perhaps most importantly, as a Florentine diplomat he was able to travel with Pope Julius II in battle; and he travelled to the German Holy Roman Emperor Maximilian I on behalf of Florence.

Machiavelli's writings prove very important for understanding the future fate of modern biblical criticism.[33] In *The Prince*, Machiavelli seeks to

---

31. Lawee, "Isaac Abarbanel," 203–4; Eriksen, "Some Sociopolitical," 102; Fried, *Donation of Constantine*, 28 and 30–32; Snobelen, "To us there is but one God," 116–17; Maddox, "Secular Reformation," 539–62; Geerken, "Machiavelli's Moses," 579–95; Marx, "Moses and Machiavellism," 551–71; Fubini, "Humanism and Truth," 79–86; Kugel, "Bible in the University," 143–65; and Goshen-Gottstein, "Christianity," 69–88.

32. In my analysis of Machiavelli that follows, I draw heavily from Hahn and Wiker, *Politicizing the Bible*, from their fourth chapter, "Machiavelli," 117–46; as well as from Hammill, *Mosaic Constitution*, 31–66; Viroli, *Machiavelli's God*; Del Lucchese, *Conflict, Power, and Multitude*, 11–37 and 45–111; Lynch, "Machiavelli on Reading the Bible," 29–55; Eriksen, "Some Sociopolitical," 102; Maddox, "Secular Reformation," 539–62; Geerken, "Machiavelli's Moses," 579–95; and Marx, "Moses and Machiavellism," 551–71.

33. With the notable exception of Hahn and Wiker, *Politicizing the Bible*, wherein

effect a transformation of politics from its ancient otherworldly orientation (as in Plato's *Republic*) to a wholly this-worldly focus where the ultimate purpose is to preserve political authority, temporal power. Machiavelli seeks to secularize all politics for the very Marsilian goal of terrestrial peace. In order to do this, Machiavelli effects a wholesale transformation of biblical interpretation. The biblical Moses is placed in the context of pagan political leaders, effectively secularizing his role within Scripture. Moses is no longer a leader called by God to mediate God's covenant with the Israelites, but is transformed in Machiavelli's exegesis into solely a civil leader, a secular prince. With his *Discourses on Livy*, Machiavelli is consciously trying to create a modern critical history. Within this account, Machiavelli shifts the question from religious veracity to its political utility. In Averroist fashion, Machiavelli sees religion as politically useful to keep order and control of a population, even though it is false. Whereas Averroës had a hierarchy of knowers (with philosophers at the top of the pyramid), Machiavelli focused on the political use of religion by princely rulers who use religious concepts to keep people in check.

With its emphasis on *sola scriptura*, the Protestant Reformation, which began during Machiavelli's lifetime, took trends, particularly from Ockham, and then went further than Renaissance thinkers in challenging the contemporaneous understanding of patristic interpretation. The Reformation itself played an important role in continuing the trajectory set by Nominalism and Renaissance philology. With their emphasis on the literal sense and their denigration of traditional Catholic spiritual exegesis, Protestant Reformers furthered the move towards modern biblical criticism, severing ties with the Catholic Magisterium as the locus of biblical interpretive authority.[34] The Reformation attack on allegorical interpretation furthered the

---

they devote an entire chapter to Machiavelli, few histories of modern biblical scholarship even mention Machiavelli in passing. Indeed, the most mention he receives in the standard works on the history of biblical scholarship, is in Sæbø's ed., *Hebrew Bible/Old Testament II*, specifically in Eriksen, "Some Sociopolitical," 102, where we read about Machiavelli, only in passing: "Only with Francesco Guicciardini (1483–1540) and Niccolò Machiavelli (1469–1527) do we encounter a more modern form of historiography that concerns itself with how causes work together to produce historical events. . . . In Machiavelli the study of history was motivated by an interest in the natural regularities that steer social and political processes. If factual accounts did not accord with a basic standard of accuracy, then one could not learn anything from history. Writers did not use history to exemplify wisdom they already possessed, but to find still hidden causal connections." Thus the following analysis of Machiavelli's writings in regard to his place in the early formation of what would become modern historical biblical criticism draws heavily upon the discussion in Hahn and Wiker, *Politicizing the Bible*, 127–42.

34. Barron, "Biblical Interpretation," 180; and Frampton, *Spinoza and the Rise of Historical Criticism*, 23–42.

drive toward historical criticism, and the Reformation itself was not void of politics.[35] As Travis Frampton makes clear:

> the Reformation was, at heart, politically engendered. What were the *protests* of Magisterial Reformers, if not political? Did Catholicism or Protestantism represent the *kingdom* of God on earth—and if the latter, which of its divergent forms would be representative? What part were churches of the Reformation to have in the numerous, religiously disparate European states? In the end, were leaders like Luther, Zwingli, and Calvin satisfied with the Catholic Church, wanting only to reform church practice and dogma? Why did so many Lutheran and Reformed churches vie against Catholicism—and at times against each other—in order to become the established church of the (representative) state? Certainly the vision of Protestants did not exclude the political sphere![36]

Indeed, it seems unlikely that it is a mere coincidence that the regions of Europe which remained Catholic through the Reformation had prior concordats limiting the pope's authority in their realms, and that the Protestant Reformation was most successful in realms where no such means of limiting the pope's reach existed.[37] At its core, however, the Protestant Reformation could never be completely severed from the changing political order. Western Europe was undergoing its bloody transformation from complex feudal space to modern centralized states which would ultimately subordinate the Church to the state.[38] As we shall see further below, the case of England is paradigmatic where support for the Reformation was driven by state politics, and all opposition was crushed.[39]

---

35. It should be noted, however, that it might be more accurate to say that the Reformers broadened the *sensus literalis* rather than completely abolished the spiritual sense of Scripture, even when, like Calvin, they explicitly attacked the idea of a spiritual sense. See, e.g., Raeder, "Exegetical and Hermeneutical Work," 371–73; Steinmetz, "John Calvin," 282–91; and Muller, "Hermeneutic of Promise," 68–82.

36. Frampton, *Spinoza and the Rise of Historical Criticism*, 13.

37. Cavanaugh, *Myth of Religious Violence*, 166–67; Duffy, *Saints & Sinners*, 175 and 199; Cavanaugh, "Fire Strong Enough," 400–1; and Skinner, *Foundations*, 59–60.

38. Cavanaugh, *Myth of Religious Violence*, 123–80; Frampton, *Spinoza and the Rise of Historical Criticism*, 13; Cavanaugh, "Killing for the Telephone Company," 243–74; and Cavanaugh, "Fire Strong Enough," 397–420.

39. Duffy, *Stripping of the Altars*, 377–523; Marx, *Faith in Nation*, 128–39, 153–61, and 175–84; Duffy, *Voices of Morebath*, 84–151; and Tumbleson, *Catholicism in the English Protestant Imagination*, 41–125 and 157–207.

In this context, Luther's role in the Reformation and in the transformation of biblical interpretation is important to consider, even if only briefly.[40] Luther confessed Ockham to be both the greatest philosopher and Luther's own master, among whose followers Luther numbered himself, and whose teachings he claimed to have completely imbibed. Such nominalism aided in Luther's severing of faith and reason, which eventually would lead to modern biblical scholars de-Hellenizing Scripture. The primary political context with the German Reformation was an extension of the throne vs. altar conflict we already encountered with Marsilius and Ockham, who were likewise embroiled in the Germanic politics of Ludwig of Bavaria. In Luther's time, the Holy Roman Emperor Maximilian I had machinations of ruling the region that would later become Italy, including the Papal States, but was also in conflict with the German electors, including Frederick III, Elector of Saxony and soon to be protector of Luther. Frederick was also frustrated by the papal taxes and other financial revenue that was redirected to Rome, and was likewise in conflict with his local bishops, most of whom were from the German nobility.

In light of this historical situation, and the long history stretching back to Marsilius and Ockham, Luther's *Ninety-Five Theses* and his call to reform must be situated within the broader context of the history of the call to reform already recounted, beginning with the poverty debate. The *Ninety-Five Theses* fit quite well within the guideposts of Catholic orthodoxy.[41] The complicating economic and political factor was that moneys for indulgences bled out of German regions and flowed to the papacy. Thus, Luther's challenges to reform on that matter of indulgences fit conveniently into German national aspirations and to anger against Rome that had been fomenting for quite some time. It was with Luther's turn to Scripture as sole authority (the Protestant principle of *sola Scriptura*) that the search for a method to replace Catholic tradition became earnest, and it was in the wake of theological divisions, each faction defending itself through Scripture that Luther handed over the body to the state. Luther turned to the state, much like Wycliffe before him, to control the public secular realm. But it was because of Luther's understanding of the "priesthood of all believers" and

---

40. In what follows on Luther, I draw heavily from Hahn and Wiker, *Politicizing the Bible*, their fifth chapter, "Luther and the Reformation," 147–219; Frampton, *Spinoza and the Rise of Historical Criticism*, 23–42; Scribner and Dixon, *German Reformation*; Marius, *Martin Luther*; Brecht, *Martin Luther*; García de Haro, *Historia teológica del modernismo*, 119–29 and 157–234; and McSorley, *Luthers Lehre*.

41. See, e.g., Hahn and Wiker, *Politicizing the Bible*, 158–59 and 159n55; Anderson, *Sin*, 162–63; and Anderson, "Redeem Your Sins," 66–69 and 68–69n71.

his grounding in no authority aside from Scripture, that the peasants who rebelled saw Luther as their inspiration.

Luther's declaration *sola fide* (justification by faith alone) became his hermeneutical key for unlocking Scripture's meaning, and thus Luther's idea of "promise" replaced the traditional role of typology. Upset with justifications of papal authority from spiritual exegesis, against which Ockham had earlier written as well, Luther severed Scripture's intimate bond with the liturgy, and erected sharp dichotomies between the "letter" and the "spirit," the "law" and the "gospel," and, importantly, the "Old" and "New" Testaments. Although Luther explicitly placed an exegetical emphasis on the literal sense, Hahn and Wiker rightly caution that, "It is misleading . . . to assume that the importance of Luther as an exegete is his focus on the literal account of Scripture; rather, his importance consists in substituting the dialectical mode of exegesis for the traditional fourfold meaning of Scripture."[42] Luther began to support state involvement in enforcing his version of orthodoxy. He found this necessary in the wake of the multiple radically diverse interpretations and positions that were emerging, at least ostensibly inspired by him. Luther thus began to affirm a form of Erastianism, wherein the state controlled the church, at least in the appointment of ecclesiastical officials. This is the origin of Luther's doctrine on "two kingdoms," church and state. Luther separated the realm of the secular from the realm of the sacred, as had Marsilius and Ockham before him, and thereby unwittingly aided in the construction of a newly emerging secular realm where the political could be severed from the ecclesiastical and wield autonomous temporal authority.[43] Given this, it should come as no surprise that many German princes welcomed Luther's teachings. After all, in the wake of the Peasants' Revolt (which claimed to be inspired by Luther), Luther advised the civil rulers to demolish rebels without clemency. R.W. Scribner and C. Scott Dixon provide an interesting comment on the reception of Luther and the sociology of the fate of the Reformation in Germany:

> After a brief period of mass enthusiasm, it [support for the Reformation] retreated to being a minority phenomenon. At a crude estimate, during the first generation of the Reformation, up to mid-century, and perhaps even during the second, probably no more than 10 percent of the German population ever showed an active and lasting enthusiasm for reformed ideas. Where massive numbers were "won" after 1526, to what became

---

42. Hahn and Wiker, *Politicizing the Bible*, 177.

43. See, e.g., ibid., 201–6; Cavanaugh, "Fire Strong Enough," 399–400; Skinner, *Foundations*, 15; and Figgis, *From Gerson to Grotius*, 6.

the new church, it occurred involuntarily, through a prince deciding that his territory should adopt the new faith. When we speak of the extensive hold "Protestantism" had on Germany by the second half of the sixteenth century . . . this was because there were large numbers of "involuntary Protestants" created by the princes' confessional choices.[44]

In the context of Luther's contribution to later biblical criticism, it is also significant that Luther developed a notion of a "canon within the canon." He explicitly exalted the Gospel of John, St. Paul's epistles (particularly Romans, Galatians, and Ephesians), and First Peter, above all other portions of Scripture. After the Reformation (i.e., later within the history of modern historical biblical criticism), exegetes progressed from Luther's sifting through the canon to distinguish authentic books from less authentic (or even inauthentic) books, to sifting through individual biblical books themselves, for the authentic "kernels." Luther's task was doubtless already made possible by earlier works like Abelard's *Sic et Non* relating to the authenticity of sayings from Scripture and the church fathers.[45] As we already saw, however, in Luther's attempt to aid the German princes in their battle with the papacy he unwittingly handed over interpretive authority to secular rulers. Hahn and Wiker underscore the ironic result:

> [I]nterpretive differences created a kind of industry of textual scholarship, producing more and more questions that only scholars had any hope of resolving. This had the interesting but entirely unintended effect of removing biblical interpretation from the hands of the common man to whom it had just been given, and handing it to academic experts, thereby creating an exegetical elite that duplicated the function of the Catholic *traditio* in defining interpretation authoritatively.[46]

From Luther we must turn briefly to the English Reformation that erupted during his era.[47] It is often forgotten that historical criticism was born in the

---

44. Scribner and Dixon, *German Reformation*, 34. Something similar can be said for the English Reformation, as we shall see below, and as is illustrated in Duffy, *Stripping of the Altars*.

45. For a critical edition, see Abelard, *Sic et Non*. See also the comments in Pernoud, *Héloïse et Abélard*.

46. Hahn and Wiker, *Politicizing the Bible*, 218.

47. In what follows I draw heavily from ibid., in their sixth chapter, "England and Henry VIII," 221-55; Duffy, *Stripping of the Altars*; Vázquez de Prada, *Sir Tomás Moro*, 164-209, 233-82, 307-17, and 354-70; Wegemer, *Thomas More on Statesmanship*, 161-82; Wegemer, *Thomas More*, 97-108, 128-70, 182-92, and 210-17; and Reventlow, *Bibelautorität*, 161-312.

world of English Deism prior to its entrance into the German academy in the eighteenth and nineteenth centuries. From the English Reformation (inspired in part by the German Reformation and the earlier Wycliffite trends of the Lollards in late medieval England) emerged Deist biblical criticism that would later transplant itself in the academic culture of Germany in the Enlightenment and nineteenth century. One of the elements, although certainly not the only one by any means, which proves important for understanding the English Reformation is King Henry VIII's "Great Matter," concerning his desire to marry Anne Boleyn. In this context it is important to recognize, as Hahn and Wiker point out, that, "the infamous divorce from Henry's first wife was not the cause but the occasion for the creation of the official Church of England."[48]

The king's "Great Matter" has several ironies, not least of which is that Henry VIII had previously argued against divorce. The Christian ban on divorce was one of the chief marks, according to Henry, that set apart Christian marriage from non-Christian marriage. Henry entered into this early debate on account of Luther. Luther and other Protestant Reformers (including Philip Melanchthon and Martin Bucer) had been considering divorce and even polygamy (or at least bigamy) as permissible under certain circumstances. One infamous case in this regard involved Philip of Hesse's desire to marry a second wife. The Reformers were able to make arguments in favor or divorce and bigamy precisely by desacramentalizing marriage. In this context Henry VIII wrote a robust defense of marriage as a sacrament. Henry of course had numerous mistresses, and his "Great Matter" became so great when Anne Boleyn refused to be his mistress, settling for nothing less than the crown as his bride.

The early English translation of the Bible and the work of William Tyndale was likewise an important contribution to the English Reformation, and it further aided Henry VIII's politics. Influenced by Luther and Melanchthon, with whom he spent time in Wittenberg, Tyndale propagated Protestantism in England from abroad. His English translation of Scripture became hugely influential, but was suspect within Catholic circles because of the theological bent of his translation. Henry VIII initially opposed Tyndale's translation. Because of the influence of Anne Boleyn, upon whom Henry had already cast his eyes, however, Henry VIII read (at least portions of) Tyndale's 1528 *The Obedience of a Christian Man*, which argued that a Christian had an obligation, laid upon them by none other than God, to obey his temporal sovereign, even over and against the papacy. Unsurprisingly, Henry became most pleased with this treatise.

48. Hahn and Wiker, *Politicizing the Bible*, 223.

A significant turning point in this history was when King Henry became convinced that he had biblical backing for annulling his marriage to Queen Catherine and taking Anne Boleyn as wife, namely Lev 18:16's prohibition of taking a brother's wife (since Catherine had been the wife of his late brother), with the added punishment that the couple in such a sinful state shall remain childless (Lev 20:21). Thus, Henry blamed his lack of a male heir through Catherine as due to God's punishment for his having taken his brother's wife, even though his brother was dead. This "Great Matter" unleashed a torrent of exegesis, both in England and on the continent, over what course Henry could and should take. Due to Anne's becoming pregnant with Henry's child, the king married her out of the public's eye, and later, through the aid of Thomas Cranmer, then Henry's appointed Archbishop of Canterbury, the English state annulled Henry's marriage to Catherine. It is difficult to overestimate the dramatic shift that took place with this action: Henry's marriage was annulled by the state and not by the papacy. As Hahn and Wiker underscore, this "marks the turning point at which the Church *in* England becomes the Church *of* England."[49]

Although almost completely ignored in the scholarship, with some notable exceptions as in the work of Hahn and Wiker, the available evidence suggests the strong influence of both Machiavelli and Marsilius on Henry's English Reformation. A number of the apologists of the Henrician reform policies utilized Machiavelli's and Marsilius' works, e.g., Richard Morison, who used Machiavelli in Morison's attempts at helping to create and then to legitimize Henry's reform, and also Thomas Starkey, who turned Marsilius of Padua's *Defensor Pacis* into a blueprint of Henry's political reform agenda. Furthermore, many of these future Henrician apologists congregated around Reginald Pole in Averroist Padua where they were immersed in such political philosophical discussions. Thomas Cromwell, one of the key members of Henry's inner circle, was likely influenced by Machiavelli as well, and Cromwell himself was responsible for getting Marsilius' *Defensor Pacis* published in English. The Marsilian program of subordinating the Church to the state found complete expression in Henry's state church. Thus we see how Marsilius,' Machiavelli's, and Wycliffe's combined influences set the stage in England for Henry's reform, which would in turn lay the seedbed for Hobbes and the future Deist exegesis which would follow upon John Locke and John Toland.

It is in the seventeenth century, however, that we find the most important transition which led to the rise of the historical critical method for

---

49. Ibid., 236.

interpreting Scripture.⁵⁰ The works of Isaac La Peyrère, Thomas Hobbes, Baruch Spinoza, and Fr. Richard Simon are pivotal here.⁵¹ These four figures would build a foundation to launch modern biblical interpretation far into the future, into the twenty-first century. This present volume focuses on the first of those four figures, La Peyrère, Hobbes, and Spinoza. I will thus only mention a few important highlights concerning those three figures below, since the remaining chapters in the volume will treat them more extensively. Before turning to these exegetes, however, we should note one further intellectual contribution that undergirds modern biblical criticism, namely René Descartes (1596–1650).⁵²

Descartes emerges as important particularly for his role in laying the intellectual groundwork for the hermeneutics and exegesis that would develop in his wake, and he is far more important here than for his particular use of Scripture, especially since Descartes blatantly laid aside the Bible in his philosophical program. It is his emphasis on method itself, as well as for the particulars of his method that constitute the significance of Descartes. The political focus of what came before, in figures like Marsilius and Machiavelli, now received a cosmological and epistemological foundation from thinkers like Galileo and Descartes. The seventeenth century "wars of religion" is extremely important for understanding Descartes, but also the figures who came after, especially Hobbes and Spinoza.

The "wars of religion" emerge as an essential context for understanding the biblical criticism that was generated and forged in the seventeenth century.⁵³ As Jon Levenson explains:

> It is no coincidence that the early pioneers of biblical criticism—Hobbes, Spinoza, Richard Simon—lived in the aftermath of the Thirty Years' War. Through the famous formula *cuius regio, eius religio* (whoever's realm, his religion), the Treaty of Westphalia (1648), which ended that war, established the superiority of the state over religion in fact and provided a hospitable climate for a theory to the same effect.⁵⁴

50. Goshen-Gottstein, "Foundations of Biblical Philology," 77–94.

51. Goshen-Gottstein, "Textual Criticism," 376.

52. In what follows on Descartes, I draw heavily from Hahn and Wiker, *Politicizing the Bible*, from their seventh chapter, "Descartes and the Secular Cosmos," 257–84; Kennington, *On Modern Origins*, especially 105–22; Klein, *Greek Mathematical Thought*, especially 197–211; Gaukroger, "Nature of Abstract Reasoning," 91–114; Lachterman, *Ethics of Geometry*; and Popkin, "Cartesianism and Biblical Criticism," 61–81.

53. In this discussion on the European "wars of religion," I draw on an earlier conference presentation, Morrow, "Revisiting the Seventeenth-Century," 66–80, as well as on Cavanaugh, *Myth of Religious Violence*, 123–80; Cavanaugh, "Killing for the Telephone Company," 243–74; and Cavanaugh, "Fire Strong Enough," 397–420.

54. Levenson, *Hebrew Bible*, 117.

In order to understand what happened in these so-called "religious wars," and the effect they had vis-à-vis Scripture scholarship and the relationship between church and state, I especially turn to the work of William Cavanaugh, both his now famous 1995 article, "'A Fire Strong Enough to Consume the House': The Wars of Religion and the Rise of the State," as well as his more recent 2009 book, *The Myth of Religious Violence*.[55]

Cavanaugh begins by recounting the familiar tale, a common founding myth of modern western nation states, namely, that in the wake of the Protestant Reformation, Europe's once unified Christendom was instantly fragmented into vying religious factions, distinguished by their divergent sets of privately held beliefs. Such a scenario proved combustible, igniting the bloody wars of religion. The modern western centralized states, and eventually nation states, emerged from the carnage in order to protect citizens from each other. The centralized state would thus be the guarantor of peace in light of the inherent dangers of violence resulting from the newfound diversity of religious beliefs held among Post-Reformation western citizens.[56]

Cavanaugh deconstructs this widespread myth, showing in his works the complexity of the history. He shows how such myths get the story backwards: "The 'Wars of Religion' were not the events which necessitated the birth of the modern State; they were in fact themselves the birthpangs of the State."[57] The standard version of the mythical history would lead us to believe that wars broke out between Catholics and Calvinists and Lutherans, and that these wars were primarily motivated by the different religious doctrines which distinguished these Christian traditions from each other. Cavanaugh shows in contrast, however, that, "These wars were not simply a matter of conflict between 'Protestantism' and 'Catholicism,' but were fought largely for the aggrandizement of the emerging State over the decaying remnants of the medieval ecclesial order."[58] Cavanaugh's work establishes three main points. He demonstrates that state centralization had a long history stretching back well before the seventeenth century, and this history culminated in the so-called "wars of religion." Thus such centralization could not be the results of such wars, and in fact, the wars were in large part bound up

---

55. Cavanaugh, "Fire Strong Enough," 397–420; and Cavanaugh, *Myth of Religious Violence*. For an important and fair critique of Cavanaugh's accounts in various of his works, see Shadle, "Cavanaugh on the Church," 246–70.

56. Cavanaugh, *Myth of Religious Violence*, 3–4, 15, 17–54, 123–42, and 181–226; Cavanaugh, "City," 190–91; and Cavanaugh, "Fire Strong Enough," 397–98, 408–9.

57. Cavanaugh, "Fire Strong Enough," 398.

58. Ibid.

with the process of state centralization itself.[59] The second point Cavanaugh drives home is that the very understanding of "religion" as pertaining primarily to divergent privately held beliefs, e.g., Judaism, Calvinism, Catholicism, Hinduism, etc., is a modern construct, one whose origins only barely predate the so-called religious wars, and a concept which gained currency after those wars. Thus, calling them "religious," in this modern sense, is anachronistic.[60] Finally, Cavanaugh demonstrates that, far from these wars being fought primarily between Catholics and Protestants, they were mostly fought between Catholics, with Protestants fighting on both sides.[61]

Prior to the early modern period, states were more relational in nature, based on bonds like kinship etc. With Machiavelli and later thinkers in the early modern period, the notion of state became more abstract.[62] State centralization enabled rulers more effectively to wage and to win wars.[63] A key stage in the history of state centralization, even prior to Reformation, was the ability of rulers effectively to wage wars but also effectively to extract taxes from a population.[64] This history reaches back as far, perhaps, as the eleventh century. Royal courts began to usurp the authority of guilds and ecclesiastical courts. Princes and nobles waged war. Those who were better able to extract resources, in the form of taxation, from their populace, and procure mercenary forces, tended to win wars, and thereby solidify their claims to sovereignty and border creation and control. This is the process that culminated in the wars after the Reformation.[65]

---

59. Cavanaugh, *Myth of Religious Violence*, 162–77; Cavanaugh, "Killing for the Telephone Company," 246–50; and Cavanaugh, "Fire Strong Enough," 398–403.

60. Cavanaugh, *Myth of Religious Violence*, 5, 7–10, 57–122, and 159; and Cavanaugh, "Fire Strong Enough," 398 and 403–8.

61. Cavanaugh, *Myth of Religious Violence*, 11–12, 142–53, 155, 160, 164–6, 169–74, and 177; and Cavanaugh, "Fire Strong Enough," 401–3.

62. Asad, "Where Are the Margins," 280; Philpott, *Revolutions in Sovereignty*, 16–17; Giddens, *Nation-State and Violence*, 1–2 and 52–53; Gellner, *Nations and Nationalism*, 8–18 and 21; and Skinner, *Foundations*, 352–58.

63. Howard, *Invention of Peace*, 15; and Porter, *War and the Rise of the State*, 7, 24, and 60–61.

64. Herbst, "States and War," 167–70; Ertman, *Birth of the Leviathan*, 4, 15, and 26–27; Burke, *Clash of Civilizations*, 122, 124, and 126; Collins, "State Building," 603–4, 609, 611, and 624–25; Spruyt, *Sovereign State*, 79; Mallia-Milanes, *Louis XIV*, 2; Tilly, "War Making," 170 and 172–73; Finer, "State- and Nation-Building," 84–163; Ardant, "Financial Policy," 164–242; Braun, "Taxation," 243–327; Tilly, "Reflections on the History," 3–83; and Strayer, *On the Medieval Origins*, 15–27 and 58–68.

65. Philpott, *Revolutions in Sovereignty*, 75–122; Ertman, *Birth of the Leviathan*; Burke, *Clash of Civilizations*; Spruyt, *Sovereign State*; Tilly, "Reflections on the History," 3–83; Finer, "State- and Nation-Building," 84–163; Ardant, "Financial Policy," 164–242; Braun, "Taxation," 243–327; and Strayer, *Medieval Origins*.

Prior to the early modern time period, *religio* was understood in the medieval period and within late antique Christianity as pertaining to the worship due God, or to monastic discipline, or to specific religious orders themselves. It was only with the emergence of figures like Nicholas of Cusa (1401–1464), Marsilio Ficino (1433–1499), Jean Bodin (1530–1596), and especially Thomas Hobbes (1588–1679), Baruch Spinoza (1632–1677), John Locke (1632–1704), and Jean-Jacques Rousseau (1712–1778), that religion was redefined in its more modern sense of pertaining to private belief, or sets of doctrines that are to be believed, which can then be studied by scholars.[66]

Finally, Cavanaugh notes the banal fact that, "the principal promoters of the wars in France and Germany were in fact not pastors and peasants, but kings and nobles with a stake in the outcome of the movement toward the centralized, hegemonic state."[67] Moreover, and just as significantly, the sides were often difficult to divide neatly between religious factions.[68] This is even the case in the sixteenth century, although not always. Sometimes the battles divided fairly clearly along religious factions. But even when they did, as in the case of the St. Bartholomew's Day Massacre of 1572, it is clear that doctrinal disputes were not Catherine de Medici's main concern, but

66. Morrow, "Secularization, Objectivity, and Enlightenment Scholarship," 14–32; Nongbri, *Before Religion*, 65–105 and 132–53; Masuzawa, *Invention of World Religions*, xi–xiii, 19, 46–53, 64; Griffiths, *Problems of Religious Diversity*, 2–7; Pickstock, *After Writing*, 146–54; Asad, *Genealogies of Religion*, 37–45; Harrison, "Religion," especially 5–17 and 19–44; Southern, *Western Society*, 214; Smith, *Meaning and End of Religion*, 31–44; and Figgis, *From Gerson to Grotius*, 124. Compare with earlier uses of *religio* in, e.g., Augustine, *De Vera Religione*; Augustine, *De Civitate Dei*, X.I.; and Aquinas, *Summa Theologiae* I–II.49–55 and II–II.81.7–8. Latin texts for Augustine are taken from the Patrologia Latina Database.

67. Cavanaugh, *Theopolitical Imagination*, 31.

68. The examples that follow are taken from Cavanaugh, *Myth of Religious Violence*, 142–50; Maltby, *Reign of Charles V*, 53, 56, 58, 62–64, and 112–13; Blockmans, *Emperor Charles V*, 41, 75, 77, 94–95, 110, and 139; Tracy, *Emperor Charles V*, 32–34, 45–47, 209–15, and 306–7; Gritsch, *History of Lutheranism*, 110–11; Kamen, *Early Modern*, 75; Jaitner, "Popes and the Struggle," 62 and 65; Israel, "Dutch-Spanish War," 112–4; von Greyerz, "Switzerland," 135; Oresko, "House of Savoy," 143–46; Langer, "Royal Swedish War," 189; Repgen, "Negotiating the Peace," 355; Hughes, *Causes of the English Civil War*, 42; Holt, *French Wars*, 50–51, 99, 103, 117–19, and 156–57; Collins, *State in Early Modern*, 29 and 115; Cavanaugh, "Fire Strong Enough," 401–3; Heller, *Iron and Blood*, 53, 61–65, 91–92, 95, 126–27, and 209–11; Hsia, *Social Discipline*, 85; Parker, ed., *Thirty Years' War*, 29–33, 59–64, 70–71, 76, 94, 123–24, 127–28, 136, 142–44, 174, 182, and 194–95; Salmon, *Society in Crisis*, 176, 183–85, 197–98, 204–5, 234, 243–57, 277, and 282–91; and Dunn, *Age of Religious Wars*, 6–7, 49–51, and 71–72. All of these can be found in Cavanaugh, *Myth of Religious Violence*, 142–50, which represents a greatly expanded version of Cavanaugh, "Fire Strong Enough," 401–3. These examples are not exhaustive, nor does Cavanaugh's account pretend to be exhaustive.

rather such disputes were used in order to protect her sovereign control. The various wars of the 1520s, however, were primarily between Catholics, initially between the Holy Roman Empire and the Papacy, over the control of the territories that would eventually become Italy and also German realms. The Four Years' War (1521–1526) found the Catholic Holy Roman Emperor, Charles V, in battle against Catholic France. Catholic France aided Catholic Venice, and the Muslim Ottoman Empire joined their forces. On the side of the Holy Roman Empire in these battles was England (Catholic at that time), as well as some German Protestant princes.

Both of the Italian Wars (those of 1536–1538 as well as those of 1542–1546), found the Catholic Holy Roman Empire again embroiled in battle with Catholic France. Muslim Ottomans joined forces with France, and German Lutheran princes teamed up with the Holy Roman Empire, as did England, which had severed ties with Rome at this point. The 1552 attack on the Holy Roman Empire had Catholics and Protestants fighting on both sides. The Catholic Holy Roman Empire utilized Protestant (as well as Catholic) mercenaries, and France teamed up against them with German Lutheran princes. The Carafa War (1556–1557) was primarily waged between the Papal States and Spain, both obviously Catholic. Even the apparently Catholic versus Protestant Huguenot Revolt of 1562, where the French Calvinists revolted against the Catholic Baron François de Fumel's ban on Calvinist religious services, found the Catholic Baron in battle against both Catholic and Protestant peasants.

With regard to the majority of the French Civil Wars (1562–1598), which of course inspired the Holy Roman Empire to launch the later Thirty Years' War when the Holy Roman Emperor saw how successful centralized France emerged from their civil wars, it is notoriously difficult to disentangle sides based on religious affiliations. Many of these skirmishes were between the Catholic League and the Catholic Guises, on the one hand, versus the Catholic group Politiques, the Catholic Catherine de Medici, the Protestant Henry of Navarre (who later became Catholic), the Protestant Prince of Condé, a number of other Calvinists, and the Catholic King Henry III of France, on the other hand. Even when the sides were predominantly Protestant versus Catholic, we find Catholics teamed up with the Protestants against other Catholics. In the Dutch Revolts of 1580, Catholic France came to the assistance of the Dutch Calvinists in their battle against Catholic Spain.

The Thirty Years' War (1618–1648), the paradigmatic "war of religion," which was brought to a close by the 1648 Treaty of Westphalia, was an incredibly messy affair, not only in regard to the brutality and the number of lives lost, but also as concerns the religious sides. Again and again, Catholics and Protestants joined forces combating other Catholics and Protestants. The final half of the Thirty Years' War was mainly between the Catholic Habsburgs and the Catholic Bourbons, again, with Protestants fighting on both sides. In what sense are these "religious" wars? In 1618 Protestant Bohemians fought against the Catholic Holy Roman Empire, enlisting the aid of Frederick V, a founder of the Protestant Union. In this instance, however, the Protestant Union refused to enter the fray. Then, in 1626 the Lutheran John George, the Elector of Saxony, joined forces with the Catholic Holy Roman Empire to retake primarily Protestant Bohemia. Later in these conflicts, however, he attacked the Holy Roman Empire. Catholic France also came to the aid of the Protestant Grisons in Switzerland during their battle against the Catholic Habsburgs. In 1628 Dutch Calvinists came to the aid of Catholic France in their fight with French Calvinists (Huguenots) at La Rochelle. In his battles the Calvinist Elector of Brandenburg, George William, used the Catholic Count Adam of Schwarzenberg as his main military advisor. Albrecht von Wallenstein, who was Catholic at the time and leader of the soldiers of the Catholic Holy Roman Empire, utilized the Lutheran Hans Georg von Arnim as one of his main commanders, and von Wallenstein's soldiers were composed of both Catholics and Protestants. Finally, from 1634–1635, Catholic France, under the authority of the Catholic Cardinal Richelieu, sent soldiers to aid the Protestant Swedes in their battle against the Catholic Holy Roman Empire.

Moreover, this terse summary masks the religious complexity of the various characters involved, who often convert to different religious traditions. Henry of Navarre (Henry III of Navarre), the son of Huguenots, was Protestant like his parents, during his initial reign, but then he converted to Catholicism when he became King Henry IV of France. Jacques de Crussol, the Duke of Uzès, was a Calvinist in France who participated in ransacking Catholic churches in France, leaving them severely damaged, but later he converted to Catholicism. The German prince, Wolfgang Wilhelm, the Count Palatine of Neuburg, who was intimately involved in the Cleves-Jülich crisis (1609–1610), was another Protestant who later converted to Catholicism. John Sigismund, the Elector of Brandenburg, who was also involved directly in the Cleves-Jülich crisis, converted from Lutheranism to Calvinism. Finally, Albrecht von Wallenstein, who headed up the Catholic Holy Roman Empire's army, began as Lutheran (the affiliation of his parents, who were Lutheran and Hussite), and then he became Bohemian Brethren (the affiliation of his uncle with whom he lived after the death of his parents), and only later became Catholic after coming into contact with Jesuits during von Wallenstein's studies at the University of Olomouc.

Michael Gillespie describes the severity of these conflicts:

> the Wars of Religion were conducted with a fervor and brutality that were not seen again until our own times. Indeed, the ferocity of the combatants may even have exceeded our own, for almost all the killing took place at close quarters, often in hand-to-hand combat, and thus without the emotionally insulating distance that modern technologies make possible. . . . During the Peasants Rebellion in the 1520s, over one hundred thousand German peasants and impoverished townspeople were slaughtered. . . . In 1572, seventy thousand French Huguenots were slaughtered in the St. Bartholomew's Day Massacre. . . . Cromwell's model army sacked the Irish town of Drogheda in 1649, killing virtually everyone. They burned alive all those who had taken refuge in the St. Mary's Cathedral, butchered the women hiding in the vaults beneath it, used Irish children as human shields, hunted down and killed every priest, and sold the thirty surviving defenders into slavery. . . . By conservative estimates, the wars claimed the lives of 10 percent of the population in England, 15 percent in France, 30 percent in Germany, and more than 50 percent in Bohemia. By comparison, European dead in World War II exceeded 10 percent of the population only in Germany and the USSR. Within our experience only the Holocaust and the killing fields of Cambodia can begin to rival the levels of destruction that characterized the Wars of Religion.[69]

Such strife as described above, so often attributed to violent and intolerant religious factions, is the ultimate context for Descartes's method in his *Discourse on Method*. Descartes's method shaped modernity and effected the new cosmological understanding of the world in which seventeenth century (and beyond) historical criticism would develop and operate. Descartes's method in his *Discourse* is nothing other than a strategy for achieving his goal of providing a solid foundation upon which humanity could build, unspoiled by violent conflicts, like that which Descartes lived through.

In Descartes' mechanistic universe, the miraculous began to seem impossible. So, even though Descartes did not apply his methodic doubt, that is, his Cartesian skepticism, to the Bible, he cleared the way so that others could do this, and moreover, as we will perceive especially in Spinoza, those that followed Descartes did apply Cartesian methodic doubt to the Bible. Descartes's methodic doubt is a key to his strategy. He situates his methodic doubt in such a way that it appears naturally to follow his version

---

69. Gillespie, *Theological Origins*, 129–30.

of philosophy. In fact, however, his philosophy, his notion of mathematics, determined the necessity of methodic doubt.[70]

As we will see in the next chapter, the seventeenth century exegetical story about modern biblical criticism really begins with Isaac La Peyrère (ca. 1596–1676), who was a French Calvinist serving as the secretary for the Prince of Condé. At the bequest of Queen Christina of Sweden (Renée Descartes's patroness), La Peyrère published his controversial *Prae-Adamitae*, which had already circulated widely throughout Europe, and had been criticized in print over a decade before it was itself formally published.[71] La Peyrère's *Prae-Adamitae* was an attempt to argue that rather than being divine revelation, the Old Testament was in reality just the history of the Jewish people. It appeared to be universal human history, but in reality was mistaken on this account. Adam was simply the ancestor of the Jewish people. The people before Adam, pre-Adamites, were the ancestors of the Gentiles, and importantly, the French. The Old Testament itself was riddled with errors, as one might expect from any ancient historical document. As with Ibn Ḥazm, La Peyrère challenged the Mosaic authorship of the Pentateuch in order to undermine any claims that the Pentateuch represented divine revelation.[72] La Peyrère focused his criticism on repetitions in the text, alleged contradictions, as well as the death of Moses in Deuteronomy. It is clear that in the medieval period and before, the Mosaic authorship of the entire Pentateuch was not seen as a necessary requirement of fidelity to tradition, either within Judaism or within Christianity.[73] In the seventeenth and eighteenth centuries, however, the Mosaic authorship of the Pentateuch became a foundational issue in theological debates over biblical criticism. In general, both those who challenged and those who defended Mosaic authorship understood the respective attributions as a safeguard for divine inspiration.[74]

We must keep in mind that La Peyrère served as secretary to the Prince of Condé. As we will see in the next chapter, and by way of preview,

---

70. I am particularly indebted to Hahn and Wiker's discussion here in *Politicizing the Bible*, 267–75.

71. Parente, "Isaac de La Peyrère," 161–82; Popkin, *Isaac La Peyrère*, 2, 5–6, 12–13, 45, 72, 80–81, 180n50, 182n76, 194–95nn2–44, and 199n20; Popkin, "Spinoza and La Peyrère," 172–95; and Popkin, "Marrano Theology," 97–126.

72. Significantly, pre-Adamite type theories predate La Peyrère, and may even be found among some earlier medieval Muslim sources, including Averroist ones. It also appears that La Peyrère was influenced by earlier Averroist writers. Popkin, *Isaac La Peyrère*, 1–2, 26, 30–32, 42, 48–49, 71–72, 88, 185nn15 and 21.

73. Levenson, "Eighth Principle," 205–25.

74. Kugel, *How to Read the Bible*, 29; and Popkin, *Isaac La Peyrère*, 50 and 71–74.

it appears that Queen Christina, Oliver Cromwell, and the Prince of Condé were involved in a plot to overthrow Louis XIV and place the Prince of Condé on the French throne. La Peyrère's biblical criticism appears to have been at the service of his political machinations. In his other work of biblical interpretation, *Du Rappel des Juifs*, La Peyrère envisioned the Prince of Condé as the King of France, ruling the world alongside the Messiah. This King would gather the Jews from across the globe to France, that land of *liberté* (at that time there were no slaves there), and return them to the Holy Land upon Jesus' return, after the Jews have converted to La Peyrère's version of a Christianity devoid of anything that he feared might offend Jewish sensibilities. It should come as no surprise that La Peyrère's work was condemned, and that he was forced to convert to Catholicism. He spent the remainder of his days with the French Oratorians.[75]

Next comes Hobbes, who wrote his *Leviathan* while in self-imposed exile in Paris. He fled to France to escape the conflagration which consumed England during its civil war. The Thirty Years' War, which he also lived through, was fresh in his mind. Hobbes's entire political theory was grounded in an ontology of violence, of a "warre, as is of every man, against every man."[76] The absolute sovereign was Hobbes's solution to such violence. This absolute sovereign had to be the head of both the state and the church. For Hobbes, the sovereign, or the officials she appointed, became *the* authority on matters of biblical interpretation. Central to such a hermeneutical task, in Hobbes's mind, was curtailing allegorical interpretations, which he saw often supporting Catholic transnational pretenses, judging Scripture through the proper use of reason, and focusing exclusively on a historical reading of the texts.

As we shall see in chapter three of this present volume, Hobbes's biblical exegesis was an attempt to justify the status quo before the war, where the state sovereign was both head of the church and the state. In addition to his nearly complete denial of the Mosaic authorship of the Pentateuch based solely on an anemic argument involving three verses (Gen 12:6; Num 21:14; Deut 34:6), Hobbes interpreted the Bible in such a way that no eternal fate was better or worse than what the state sovereign could grant. Hobbes saw the concept of hell as a threat to the security of the state, since such security

---

75. Popkin, "Millenarianism and Nationalism," 78–82; Åkerman, *Queen Christina*, 11, 32, 186, 202–4; and 213–5; Popkin, *Isaac La Peyrère*, 2–3, 5, 8–9, 12, 18, 40, 52–54, 58–62, 66–68, 78, 87, 96, 99, 103, 105, 180n49, and 199n20; Popkin, "Menasseh ben Israel II," 12–20; and Katz, "Menasseh ben Israel's Mission," 57–72.

76. Hobbes, *Leviathan* 2, 192.

rested upon the fear of physical death the power of which must lie in the hands of the sovereign.[77]

The similarities between Hobbes's project and La Peyrère's are not likely to be the result of mere coincidence, particularly since Hobbes walked in the same circles as La Peyrère. Hobbes may have in fact been motivated by theological concerns; in the England of his time, at least his views concerning church and state relations would not have been viewed as heterodox, even if his was denounced as an impious atheist because of other less orthodox views in his work. As we will see in chapter four of this volume, the ways in which Spinoza would elaborate on Hobbes's project, even where Spinoza preferred democracy to Hobbes's ideal of monarchy, guaranteed Hobbes's turn to history would survive into the next century.

Spinoza wrote his famous *Tractatus Theologico-Politicus* as an attempt to support his political program. Spinoza not only relied upon the works of both Hobbes and La Peyrère (whose books have been preserved in Spinoza's library), but rather it is also possible that he drew upon the medieval Muslim polemical literature of Ibn Ḥazm. At least fourteen of Spinoza's arguments concerning biblical criticism are found in sixteen (of over 1,000) pages of Ibn Ḥazm's *Al-Faṣl*.[78] As with Ibn Ḥazm, Spinoza too thought it was important to see the Torah abrogated so that it only applied to the Hebrew nation of the Old Testament. Part of Spinoza's motivation may have been to get revenge on the Jewish community in Amsterdam that had banned him from their community.[79]

Spinoza was kicked out of the Jewish community in Amsterdam at a very young age. We do not know the precise theological reasons, or even if there were clear ones, for his ban. The archival evidence suggests that Spinoza was banned at the very least in part because he jeopardized the relative autonomy of Amsterdam's Jewish community by circumventing

77. Hobbes, *Leviathan 3*, 698–729; Malherbe, "Hobbes et la Bible," 691–99; Pacchi, "Hobbes and Biblical Philology," 231–39; and Pacchi, *Filosofia e Teologia*, 16–17, 29–30, 34–41, 47, 49–50, 116, and 125–6.

78. Freedman, "Father of Modern Biblical Scholarship," 31–38. Freedman isolates twenty arguments Spinoza employs to make his methodological case for modern biblical criticism. Fourteen of these arguments, a full two thirds, Freedman traces back to sixteen pages of Ibn Ḥazm's 1050-page *Al-Faṣl*. It is clear that Spinoza's work bears some of the marks of medieval Muslim scholarship. See, e.g., the comments in Guerrero, "Filósofos hispano–musulmanes," 125–32; and Arnaldez, "Spinoza et la pensée arabe," 151–74.

79. We do not know for certain the exact reasons for his ban. The archival evidence suggests that Spinoza went outside of the traditional community boundaries and turned instead to the secular Amsterdam authorities to deal with multiple instances concerning debt. See Vlessing, "Excommunication of Baruch Spinoza," 15–47; and Vlessing, "Jewish Community," 209–10.

their authority structures in the matter of debts. In order to free himself from the debts he owed, he went to the secular Amsterdam authorities to request a legal guardian, which was granted him, as opposed to turning to the synagogue to settle the matter, which was the expected route of addressing the situation.

Part and parcel of his hermeneutical program is the historical method articulated by Spinoza, which provided the foundation upon which historical criticism would thenceforth build. His method called for discovering the complete histories of textual transmission, canonization, original meaning and content of each biblical book and author, before any theological interpretation could begin; what amounts to an impossible task.[80]

Spinoza may in fact have had genuine theological concerns.[81] Those who followed in his wake, however, sought to distance themselves from Spinoza, even as they relied upon his methodological framework. Indeed, as David Dungan points out, "Spinoza and his followers multiplied questions about the physical history of the text to the point that the traditional theological task could never get off the ground."[82] The new historical biblical methodology in Spinoza's *Tractatus Theologico-Politicus* served his political theory expressed in that text. The fact that he was offered a pension to dedicate another work to King Louis XIV of France, and that (no-longer Queen) Christina of Sweden's brother offered him a professorship at the University of Heidelberg, both of which Spinoza turned down, shows how the political project had broad appeal for emerging modern European states.

The Oratorian priest Richard Simon (1638–1712) followed La Peyrère (whom he befriended when they both lived among the Oratorians in Paris), Hobbes, and Spinoza, even when he took them further and disagreed with them at many points.[83] Simon developed much of his criticism while in

---

80. See the seventh chapter of Spinoza's *Tractatus Theologico-Politicus*. On Spinoza's biblical interpretation in general, its political background, and especially his pivotal role in steering the course for later historical criticism, see Nadler, "Bible Hermeneutics," 827–36; Preus, *Spinoza and the Irrelevance of Biblical Authority*; and Lagrée and Moreau, "La lecture de la Bible," 97–115.

81. For situating Spinoza in a theological context, see especially Polka, *Between Philosophy and Religion I*; and Frampton, *Spinoza and the Rise of Historical Criticism*.

82. Dungan, *History of the Synoptic Problem*, 172. For the importance of Spinoza's Marrano background in explaining his implicit skeptical positions sometimes couched in more traditional sounding language, see especially the 5th and 6th parts of Yovel, *Other Within*, 227–377; and Yovel, *Spinoza and Other Heretics 1*.

83. In what follows on Simon I draw heavily from Morrow, "Faith, Reason, and History,"; Hahn and Wiker, *Politicizing the Bible*, from their tenth chapter, "The Ambiguous Richard Simon," 395–423; Barthélemy, *Studies in the Text*, especially 58–81; Bernier, *La critique du Pentateuque*, especially 33–41, 44–47, 49–69, 71–114, 117–26, 162–67, 186–208, 210–12, 214–16, 222–24, 277–79, and 281–4; Müller, *Richard Simon*; Müller,

dialogue and debate with French Calvinists. In many ways, his work was partially an apologetic for the Catholic tradition. Simon attempted to demonstrate the numerous historical and textual problems found in the biblical texts and manuscripts, and thereby to highlight the importance of infallible Catholic tradition which alone is able to preserve God's truth when faced with so many historical and textual problems as the Bible contains.

At the same time, however, Simon appears to have been a state supporter, over and against the papacy. He attempted to dedicate his controversial *Histoire critique du Vieux Testament* to King Louis XIV, but was blocked by Bishop Jacques-Bénigne Bossuet (1627-1704). His book was suspect, so he was asked to send it to the ecclesiastical authorities, but he excised the controversial portions, mainly the sections calling the Pentateuch's Mosaic authorship into question, before sending the authorities a manuscript. When he was forbidden to publish his book in France, and it was placed on the Index of Forbidden Books, he sought publishers outside of Catholic France, and published the book in the Dutch Republic. He was eventually expelled from the Oratorian Order.

On the one hand, Simon appeared to be defending Catholic tradition against the more skeptical Spinoza et al., but on the other, he clearly took their work further, and this had a long-lasting effect both on biblical interpretation and on the tradition he was so adamantly trying to defend. Simon clearly built upon Spinoza's exegetical project.[84] The irony is that Simon's *Histoire critique du Vieux Testament* was an attempt, at least ostensibly, to combat Spinoza's exegetical method. Simon hoped to defend Catholic tradition and at the same time demolish the Protestant assumption of *sola Scriptura*. In order to do so, however, Simon took Spinoza's arguments even further, multiplying problems with the biblical text. In many places, Simon followed the lead of La Peyrère, who was a close friend of Simon's ever since La Peyrère joined the Oratorians, for whom *Fr.* Richard Simon was a priest.

Simon's work was used in England as a tool to dismantle the authority of the Bible. Indeed, John Locke, who was already quite familiar with Hobbes's work, was captivated by Simon's biblical criticism, and annotated more than one edition of his *Histoire critique du Vieux Testament*.[85] This is significant, since German biblical scholarship would initially feed off

---

Kritik und Theologie; Stroumsa, "Richard Simon," 89-107; Nichols, "Richard Simon," 115-68; Woodbridge, "Richard Simon," 193-206; McKane, *Selected Christian Hebraists*, 111-50; and Hazard, *La Crise de la conscience*, 125-36.

84. On this point, see Hahn and Wiker, *Politicizing the Bible*, 395-99, 406-7, 411-12, and 421-23; Barthélemy, *Studies in the Text*, 60-62; Mirri, *Richard Simon*, 29-84; and Auvray, "Richard Simon et Spinoza," 201-14.

85. Champion, "Père Richard Simon," 39-61.

of English biblical criticism, even as later English biblical criticism often grounded itself on nineteenth century German scholarship.[86] Simon's philological and historical analyses became the foundational work in France and Germany for the kind of close philological analysis that would emerge in the eighteenth century as the dominant historical method, transforming the Bible from a primarily theological text to an ancient cultural source with the potential to be used to shape and form servants of colonial states.

Locke's contribution to exegesis merits some attention at this point.[87] Locke's context is the English Civil Wars. The English Parliament's rebellion against the king was a rather complex event involving economical, political, and religious issues that were impossible to disentangle completely and isolate from each other, so intertwined were they. Locke's family was found on the side represented by Parliament, which was basically recently landed or propertied. Locke was about ten years old when this First Civil War erupted. The Second Civil War found Locke at Westminster School, at age fifteen. Locke was studying at Oxford during the tumultuous transition from the Third Civil War and the chaos which ensued to Oliver Cromwell's military rule.

This context of violent strife and the "nearly anarchic radicalism" that was rampant throughout England profoundly shaped Locke, who proved himself "deeply influenced" by Hobbes' *Leviathan*. Locke also was influenced by Robert Boyle (a prominent member of the Royal Society) who was another mechanist like Hobbes, popularizing Epicurean atomism in England. Locke's political machinations forced him into exile as he was trailed by royal spies on the continent. Initially, Locke served as secretary for the Elector of Brandenburg on a diplomatic mission to the European continent. Locke later became intimately acquainted with Anthony Ashley Cooper, who became the Earl of Shaftesbury. Locke even served as his personal physician. As a Whig, Locke was constantly involved in political plots and intrigue, including a plan for violent rebellion. Indeed, the evidence seems to indicate that Locke may have been personally involved in the Rye House Plot, a plan to kidnap and then murder King Charles II (whom Locke earlier supported) and the king's brother.

In self-imposed exile Locke remained in the Dutch Republic, within six years of Spinoza's death. In the Dutch Republic, Locke was exposed to radical intellectual traditions, including the critic of Richard Simon, Jean Le

---

86. Sheehan, *Enlightenment Bible*, xii, xiv, and 89.

87. In discussing Locke here I rely primarily upon the fine account in Hahn and Wiker, *Politicizing the Bible*, in their eleventh chapter, "The English Civil Wars, Moderate Radicals, and John Locke," 425–86, from which are taken the partial quotes in the next paragraph; but also Ashcraft, *Revolutionary Politics*.

Clerc, who would become a good friend of Locke's. Locke likewise assiduously studied Spinoza and Simon. It was also at this time that Locke created a private intellectual meeting group, which involved figures in Benjamin Furly's radical circle of intellectuals. After the Rye House Plot failed, the English crown, on many occasions, attempted to capture Locke and bring him back to England for trial and punishment. Meanwhile, Locke was busy plotting a coup which would bring down King James II and place William of Orange in his stead. After the success, the "Glorious Revolution," Locke was able to return to England a hero.

Locke's *Epistola de Tolerantia* is a clarion call for toleration amidst a turbulent moment in English political life. Locke's *Epistola* duplicates the sort of "political Averroism" (Hahn's and Wiker's words) of Marsilius' *Defensor Pacis* through Locke's particular call for toleration. Like Spinoza before him, a core morality, which has been obscured by so much attention to doctrine, became Scripture's central message for Locke. For Locke, the Bible, at its core, is a rule book, providing moral guidance, each rule of which is dictated by reason. Locke's vision of toleration required a secular governing authority and the complete privatization of religion.

Locke's *An Essay Concerning Human Understanding* forms an important part of his overall political project. It is one of several attempts to diminish the scope of faith and at the same time expand the scope of reason. Locke is privatizing faith, while uniting Cartesian rationalism with the empiricism of the science. In the *Essay*, Locke devotes significant time to discussing the nature of reason. What he seeks to do is limit reason's abilities, and then expand the power and capability of this new anemic reason. For Locke reason has to do with clear ideas that are precisely distinct, and thus reason is capable of judging revelation. If something cannot be clearly detected using the senses, then it is nothing at all, sheer nonsense. Locke thereby transformed the Protestant notion of sole reliance on Scripture as an authority (*sola Scriptura*) to the more Enlightenment approach of sole reliance on disinterested reason as the locus of ultimate authority. It is in his discussion of judging the authenticity of manuscripts (and his discussion here makes it clear he has the Bible in mind), that Locke is most indebted to Simon's prior work with its multiple editorial layers.

In Locke's *First Treatise of Government* we find a quite radical articulation of modern individualism. As Hahn and Wiker note, this individualism takes the place of the more natural authority found in families. This served Locke's more significant political and economic goal of placing rule in the propertied classes, as represented by the Parliament which emerged after the English Civil Wars, rather than the more familial monarchy style of ruling of an earlier age. His *Second Treatise of Government* finished the job of the first, rooting all rights in what he took to be the fundamental right, namely private property. Locke's argument here might be viewed as a biblical defense of Francis Bacon's conquest of nature with the goal of earthly comfort and security as the reward for such scientific labor, but also an exegetical defense of Boyle's Royal Society.

Locke's scriptural work was intended to minimize faith commitments to the barest minimum possible, in order to further his political goals. Indeed, his *The Reasonableness of Christianity* basically boils down to an apologetic for the notion that the only really important thing for which Scripture demands the adherence of faith is that Jesus was in fact the Messiah. With such a doctrinal reduction, there would no longer be any reason for violent religious controversies. Borrowing Hahn's and Wiker's phrase, the important thing for Locke was "civic morality." In *A Paraphrase and Notes on the Epistles of St. Paul*, Locke focuses at the outset on demonstrating how incredibly "obscure" Paul appears to be at first glance. Locke provided a solution to penetrating Paul's apparent obscurity. He urged the readers to discard commentaries and just read the epistles themselves. He moreover cautioned against any attempt to a unified, or we might say canonical, biblical interpretation. Rather, each text must be taken on its own, apart from the others. In his own commentary, which would prove incredibly influential, Locke prepared the way for the emphasis in modern biblical criticism of the New Testament for assuming a sharp distinction between Judaizing factions within early Christianity and those opposed to them. Locke's Pauline commentary was influential and paved the way for future Pauline scholarship. As just one example of this, the great eighteenth century German biblical scholar Johann David Michaelis penned the preface for the German edition of Locke's *Paraphrase*.

An important transitional figure standing in both the seventeenth and eighteenth centuries, is John Toland (1670-1722), born the year Spinoza published his *Tractatus Theologico-Politicus*.[88] Examining Toland shows how so many of the skeptical conclusions of late eighteenth and nineteenth century historical critics were already firmly in place in the seventeenth century. Toland's 1704 *Letters to Serena* establishes what Hahn and Wiker label a "method of equivocation" in Toland's notion of "two doctrines," the idea that the enlightened philosopher must hide some things from the more ignorant masses, which hearkens back to (possibly Locke), Spinoza, Hobbes, Descartes, Machiavelli, Marsilius, and, we might add the Latin Averroist tradition more broadly. Toland continued his "method of equivocation"

---

88. In this portion on Toland, I draw extensively from Hahn and Wiker, *Politicizing the Bible*, in their twelfth chapter, "Revolution, Radicals, Republicans, and John Toland," 487-541.

in his 1720 *Pantheisticon* which attempted to explain Toland's pantheism. In it he clearly called for the enlightened philosopher to separate from the unenlightened masses. Such an enlightened philosopher could speak with the people in the crowds, but must only reason with other enlightened philosophers.

The same year Toland published his *Pantheisticon* he also published his *Clidophorus, or Of the Exoteric and Esoteric Philosophy*, wherein he continued his hermeneutical discussion of the role of his "double philosophy," this time because of the threat of potential persecution. Toland was a careful reader of Machiavelli, and here Toland lashes out against priestcraft and religious hypocrisy, which Machiavelli had so praised as the dissembling necessary for a good ruler. For Toland, clergy abuse their positions of authority and use the ignorance and naiveté of the crowds to amass wealth for themselves, and all under the guise of sacred "mysteries." Toland apparently hoped to construct a secular theology based on rewriting superstitious religious "myths" and reducing the supernatural to the natural.

Resembling Locke, Toland spent time among radical and skeptical intellectual groups in the Dutch Republic. And as with Locke, Toland inserted himself into the active politics of his day. In particular, Toland became an apologist for the Hanoverian succession. Toland hoped to intervene in political matters, making a long-lasting difference in the secular realm of politics for future generations. In this context he decided to teach the House of Hanover the radical skeptical philosophy he had imbibed, so that he could teach the future rulers his secular theology. He thus began his brief friendship with Sophia of Hanover, as well as with Sophie, her daughter, who would become Queen of Prussia. Although he failed, Toland had viewed the Hanoverian succession as the way to achieve a secular theology that would spread through England and transform Christianity by secularizing it.

Similar to Spinoza and Machiavelli before him, Toland put forward natural explanations to explain away any apparent miracle in Scripture. Any explanation would do so long as it was natural and not mysterious or supernatural. For Toland, reason alone was sufficient to understand Scripture, which must be studied as any other book. Moreover, since there was no supernatural, no miracles, nothing mysterious, there was no need for priesthood nor for priestly mediation. His assumptions here would govern the rest of modern historical–criticism, with its transformation of the Bible into a book like any other, its refusal to allow for the supernatural and instead seeking out a natural, any natural, explanation in its place, and its view of priesthood as a devolution or corruption of what came before. Toland, as with later historical critical exegetes, would understand history as a decline into superstition and priestly corruption from an earlier purely rational faith. The hope was to climb out of the superstition and return to the rational faith aided by secular reason.

BETWEEN ATHENS AND JERUSALEM: THE ENLIGHTENMENT AND STATE SPONSORED BIBLICAL CRITICISM

It is in the eighteenth century that we find exegesis recognizable today as historical criticism consciously severed from ecclesial or theological foundations. Johann Salomo Semler (1725–1791), one of the first to engage in such criticism, brought Simon's works into the German language.[89] By translating his posthumously published *Ethics*, Johann Lorenz Schmidt (1702–1749) brought Spinoza into the German reading world. Schmidt's goal, as Jonathan Sheehan explains, was "to tear the Bible out of the hands of traditional Christian theology."[90] Johann David Michaelis (1717–1791) emerged as the paragon of philological analysis, and brought such analyses into the modern world bereft of explicit theological concerns. Michaelis himself was committed to his theology, but with his work, we find the transformation of the Bible into a cultural artifact, and biblical studies transformed into a form of cultural historical studies.[91]

What was occurring, at least in the German speaking world of the eighteenth and nineteenth centuries, was the supplanting of moral, theological, and authority structures and discourse which located its foundation in the Old Testament, with Classical Greek and Roman cultural values and civic authority structures. The culmination of such attitudes, of course, can be found in Julius Wellhausen's friend and colleague Ulrich von Wilamowitz-Moellendorff (1848–1931).[92] The founding purpose of particular universities in the eighteenth century German speaking world was often explicitly connected with matters of state. As an example, the Georg-August-Universität in Göttingen, where Wellhausen was later a student and then a professor until his death, began to produce qualified state officials for King

---

89. Sheehan, *Enlightenment Bible*, 103–4, 114–15, and 180; and Woodbridge, "German Responses," 65–87.

90. Sheehan, *Enlightenment Bible*, 126.

91. Legaspi, *Death of Scripture*, especially ix–xii, 79–153, and 155–65; and Sheehan, *Enlightenment Bible*, 186–220.

92. Legaspi, *Death of Scripture*, 56–61 and 64–68; Sheehan, *Enlightenment Bible*, 213; Williamson, *Longing for Myth*, 1–18, 22–25, 35–41, and 56–71; and the comments in Horkheimer and Adorno, *Dialektik der Aufklärung*, 370n42, 372–73n46, 376n77, and 378n97.

George II, for whom the university was named. In general, the production of faithful state servants was the very *raison d'être* of German universities; the German university was in a very real way a tool of the state.[93]

During this time, we find the works of a number of scholars, universally recognized as founding figures of modern historical biblical criticism, clearly building on what came before. We have, for example, Gotthold Lessing (1729-1781), whose famous Wolfenbüttel Fragments, written by Hermann Samuel Reimarus (1694-1768), are popularly associated with the advent of historical Jesus research. The history and figures we have already covered up to this point, tremendously influenced Reimarus. As just a few examples, Reimarus' doctoral dissertation was actually on Machiavelli, and it was on the basis of this dissertation that Reimarus became a professor of philosophy. Moreover, Reimarus was a close reader of Toland, following Toland's advice to keep his true beliefs secret. He further supported the Locke-influenced Christian Wolff. What Lessing published of Reimarus, however, were his more radical private views. Reimarus was not alone in his radical views; Spinoza exerted a far more thoroughgoing influence on intellectual life in Germany from the end of the seventeenth century and well into the eighteenth century. This was not only through more obscure (to historians of biblical scholarship) figures like Johann Georg Wachter (1663-1757), Matthew Knutzen (1646-1764), and Friedrich Wilhelm Stosch (1648-1704), but also to more significant figures within the standard histories of biblical scholarship like Schmidt and Semler, whom we have already mentioned, and thus Johann Gottfried Eichhorn (1752-1827). As we mentioned above, Schmidt, responsible for the Werthheim Bible, was the first to publish a German translation of Spinoza's *Ethics*. Lessing completely assimilated Spinoza via Schmidt's German text of Spinoza's *Ethics*.[94]

Historical Jesus scholarship was to take another bound, again grounded in Reimarus, the Machiavelli specialist, through the work of David Friedrich Strauss, but the biblical work of Semler was likewise important for the future of modern biblical criticism. Semler was a devotee of Richard Simon, whose work he brought into German translation. Semler also published an edition of Lodewijk Meyer's (Spinoza's friend) *Philosophia* in Latin and Semler placed Spinoza's *Tractatus* in Latin bound together with this work

---

93. Legaspi, *Death of Scripture*, 27-51. See similar comments on the development of the modern university from the 19th century to the present in Hauerwas, *State of the University*, 6 and 12-32.

94. Hahn and Wiker, *Politicizing the Bible*, 547-52 and 555-62; Vaysse, "Spinoza dans la problématique," 65-74; Muslow, "Libertinismus," 37-71; Israel, *Radical Enlightenment*, 628-63; Wollgast, "Spinoza und die deutsche," 163-79; and Bell, *Spinoza in Germany*.

by Meyer. This is important because it emphasizes the way in which Semler (and the others who juxtaposed these two texts in the same published bound volume) intended to see Meyer's work as a prolegomenon to Spinoza's. Furthermore, Semler was incredibly influential on Lessing, and even more so on his student Johann Jakob Griesbach (1745–1812) who would set the synoptic problem and the historical study of the Gospels on a whole new track with a version of the two source hypothesis.[95]

Michaelis, however, was the premier Bible scholar of the eighteenth century and was one of Göttingen's early professors. He played an immensely important role in the transformation of the study of the Bible from primarily a theological task to a cultural and historical artifact, and if politics played less of an explicit role in Michaelis's work than it had in the previous century for Hobbes and Spinoza, it nevertheless provided an underlying framework, involving a complex network of assumptions, within which Michaelis operated.[96]

Michaelis's work was profoundly shaped by classical philology, as practiced within the general neo-humanist movement then reigning in the German-speaking world, and particularly as advanced by his teacher Johann Matthias Gesner (1691–1761) and colleague Christian Gottlob Heyne (1729–1812). Gesner's famous Seminarium Philologicum at Göttingen set the standard for rigorous classical philology, and would influence the practice of ancient philology up to the present. The key context in which the Philological Seminar operated, and which it developed further, was one where the humanistic discipline of philology itself formed scholars in a particular way that was intended to shape them into productive useful civic gentlemen. Philology became an important component in a wider cultural process of building up a robust civil society. Michaelis was instrumental in carrying the type of philological methodology epitomized both by Gesner and his successor Heyne into the realm of biblical studies, justifying such study apart from any explicit theological rationale.[97]

We find the epitome of such modern endeavors in the work done at the University of Berlin.[98] Schleiermacher and his only son's godfather Wilhelm Martin Leberecht de Wette (1780–1849) radically transformed the theological curriculum at the Friedrich-Wilhelms-University (founded in

---

95. Hahn and Wiker, *Politicizing the Bible*, 355–56, 404, and 553–55.

96. On Michaelis, see e.g., Legaspi, *Death of Scripture*, especially 79–153; Smend, *From Astruc to Zimmerli*, 30–42; and Sheehan, *Enlightenment Bible*, 184, 186–87, 190, 197, and 210–15.

97. Legaspi, *Death of Scripture*, 53–78; and Vick, "Greek Origins," 483–500.

98. D'Costa, *Theology in the Public Square*, 8–20.

1810) as members of its first theological faculty.[99] Building on the model of the Enlightenment university, namely Göttingen, the University of Berlin set the standard for western universities devoted to the concerns of the modern project. Sheehan has emphasized how both Schleiermacher and even more so de Wette excluded Jews and Catholics from their modern endeavors, which, in the case of Schleiermacher, was an attempt to refashion Christianity apart from any biblical moorings.[100] The *Wissenschaft des Judentums* movement is one nineteenth century pinnacle of these trends within the German-speaking academy.[101]

During this time, Christianity became ever more associated with the Greco-Roman world in German-speaking scholarship, at the same time that German culture represented in the academy was attempting to find inspiration from Greco-Roman antiquity. A sharp dichotomy was beginning to take shape, influenced by comparative philology, between what would be called Aryan or Indo-European (Greek, Indian, etc.) and Semitic (especially Jewish and Muslim). Scholars began severing Christianity from its Jewish roots and presenting it, along with newly "discovered" Buddhism, as an Aryan or Indo-European (Greek) religious tradition distinct from the wholly Semitic Judaism, and Islam which, although the majority of Muslims then as now were and are non-Arabs, was viewed as completely Semitic.[102]

Wilamowitz's work in classical philology became an attempt to conquer the classical world through his scholarship, and uphold classical antiquity as a model for German culture. His work cannot be completely separated from the Prussian nationalism which inspired him.[103] Prussian and German nationalism was at the heart of most such endeavors to secularize the study of the Bible in the German academy.[104]

Secularization, in this context, should not be confused with the more common understanding entrenched in some post-Enlightenment desire to see the end of "religion," but rather in the privatization of 'religion' begun with the Nominalist movement and the Reformation itself, notwithstanding how theological and "religious" such movements may have been, and epitomized in the dissolution of the monasteries in the Reformation and

---

99. Smend, *From Astruc to Zimmerli*, 50–51.

100. Sheehan, *Enlightenment Bible*, 230, 234–36, and 238–39.

101. Ibid., 239.

102. Masuzawa, *Invention of World Religions*, xii–xiii, 24–26 and 145, 147, 149, 152 and 179–206; and Sheehan, *Enlightenment Bible*, 238–39.

103. Legaspi, *Death of Scripture*, 57; Sheehan, *Enlightenment Bible*, 213; and Momigliano, "Religious History," 49–64.

104. Sheehan, *Enlightenment Bible*, 233.

early modern period.[105] After all, the primary definition the *Oxford English Dictionary* has for "secularization" is the transformation of religious institutions and property for non-religious use and ownership.[106] Thus, religious and theological concerns do not preclude such drives for secularization, in fact, as Michael Gillespie has recently shown, what is often called the modern secular project has always been undergirded with theological concerns.[107]

Religionswissenschaft and its philology, as well as *Religionsgeschichte* and its philhellenism, developed in contexts that upheld what was understood as Aryan (Greco-Roman, Indo-European), in which was placed a de-Judaized New Testament and early Christianity, and which denigrated Semitic culture, especially the Old Testament and Islam.[108] Julius Wellhausen (1844–1918), a Bismarck admirer, entered the scene in this broader cultural context.[109] One result, intended or unintended, of the biblical historical scholarship of the time, was an anti-Semitism among certain scholarly circles in Germany that worked its way well into the twentieth century. Such anti-Semitic sentiments initially pushed for the removal of the Old Testament from Christian Scripture (Adolf von Harnack), to the Old Testament's replacement with German folklore (Friedrich Delitzsch), to the legal separation of Jews from Gentiles within the German state (Gerhard Kittel).[110]

Such anti-Semitic leanings were present already in Wellhausen's work.[111] In nations where governments and peoples adopted a hostile stance toward the Catholic Church, and particularly toward the papacy, anti-Semitism often went hand-in-hand with anti-Catholicism. Stanley Hauerwas insightfully remarks that:

> Catholics understood they often became for Protestants the Jews, that is, Catholics had been surpassed. Nowhere was this more

---

105. Duffy, *Stripping of the Altars*, 383–85, 397, 402–3, and 462; MacCulloch, *Reformation*, 163, 200–1, 227, 289, 292, 353, 379, 452, 559, and 661; and Baskerville, *English Monks*.

106. *Oxford English Dictionary XIV*, 849.

107. Gillespie, *Theological Origins*.

108. Masuzawa, *Invention of World Religions*, xii–xiii, 24–26 and 145–206.

109. Smend, *From Astruc to Zimmerli*, 91–102; and Momigliano, "Religious History," 49–64

110. Meeks, "Nazi New Testament Professor," 513–44; Arnold and Weisberg, "Centennial Review," 441–57; and O'Neill, "Adolf von Harnack," 1–18.

111. Weinfeld, *Normative and Sectarian Judaism*, 286–90; Levenson, *Hebrew Bible*, 11–13, 15, and 42; and Smend, "Wellhausen und das Judentum," 249–82, although Smend is careful to distinguish what is present in Wellhausen from anti-Semitism, which Smend distances Wellhausen from.

apparent than in the scholarly guilds surrounding the study of scripture in which Second Temple Judaism became the dead priest-ridden religion that the charismatic Christianity of the New Testament replaced. Protestant biblical scholarship simply reproduced that story with their triumph in the Reformation.[112]

A TALE OF TWO CITIES?: CHURCH AND STATE

An important factor in understanding the political context discussed above is the role of the papacy as a transnational institution. The story of the papacy's rise to political power out of perceived necessity following upon Constantine's relocation of the heart of the Roman Empire to Constantinople is well known. Since at least the eleventh or twelfth century, however, local rulers, princes, nobles, and kings began the long process of state centralization which culminated in the birth of modern states which many date to the Treaty of Westphalia in 1648, as we have already seen. As rulers attempted to centralize, strengthening royal tribunals over and against ecclesiastical courts, extracting resources from the peasantry, liquidating or subsuming guilds and waging and winning wars, the papacy became ever more an obstacle to various rulers' desires for sovereignty.[113]

Religious orders, particularly those that circumvented the authority structures of state appointed national bishops, became signs of the transnational authority of the pope who was viewed as a threat to state autonomy. As late as 1829, the bishops of 555 of the 646 dioceses spread across the globe were appointed by heads of state.[114] Resistance to the transnational Catholic Church was named differently in different regions of Europe: e.g., Josephism in Austria and Pombalism in Portugal. These movements began with real theological concerns in a growing medieval Conciliarism that found an answer to the question of ultimate authority in ecumenical councils as opposed to the papacy.[115]

French Gallicanism became the paradigmatic expression of Conciliarism, just as France emerged victorious from its violent civil wars as the paradigmatic modern state. What began as a theological debate quickly became a political tool in the form of the Gallican Articles which would elicit a formal response from the papacy in the First Vatican Council's document,

112. Hauerwas, *State of the University*, 73n46.

113. Cavanaugh, "Killing for the Telephone Company," 243–74; Ertman, *Birth of the Leviathan*; and Cavanaugh, "Fire Strong Enough," 397–420.

114. Costigan, "State Appointment," 82–96.

115. Portier, "Church Unity," 27–37.

Pastor Aeternus.[116] In an international church where the majority of bishops were appointed by heads of state, it is easy to see how the call for a council of bishops trumping the papacy was a thinly veiled argument for state dominance over the Church.[117] It is in this context that Ultramontanism developed as a popular transnational Catholic movement centered around the papacy, involving a complex web of devotional practices particularly focused on Marian devotions.[118] Such a response, which was both political and theological, culminated in Vatican I's dogmatic definition of papal infallibility in *Pastor Aeternus* (1870), in Pope Leo XIII's Neo-Thomistic revival represented especially in his encyclical *Aeterni Patris* (1879), and in the Church's attack on Modernism epitomized in Pope St. Pius X's encyclical *Pascendi Dominici Gregis* (1907).[119]

Already on the eve of the Reformation rulers in Europe viewed the papacy's transnational nature as a threat to their desires for sovereignty. Rulers in places like Spain, Naples, and France secured concordats limiting the pope's authority within their realms, through their ability to appoint bishops, curtail papal taxes, etc. Pre-Reformation concordats were an attempt by Catholic regions to increase their sovereign authority, just as state rulers unable to broker such concordats, used the Protestant Reformation as justification for their authority in their realms over and against the papacy.[120]

This battle between states and the Church, and particularly against the transnational nature of the Church and thus against the office of the papacy, is an important but too often neglected part of the background to the rise

---

116. Schatz, *Der päpstliche Primat*, 174-87; Portier, "Church Unity," 27-37; and Heft, *John XXII*, 214.

117. Portier, "Church Unity," 27-37.

118. Portier, *Divided Friends*, 8-9; Duffy, *Saints & Sinners*, 260-318; von Arx, introduction, 1-11; Yonke, "Cardinal Johannes von Geissel," 12-38; Padberg, "Cardinal Louis-Edouard-Désiré Pie," 39-60; Larkin, "Cardinal Paul Cullen," 61-84; von Arx, "Cardinal Henry Edward Manning," 85-102; Ciani, "Cardinal Camillo Mazzella," 103-17; Fogarty, "Cardinal William Henry O'Connell," 118-46; and Portier, "Church Unity," 27-37.

119. Portier, *Divided Friends*, 7-12, 14, 33-34, and 44-45; Jodock, "Introduction I," 3, 10-11, 14-15, and 18; Lease, "Vatican Foreign Policy," 31-55; Misner, "Catholic Anti-Modernism," 56-87; Daly, "Theological and Philosophical Modernism," 95-96 and 98-102; Tavard, "Blondel's *Action*," 143, 146, 151-58, and 167-68; Hill, "Politics of Loisy's Modernist Theology," 169-72, 176-78, and 180-89; Talar, "Innovation and Biblical Interpretation," 194, 202, and 205-11; Bernardi, "Social Modernism," 280-85; Komonchak, "Enlightenment and the Construction of Roman Catholicism," 31-59; and Hennesey, "Leo XIII's Thomistic Revival," 185-97.

120. Duffy, *Saints & Sinners*, 175 and 199; and Cavanaugh, "Fire Strong Enough," 400-1.

of modern biblical criticism.[121] As we have seen, one of the earliest occurrences of biblical criticism that laid the groundwork for modern historical criticism came from the medieval Muslim world. The Muslim polemical development of biblical criticism epitomized with Ibn Ḥazm, served a political role, particularly in relationship to the Caliphate structure. When these critical methodologies, assumptions, and conclusions are brought into the medieval world of Christendom, we see some of the ways they entered into the throne vs. altar debate we have just described. It is in the early modern and enlightenment periods especially that we see how previous work in such criticism came to be tools of statecraft, explicit claims to objectivity notwithstanding: seventeenth-century scriptural exegesis underpinned early modern monarchical and democratic politics alike; eighteenth-century biblical philology served colonial and imperial designs; and nineteenth-century historical criticism was often at the service of nationalist concerns. The remainder of this volume will look at the seventeenth century, and particularly the works of La Peyrère, Hobbes, and Spinoza, as a turning point in this history. These figures become an important bridge between the political, philosophical, and technical exegetical skills that preceded them, with the more specialized modern historical biblical criticism that emerges through the eighteenth-century Enlightenment.

---

121. Indeed, this is one of the many significant contributions that Hahn and Wiker make in their *Politicizing the Bible*, wherein their entire volume draws attention to this much neglected, but incredibly important aspect to this history.

2

The Biblical Criticism of Isaac La Peyrère in Context

ALTHOUGH ISAAC LA PEYRÈRE is not the first name Bible scholars think of when writing about the origins of modern biblical criticism, he is an important figure within this history. Julius Wellhausen, the father of the documentary hypothesis, associated biblical criticism's origins with La Peyrère.[1] In his survey of the critical study of the Old Testament, Moshe Goshen-Gottstein identifies La Peyrère, along with Baruch Spinoza and Richard Simon, as marking a turning point in the history of biblical exegesis. It was during this time period that a new type of biblical criticism emerged.[2] La Peyrère is especially associated with early anthropological and evolutionary theories, since he was the single most important figure in propagating the idea that human origins predated the biblical Adam. Although La Peyrère's work considering pre-Adamites is noteworthy for anthropological and geographical studies, it is even more essential for the birth of modern biblical criticism, as we shall see below.

This chapter consists of three major parts. The first part situates La Peyrère's life and work within its social and historical context. The second

---

1. Wellhausen, *Prolegomena*, 6. His comments here pertain specifically to the study of the Pentateuch, and significantly, Wellhausen lists Spinoza along with La Peyrère in this regard.

2. Goshen-Gottstein, "Textual Criticism," 376. Lambe makes a sharp dichotomy between what he calls "critics" and "skeptics" within the seventeenth century, placing La Peyrère squarely on the side of the skeptics, in "Critics and Skeptics," 272–92. Goshen-Gottstein is aware of La Peyrère's skeptical attitude, but still places him in an important position within the broader history of modern biblical criticism.

portion analyzes La Peyrère's hermeneutical program, including a detailed examination of specific instances of La Peyrère's biblical exegesis. The final section places La Peyrère's biblical project within the more specific cultural and political context which such a program served: primarily the political desires of the Prince of Condé, for whom La Peyrère served as secretary and diplomat. This chapter highlights La Peyrère's central place in the history of modern biblical interpretation, specifically his important contributions to the development of Pentateuchal criticism. La Peyrère's biblical criticism was rooted in his political commitment which became the very *raison d'être* of his textual analyses and the methods he forged. La Peyrère influenced the future of modern biblical criticism especially through his friendship with Richard Simon, who would become known as the father of the historical critical method.

BORDEAUX AND BEYOND: LA PEYRÈRE'S PLACE IN THE SEVENTEENTH CENTURY

The date of Isaac La Peyrère's birth and his family's historical origin are uncertain, though Richard Popkin, the modern scholar who has done the most work on La Peyrère, argues for the likely birth date 1596. We have much more reliable knowledge about his immediate family and place of birth, namely, Bordeaux, France. He comes from a wealthy Huguenot family living in a region of southern France where it was not uncommon for Protestant families to be descendants of Marranos, the Jewish converts to Christianity from the Iberian Peninsula. This fact, coupled with La Peyrère's Marrano-like theology and Marrano-sounding name (Pereira was a known Marrano name), have led many like Popkin to speculate that La Peyrère was in fact of Marrano heritage. La Peyrère's family was in business with the Prince of Condé, and beginning in 1640, La Peyrère entered the Prince's service as his personal secretary. Through this service La Peyrère became a member of the elite intellectual circle that included such important seventeenth century thinkers as Hugo Grotius, Pierre Gassendi, Gabriel Naudé, and Blaise Pascal.[3]

3. Pietsch, *Isaac La Peyrère*, 125–33 and 185–93; Gabriel, "Periegesis and Skepticism," 160–63; Nellen, "Growing Tension," 818; Wachtel, "Théologies marranes," 69–100; Popkin, *History of Scepticism*, 221 and 362n70; Popkin, *Isaac La Peyrère*, 5–6, 17, 21–25, 95–96, 177n1, and 183n106; Popkin, "Marrano Theology," 97–126; Yovel, *Spinoza and Other Heretics 1*, 81–82; Robinson, "Isaac de la Peyrère," 117–30; Oddos, "Recherches," 49; Yardeni, "La religion," 245–59; Markreich, "Notes on Transformation," 273 and 273n74; Schoeps, "Philosemitism," 141; and McKee, "Isaac de La Peyrère," 456.

La Peyrère's service to the Prince of Condé as secretary and diplomat thrust him into the middle of the complex post-Treaty of Westphalia (1648) seventeenth century politics. After the death of the Prince of Condé, Henry II de Bourbon (1646), La Peyrère remained in the service of his successor Louis II de Bourbon, although that appointment was not made until 1647. La Peyrère not only served Louis II de Bourbon, the new Prince of Condé, as his secretary, but also functioned as an important diplomat, travelling throughout Europe, to such places as the Dutch Republic and England. As Condé's diplomat and secretary La Peyrère befriended Queen Christina of Sweden, the patroness of René Descartes. Queen Christina, who abdicated her throne in 1654 and converted to Catholicism in 1655, became patroness of La Peyrère in addition to Descartes. In particular, Queen Christina supported La Peyrère in the completion of his infamous *Prae-Adamitae*.[4]

La Peyrère wrote a number of prominent works that at first glance seem simply unrelated. I argue, however, that on closer inspection these texts are intimately connected with one another. His manuscripts considered topics such as the geography of Iceland (*Relation de l'Islande*) and Greenland (*Relation du Groenland*), speculations concerning human origins and the existence of humans before the biblical Adam (*Prae-Adamitae* and *Systema Theologicum*), as well as a messianic speculation about the return of Jews to the Holy Land (*Du Rappel des Juifs*). As we shall soon see, all of these works had implications for his biblical hermeneutic, spelled out most explicitly in *Prae-Adamitae* (including *Systema Theologicum*, which was usually bound together in one volume), which was inextricably tied to his contemporary political concerns.[5]

La Peyrère was arrested on account of the publication of *Prae-Adamitae*, and he followed Christina of Sweden's lead by converting to Catholicism one year after she had, when he was advised that he should enter the Catholic Church. After his conversion, he penned a formal recantation of his views to Pope Alexander VII, and even appeared in person before the pope. Pope Alexander asked La Peyrère to consider remaining in Rome, but he refused the Pope's offer, and instead returned to Paris. In Paris, he continued working for the Prince of Condé, but no longer functioned as the Prince's

---

4. Pietsch, *Isaac La Peyrère*, 2, 69, 131, 141–42, 190, and 192–94; Weststeijn, "Spinoza sinicus," 543; Quennehen, "L'auteur des *Préadamites*," 363; Starobinski-Safran, "Raison et conflits," 97; Livingstone, "Preadamite Theory," 6; Åkerman, *Queen Christina*, 25–26, 32, 186, and 204; and Popkin, *Isaac La Peyrère*, 12–14 and 180n50.

5. Livingstone, "Cultural Politics," 207; Livingstone, *Adam's Ancestors*, 27–31; Livingstone, "Geographical Inquiry," 95–96 and 99–102; Livingstone, "Geography," 365; Gabriel, "Periegesis and Skepticism," 160, 163–64 and 170; Almond, *Adam & Eve*, 52–54; and Popkin, *Isaac La Peyrère*, 6, 10, 12, and 178n20.

secretary, but served rather as the Prince's librarian, from which service he eventually retired in 1665 at the age of 69. We do not know what became of his wife or any children. After his retirement, he joined the French Oratorians as a lay member. From the time of his retirement until his death in 1676, he resided with the Oratorians in their Oratory at the seminary Notre Dame des Vertus in Aubervilliers, just outside of Paris. There La Peyrère continued to receive his pension from his service as Condé's librarian. La Peyrère's decision to join the Oratorians proved to be instrumental in the dissemination of his method of interpretation as modern biblical criticism entered the eighteenth century because it was through the Oratorians that La Peyrère established a close friendship with the Oratorian priest Richard Simon. This friendship forged at Notre Dame des Vertus was cause for the further spread of La Peyrère's work.[6]

A PIONEER OF MODERN BIBLICAL CRITICISM: A CRITICAL EXAMINATION OF LA PEYRÈRE'S EXEGESIS

What makes La Peyrère's work so important for our discussion is the manner in which he built upon the work of others, ultimately forging a path that later biblical critics would follow as they founded the project of modern biblical criticism.[7] La Peyrère is one of the first and most significant intellectuals since the medieval period to call into question the entire Mosaic authorship of the Pentateuch; and few thinkers before the eighteenth century did so with as many textual arguments as La Peyrère. Previously, some Jewish and Christian scholars had implied that certain passages in the Pentateuch appeared post-Mosaic, and they raised questions about particular passages which seemed to point beyond Moses to a later author. Other theologians then raised questions which they answered in defense of Mosaic authorship. In rarer instances, some theologians posited a later editor of Moses' works, like Ezra. But it was not until the second part of La Peyrère's *Prae-Ada-*

---

6. Pietsch, *Isaac La Peyrère*, 14, 52, 62, 69, 154, 190, 198–200, 205, 215–18, and 231–41; Quennehen, "L'auteur des *Préadamites*," 350–51, 351n10, 364, 367–70, and 373; Wetsel, "Isaac de La Peyrère," 380n26 and 381; van Asselt, "Adam en Eva," 101; Åkerman, *Queen Christina*, 25–26; Popkin, *Isaac La Peyrère*, 14–15, 17–18, and 20; and McKee, "Isaac de La Peyrère," 459. On the importance of La Peyrère's biblical exegesis in the history of modern biblical criticism, see Gibert, *L'invention critique*; Räisänen, *Marcion*, 137–52; Grafton, *Defenders of the Text*, 204–13; Popkin, *Isaac La Peyrère*, 42–59; and Popkin, "Bible Criticism and Social Science," 339–60.

7. Legaspi describes well the path modern biblical criticism took from the seventeenth to nineteenth centuries in, "What Ever Happened," 10–11. See also Gibert, *L'invention critique*.

mitae (his *Systema Theologicum*), which was composed by 1648, that any non-Muslim scholars argued so vigorously against the Mosaic authorship of the Pentateuch as a whole. La Peyrère's stringent argument against Mosaic authorship became the origin of modern source criticism.

As Wellhausen noted above, centuries of scholarship built upon La Peyrère's foundation, driving the development of source criticism into the twentieth and twenty-first centuries. This denial of Mosaic authorship became the backbone of La Peyrère's biblical criticism, but he utilized a host of other resources to aid in his exegetical program as well. La Peyrère's famous geographical investigations were integral to his biblical hermeneutic, and he utilized these studies to help show errors in the biblical texts, just as he found inconsistencies internal to the texts themselves. For La Peyrère, "The Bible . . . comprised a set of culturally specific books aimed at local audiences, and could not be treated as a seamless, transhistorical object."[8] Finally, what drove his biblical interpretation was his unique messianic theology, which was as political as it was theological. It is to these hermeneutical edifices that we now turn.

Moses and the Authorship of the Pentateuch: An Enduring Proposal

La Peyrère denied, almost wholesale, the Mosaic authorship of the Pentateuch.[9] Although it is not entirely clear which portions of his *Prae-Adamitae* landed him in trouble, the censure of his work was almost certainly on account of his denial of Mosaic authorship and pre-Adamite hypothesis, namely that humans predated Adam. Although the denial of the Mosaic authorship of most of the Pentateuch in Hobbes' *Leviathan* (1651) was published before La Peyrère was able to publish his own more thorough critique in *Prae-Adamitae* (including his *Systema Theologicum*, 1965, which is where the critique is found), La Peyrère's text had already circulated throughout Europe long before. The first part, *Prae-Adamitae*, which he began around 1635, was circulated shortly after La Peyrère completed this section, by 1643.[10] In fact, well before either *Leviathan* or *Prae-Adamitae*

---

8. Poole, *World Makers*, 28.

9. Bernier, *La critique du Pentateuque*, 25, 27, 39, 118, 127, 132–46, 148, 149, 152–53, 157–58, 171, 174, 190, 193, 205, 222–24, 230, 242–45, 250, and 254–55; Nellen, "Growing Tension," 822; Jorink, "Horrible and Blasphemous," 429; Wetsel, "Isaac de La Peyrère," 376 and 379; van Asselt, "Adam en Eva," 106; Popkin, *History of Scepticism*, 222–23; Popkin, *Third Force*, 16–18, 32–34, 37, 159, 352 and 355; Popkin, *Isaac La Peyrère*, 1–2, 48–49, 69, 71 and 78; and Starobinski-Safran, "Raison et conflits," 99–100.

10. Quennehen, "Lapeyrère," 244. The earliest reference we have to this work is a

were published, scores of intellectuals throughout Europe were publishing refutations (of which Hugo Grotius' appears to be the first) of La Peyrère's unpublished manuscript.[11]

We cannot be sure as to how much of La Peyrère's completed work was in circulation before its publication in 1655. Noel Malcolm believes that only the first part of the work, which does not contain any explicit question of Mosaic authorship, was available, and that the second much longer portion, *Systema Theologicum*, was only completed by 1648.[12] La Peyrère's text was certainly complete by 1648, and it seems likely that the general idea of the majority of the second part was already present, even if only in inchoate form. This certainly was the case with his *Du Rappel des Juifs* which was based on ideas he incorporated in *Prae-Adamitae* and was published much earlier.

The idea that Moses wrote the Pentateuch, although usually assumed as true before La Peyrère's time, was not always viewed as essential within

---

letter from Gabriel Naudé to Cardinal Barberini 1642 (I am uncertain as to whether this reference, which I have taken from Quennehen, "Lapeyrère," 244n6, is to Cardinal Antonio Barberini [1607-1671]—who would have been the Crown Cardinal Protector of the Kingdom of France in 1642, a friend of Cardinal Mazarin, and nephew to the then current Pope Urban VIII—or his older brother Cardinal Francesco Barberini [1597-1679]—who was also Urban VIII's nephew and was the Grand Inquisitor of the Holy Roman Inquisition at the time [1633-1679]). La Peyrère's claim is that his thought and research on the contents of *Prae-Adamitae* and *Systema Theologicum* go back at least to 1635. Two nearly identical early drafts exist, one at least from 1644. Finally, an autographed French copy by La Peyrère has also been discovered, entitled, *Traité confirmatif des Préadamites. Dissertation philosophique sur les Préadamites*, but the manuscript is not dated. See ibid., 244 and 244n7-8; Quennehen, "Un Noveau Manuscrit"; and Quennehen, "À Propos," 17-20.

11. Pietsch, *Isaac La Peyrère*, 56-57, 57nn118-19, and 99-104; Wetsel, "Isaac de La Peyrère," 379; Rubiés, "Hugo Grotius's Dissertation," 238-40; and Popkin, *Isaac La Peyrère*, 6. On the complex issues involved in the composition of *Prae-Adamitae* and *Systema Theologicum*, see Gibert, *L'invention critique*, 85n1; Malcolm, *Aspects of Hobbes*, 392-94, 393nn31-32, 393-94n33, and 394n37; Quennehen, "Lapeyrère," 243-55; Quennehen, "Un Noveau Manuscrit"; Quennehen, "À Propos," 17-20; and Popkin, *Isaac La Peyrère*, 42-43. What was published as *Prae-Adamitae* is actually composed of two separate works. The first is a brief text whose long title may be shortened to *Prae-Adamitae* (Pre-Adamites). The second text, whose title might be shortened to *Systema theologicum* (Theological System), is over four times the size of the first. Although the earliest known reference that might provide a clue to the origin of La Peyrère's thought on this matter is 1642, Malcolm maintains that the reference need only refer to the first part, *Prae-Adamitae*, which, from further correspondence, Malcolm concedes was probably completed by 1643. Primarily based upon other later texts which the second work, *Systema theologicum* cites, Malcolm dates the completion of the entire bound work to around 1648. Popkin believed that La Peyrère revised *Prae-Adamitae* quite frequently during 1641-1643 (*Isaac La Peyrère*, 6).

12. Malcolm, *Aspects of Hobbes*, 392-94.

Jewish and Christian traditions.[13] By the mid-seventeenth century, and well into the eighteenth century, the concept of Mosaic authorship became a much contested issue that held an important position within the theological and philosophical debates, as can be gauged in the work of scholars and philosophers as diverse as Spinoza and Voltaire, on the one hand, and Jean Astruc and Johann David Michaelis, on the other. The issue of the Mosaic authorship of the Pentateuch became viewed as the necessary attribute protecting the Bible's divine inspiration.[14]

A Brief History of Pentateuchal Source Criticism and the Denial of Mosaic Authorship

The contestation over the authorship of the Pentateuch and challenges to Moses' revelation at Sinai can be dated back to the proto-Gnostic Nasarenes just before the onset of Christianity.[15] Although he did not deny the Mosaic authorship of the Pentateuch, Marcion (ca. 85–160) is a significant critic within this history, because he cast into question the relevance of the Old Testament (and not just the Pentateuch) for Christians. Marcion worked hard to show that the Old Testament was not for Christians, that the God of the New Testament was not to be found in the Old.[16] In a letter preserved for us in Epiphanius of Salamis's (ca. between 310 and 320–403) *Panarion*, Ptolemy the Gnostic (second century AD) questioned the Mosaic origin of certain laws within the Pentateuch, although he conceded the Pentateuch's Mosaic authorship, or at least that Moses compiled the Pentateuch.[17] Celsus (second century AD) mounted a wholesale attack on Christianity, and in doing so included criticisms of the Pentateuch and the rest of the Old

---

13. Levenson, "Eighth Principle," 205–25.

14. Bernier, *La critique du Pentateuque*, 14–15, 25, and 128–29; Legaspi, *Death of Scripture*, 137–40; Gibert, *L'invention critique*, 111–13 and 169; Kugel, *How to Read the Bible*, 29–30; Popkin, *History of Scepticism*, 195–97; Popkin, "Spinoza and Bible Scholarship," 388; Popkin, *Third Force*, 16–19; Popkin, *Isaac La Peyrère*, 50 and 70–74; and Malcolm, *Aspects of Hobbes*, 383–86.

15. Bernier, *La critique du Pentateuque*, 22; Yamauchi, *Gnostic Ethics*, 60; and Young, *Introduction*, 111–12.

16. HaCohen, *Reclaiming the Hebrew Bible*, 12; Tyson, "Anti-Judaism," 198–202 and 207–8; Löhr, "Did Marcion Distinguish," 131–46; Young, *Introduction*, 110–11; and Grant, "Historical Criticism," 187.

17. Bernier, *La critique du Pentateuque*, 23; Epiphanius, *Panarion*, 199; Young, *Introduction*, 109–10; and Grant, "Historical Criticism," 186–87.

Testament, although he did not specifically challenge the Pentateuch's Mosaic authorship.[18]

A number of early Jewish and Christian texts also seemed, at points, either to implicitly call into question wholesale Mosaic authorship or else they demonstrated awareness of such concerns. On the Jewish side, texts like 2 Esdras (also called the Apocalypse of Ezra, or sometimes 4 Esdras, ca. first century AD) seemed to imply that Ezra was the author of the Torah since the original was depicted as having perished in the Babylonian destruction of Jerusalem (2 Esdras 14:22). The Babylonian Talmud (e.g., Tractate Bava Batra 14b) included questions about the possibility of the Mosaic authorship of the final portion of Deuteronomy depicting Moses's death and burial and about Moses writing Numbers 22–24 concerning the Canaanite Prophet Balaam for which Moses was not depicted as having been present. The Talmudic responses to the questions posed were that God dictated to Moses what to write (this was Rabbi Simeon's position) or that Joshua wrote the final verses (this was Rabbi Judah's position). Although this Talmudic debate did not represent an affront to the traditional view of the Torah's Mosaic authorship—but rather a defense—it does provide evidence that very early on there were some challenges to this position.[19]

On the Christian side, the so-called Clementine Homilies from approximately the third or fourth century AD depict Moses dictating the Pentateuch to seventy elders who later wrote it down after Moses died, including the passage about Moses' death. Origen (184/185–253/254) was aware of a some challenges to the Mosaic authorship of the Pentateuch and he conceded that portions of the Pentateuch may have been penned by others. Jerome (ca. 345–420 or ca. 347–420) was likewise aware of these challenges, and especially of the claim that Ezra may have had an editorial hand in the final form of the Pentateuch, to which he posed no objection.[20]

In the third century, the anti-Christian Roman Neo-Platonist philosopher Porphyry (234–ca. 305 or 233–309) likewise challenged the Mosaic authorship of the Pentateuch as well as the revelation at Sinai. Porphyry's were the most serious challenges to the Mosaic authorship of the Pentateuch from antiquity. Unlike other critics of Judaism and Christianity of the time, Porphyry made careful study of the Bible. He gathered together all of the arguments against the Bible he could find from Gnostic, Marcionite, Manichaean and other sources. It should come as no surprise that after

---

18. Young, *Introduction*, 113; Grant, "Historical Criticism," 186; and Young, "Celsus," 192–3.

19. Homan, "How Moses Gained," 111–32; and Young, *Introduction*, 114.

20. Bernier, *La critique du Pentateuque*, 22; Homan, "How Moses Gained," 111–32; and Young, *Introduction*, 108–9 and 115.

361, when the Roman Emperor Julian took control of the Roman Empire he borrowed his major arguments against Christianity from Porphyry. One of Porphyry's main points of attack was to detail the portions of Genesis he found to be absurd. Porphyry went further than many other critics of the time in maintaining that the entire Pentateuch was composed over one thousand years after Moses by the scribe Ezra.[21]

In the medieval period, a new stage was entered in the history of Penateuchal criticism, with Jewish, Muslim, and Christian scholars, almost all of whom were influenced by Muslim works. The earliest criticisms remained polemical, in continuity with the majority of the work that had come before. The arguments grew in sophistication, however, and eventually entered the Latin Christian world. In the second half of the ninth century, the sage Ḥiwi al-Balkhi wrote attacking the Bible. Ḥiwi came from a Jewish background, but both rabbinic Jewish writers and Karaite Jewish writers condemned his works as heretical, and it is possible that he became a Gnostic by the end of his life. We know about Ḥiwi and his polemical work especially through the medieval Jewish savant Saadia Gaon's (882–942) *Polemic Against Ḥiwi al-Balkhi*.[22]

Ḥiwi's most important text, which has only survived in Saadia's response to him, was his poetical *Book of Two Hundred Questions*, wherein Ḥiwi leveled challenges to the divine inspiration of Scripture in the form of questions and highlighting what he found to be difficulties or inconsistencies in the biblical text. The brunt of Ḥiwi's criticism, especially of the Pentateuch, focused on several points concerning how the Pentateuch depicts God—(1) as unjust; (2) as having limited knowledge; (3) as having limited power; (4) as having an inconsistent will; (5) as bloodthirsty; (6) as anthropomorphic—and his criticism also focused on a host of other problems he found in Scripture: (7) Ḥiwi denied the miracles in the Pentateuch; (8) he claimed the Bible lends evidence to the existence of multiple deities; (9) he listed what he saw to be numerous contradictions within the Bible (especially the Pentateuch but in other Old Testament books as well); (10) he saw

---

21. Homan, "How Moses Gained," 111–32; Malcolm, *Aspects of Hobbes*, 400; Kofsky, *Eusebius*, 30; Dungan, *History of the Synoptic Problem*, 91–92; Droge, *Homer or Moses*, 178; Wilken, *Christians as the Romans Saw Them*, 137 and 143; Young, *Introduction*, 114–5; Young, *Prophecy of Daniel*, 317–20; and Grant, "Historical Criticism," 194.

22. Biale, *Not in the Heavens*, 63; Homan, "How Moses Gained," 111–32; Young, *Introduction*, 116; Rosenthal, *Ḥiwi al-Balkhi*; Rosenthal, "Ḥiwi al-Balkhi," 317–42; Rosenthal, "Ḥiwi al-Balkhi (Continued)," 419–30; Rosenthal, "Ḥiwi al-Balkhi (Continued)," 79–94; Marmorstein, "Background of the Haggadah," 157–204; Malter, *Saadia Gaon*, 260–71; Davidson, *Saadia's Polemic*, 11–37; Gottheil, "Some Early Jewish," 6–12; and Schechter, "Geniza Specimens," 345–44.

biblical commandments, stories, and various statements as either a-rational or irrational.[23]

What is clear from an examination of his two hundred questions is that Ḥiwi relied upon the polemical literature which preceded him, coming from Marcion, Celsus, Porphyry, Emperor Julian the Apostate, as well as both Gnostic and Manichaean sources. Furthermore, considering the influence of Muslim biblical criticism during Ḥiwi's time and location, and the similarities between his criticism and what was already ongoing in the Muslim world, it is very likely that he was influenced by such sources, sources which also relied upon the prior criticisms of Gnostics et al.[24] As with Porphyry's criticisms, a number of Ḥiwi's questions travel down through history and remain important foundation stones in Pentateuchal source criticism: e.g., the presence of passages which appear anthropomorphic, apparent contradictions within the text, and apparent inconsistencies in God's will evidenced in his commands and statements.

But it is Ibn Ḥazm's eleventh century manuscript *Al-Fasl fi-l-Milal wa-l-Ahwā wa-l-Nihal* that is arguably the most significant philological and textual analysis that calls into question the Mosaic authorship of the Pentateuch.[25] We already encountered Ibn Ḥazm in the previous chapter, and we will discuss him further in chapter four, when we take a closer look at Spinoza's contribution to modern biblical criticism. For now, it is important to emphasize that Ibn Ḥazm's work represents a thorough philological treatment of the Pentateuch, and that he relied upon the previous polemical tradition which we have just covered in the preceding paragraphs.[26]

23. Biale, *Note in the Heavens*, 63; Rosenthal, *Ḥiwi al-Balkhi*; Rosenthal, "Ḥiwi al-Balkhi," 317–42; Rosenthal, "Ḥiwi al-Balkhi (Continued)," 419–30; Rosenthal, "Ḥiwi al-Balkhi (Continued)," 79–94; Davidson, *Saadia's Polemic*, 11–37; Gottheil, "Some Early Jewish," 6–12; and Schechter, "Geniza Specimens," 345–44.

24. Rosenthal, *Ḥiwi al-Balkhi*; Rosenthal, "Ḥiwi al-Balkhi," 324n39, 325n41, 325n43, 326n45, 326–28nn47–52, 331n64, 331n68, 332–33nn70–72, 335n80a, 336nn82–83, 338n99, 340–41, and 340nn100–101; Rosenthal, "Ḥiwi al-Balkhi (Continued)," 425 and 430; Rosenthal, "Ḥiwi al-Balkhi (Continued)," 79 and 93; Young, "Celsus," 166–97; Stein, *Alttestamentliche Bibelkritik*, 38–82; Marmorstein, "Background of the Haggadah," 157–204; and Büchler, "Über die Minim," 271–95.

25. Lazarus-Yafeh, "Some Neglected Aspects," 61; Lazarus-Yafeh, *Intertwined Worlds*, 41–47, 50, 67n52, and 67–69; Freedman, "Father of Modern Biblical Scholarship," 31–38; and Powers, "Reading/Misreading," 109–21.

26. Naor, *Ma'amar*, 3–5; Sabra, "Ibn Ḥazm's Literalism," 7–40; Behloul, *Ibn Hazms Evangelienkritik*; Adang, "Medieval Muslim Polemics," 143–59; Adang, "Ibn Ḥazm's Critique," 1–15; Adang, "Eléments karaïtes," 419–41; Adang, "Some Hitherto Neglected," 17–28; Roth, "Forgery and Abrogation," 203–36; Aasi, "Muslim understanding"; Abu Laila, "An Introduction 1," 75–100; Abu Laila, "An Introduction 2," 165–71; Friedlander, "Heterodoxies," 9–11, 13, and 16–17; Friedlander, "Zur Komposition," 267–77;

The twelfth century Jewish luminary Ibn Ezra was the most famous medieval biblical commentator to, at least obliquely, call into question the Mosaic authorship of fragments of the Torah.[27] In the fifteenth century, Alfonso Tostado Ribera de Madrigal, who became the bishop of Avila in Spain, recorded a number of questions that he identified as having been leveled against the Mosaic authorship of certain Pentateuchal passages. He then responded to these questions, defending the more traditional view. In the sixteenth century, Andreas Rudolph Bodenstein von Karlstadt affirmed that certain portions of the Pentateuch did not date from Moses, and, in the same century, Andreas Masius connected much of the Old Testament with Ezra, although Masius was more cautious when he described the Pentateuch's origins. Cornelius à Lapide and Jacques Bonfrère bring us into the seventeenth century, and although Lapide supposed Joshua was responsible for at least some of the Pentateuchal redaction, and Bonfrère was well aware of problems with Mosaic authorship that had been brought up by theologians and biblical commentators in the past, both maintained the core Mosaic authorship of the Pentateuch as a whole.[28]

By the end of the seventeenth century, with Thomas Hobbes's *Leviathan* (1651), Baruch Spinoza's *Tractatus Theologico-Politicus* (1670) and Richard Simon's *Histoire critique du Vieux Testament* (1678), the denial of Mosaic authorship had become more common among critical scholars, although the issue remained controversial on the whole.[29] In the eighteenth century, by contrast, a number of the central figures involved in the development of modern biblical criticism responded to these earlier seventeenth century figures by defending the Pentateuch's Mosaic authorship. This is the case especially for Jean Astruc whose book in defense of Mosaic authorship, *Conjectures sur les mémoires originaux dont il paroit que Moyse s'est servi pour composer le livre de la Genèse* (1753), proved foundational in the

---

Hirschfeld, "Mohammedan Criticism," 225–35; and Goldziher, *Die Ẓâhiriten*, 123–24 and 132.

27. Simon, "Abraham Ibn Ezra," 382–83; Levenson, "Eighth Principle," 209–10; and Sarna, "Modern Study," 22. Though see Kugel's important caveat (*How to Read the Bible*, 30–31).

28. Malcolm, *Aspects of Hobbes*, 404–10.

29. Rogerson, "Early Old Testament," 839–40; Popkin, "Spinoza and Bible Scholarship," 1–20; Malherbe, "Hobbes et la Bible," 691–99; and Pacchi, "Hobbes and Biblical Philology," 231–39. On the changing views concerning the Mosaic authorship of the Pentateuch, especially from the beginning of the seventeenth century to the early eighteenth, see Malcolm, *Aspects of Hobbes*, 383–86. On La Peyrère's relationship with Spinoza, see especially Popkin, "Spinoza and La Peyrère," 172–95.

development of the later Documentary Hypothesis which triumphed at the end of the nineteenth century and dawn of the twentieth.[30]

Simon's criticisms which carried biblical scholarship further than his predecessors had been an apologetic response to his contemporaries like La Peyrère, Hobbes and Spinoza, and so it should come as no surprise that Johann David Michaelis, another eighteenth century defender of Mosaic authorship, likewise would carry biblical scholarship further by reacting to Astruc's *Conjectures*, which, although Astruc defended Mosaic authorship, Michaelis saw as a threat to the authenticity of Genesis.[31] And it was with Michaelis' student, Johann Gottfried Eichhorn that we see the challenge to Mosaic authorship begin to build upon the critical assessments which preceded him and develop into source critical theories like those more generally accepted by scholars today.[32]

La Peyrère's Place in the History of Pentateuchal Source Criticism on the Question of Mosaic Authorship

Unlike many of the figures who worked on these questions in the previous centuries and afterward, La Peyrère was not known for his philological abilities. In fact, Richard Simon, who knew La Peyrère personally, claimed La Peyrère knew no Hebrew or Greek. The evidence indicates, however, that La Peyrère did at least know Greek, technical details of which he discussed in his published works. He may also have had a very rudimentary understanding of Hebrew, although this is less certain than his knowledge of Greek. The evidence for these language abilities are indicated from autographed unpublished letters.[33]

Malcolm summarizes La Peyrère's arguments against the Mosaic authorship of the Pentateuch as follows: (1) the mention of "Transjordan" in Deut 1:1; (2) the death of Moses in Deut 34; (3) the mention of a new location for the "iron bed" in Deut 3:11; (4) the phrase "unto this day" throughout Deuteronomy, especially Deut 34:6; perhaps (5) the apparently anachronistic phrase "as Israel did" in Deut 2:12; and (6) the mention of the text "book of wars of Lord" in Num 21:14.[34]

30. Astruc, *Conjectures*, 123, 140, 315, 433, 489, 495 and 513–15; Rogerson, "Early Old Testament," 846–47; Smend, *From Astruc to Zimmerli*, 1–14; Smend, "Jean Astruc," 157–73; Gibert, "De l'intuition," 174–89; and Nahkola, "*Memoires* of Moses," 204–20.

31. Legaspi, *Death of Scripture*, 136–40; and Smend, *From Astruc to Zimmerli*, 30–42.

32. Legaspi, *Death of Scripture*, 136, 156, 165, and 194n30.

33. Nellen, "Growing Tension," 818; and Popkin, *Isaac La Peyrère*, 18 and 42.

34. Malcolm, *Aspects of Hobbes*, 412; La Peyrère, *Præ-Adamitæ*; and La Peyrère,

La Peyrère argues against the Mosaic authorship of the Pentateuch on account of all sorts of errors, inconsistencies, and contradictions in the texts in the first chapter of the fourth book of his *Systema Theologicum*. He begins his analysis on the Pentateuch's authorship by bringing up the question about whether or not the Old Testament texts are the originals, and concludes that they are not. He thinks it is self evident, e.g., that the Books of Joshua, Chronicles and Kings are "copies" and not originals.[35] He explains:

> And nothing more frequent in other books, *Behold they are written in the books of Nathan, or in the books of Gad, or in the books of the remembrances of the Kings of Israel, and the Kings of Judah: or in the words of Jehu, the son of Hanani; or in the words of Hosea the Prophet, or in the Prophet Isay*, every one of them having their own History, to which it had relation, now lost. Whatsoever is read in the *Kings*, or *Chronicles*, are gather'd out of the books of *Nathan, Gad, Jehu, Hosea, Isay*, &c. Whence they are taken and gather'd, as is found by the confession of the authors who wrote them.[36]

La Peyrère immediately follows this by diving into his critique of the Mosaic authorship of the Pentateuch. He begins by admitting ignorance about why anyone would think Moses wrote the Pentateuch, and is quick to mention that not everyone believes Moses to be the author. He then introduces his list of arguments by explaining that these points will illustrate the reasons why he is convinced these texts are not Moses' originals, but rather "copies."[37]

First, La Peyrère considers the death of Moses in Deuteronomy. He writes: "*Moses* is there read to have died. For how could *Moses* write after his death? They say that *Josuah* added the death of *Moses* to *Deuteronomie*. But, who added the death of *Josuah* to that book which is so call'd; and which, being written by *Josuah* himself, is reckon'd in *Moses* his Pentateuch?"[38] Thus La Peyrère not only calls into question the Mosaic authorship of that section of the Pentateuch, but he even considers specious the argument, employed

---

Systema Theologicum. All English translations taken from La Peyrère, *Men before Adam*; and La Peyrère, *Theological Systeme*. La Peyrère originally published these works anonymously.

35. La Peyrère, *Systema Theologicum*, 4.1.197–98; and La Peyrère, *Theological Systeme*, 4.1.204.

36. La Peyrère, *Systema Theologicum*, 4.1.198; and La Peyrère, *Theological Systeme*, 4.1.204.

37. La Peyrère, *Systema Theologicum*, 4.1.198; and La Peyrère, *Theological Systeme*, 4.1.204–5.

38. La Peyrère, *Systema Theologicum*, 4.1.198; and La Peyrère, *Theological Systeme*, 4.1.205.

by many including Lapide, that Joshua wrote that portion. No, for La Peyrère, this instance indicates that the text must be dated much later than that, as he will make clear in his subsequent arguments.

The second argument La Peyrère employs has to do with distinguishing which side of the Jordan Moses was when he spoke, and the narrator's refrain "beyond the Jordan":

> Besides, we read in the I. Cha. Of Deut. *These are the words which Moses spake beyond* Jordan. Which if *Moses* had spoken, he had said, *on this side* Jordan. For *Moses* had not pass'd *Jordan*; nay he never pass'd it: but he that writes *Deuteronomy*, sayes *beyond Jordan*, because it was in the holy Land, and because that place in the plains of *Moab*, where *Moses* last spoke to the *Israelites*, was beyond *Jordan*.[39]

La Peyrère's third argument pertains to the citation of the Book of the Wars of the Lord. La Peyrère asks how Moses could possibly cite this text which allegedly was a book about the very events in which Moses played a part:

> There is also a passage cited out of a Book, whose Title was, *The Warrs of the Lord*. The words in *Numbers* are these. *Whence it is said in the book of the warrs of the Lord. As he did in the red sea, so shall he do in the brooks of* Arnon. But that Book of the Wars of the Lord could not be cited by *Moses*, in which there could be mention made of those things which were done at *Arnon*, in the very place where *Moses* perform'd this exploit.[40]

It is here that La Peyrère explains his view of the general history of the Pentateuch's composition. He concedes a role to Moses, but, like many later critics afterward, he believes the original words of Moses have been corrupted and expanded upon over the years:

> Truly I believe that *Moses* made a Diarie [diurnos commentarios] of all those wonderfull things which God did for the people of *Israel*, under the conduct of *Moses*. From which collections the books of wars the Lord might afterwards be taken; Which for that cause was neither the Original, nor the Original of the Original: but indeed a Copy from a Copy [apographum apographi].[41]

39. La Peyrère, *Systema Theologicum*, 4.1.198; and La Peyrère, *Theological Systeme*, 4.1.205.

40. La Peyrère, *Systema Theologicum*, 4.1.198–99; and La Peyrère, *Theological Systeme*, 4.1.205–6.

41. La Peyrère, *Systema Theologicum*, 4.1.198–99; and La Peyrère, *Theological Systeme*, 4.1.205–6.

His fourth argument gives a clue to La Peyrère's dating of the Pentateuch, which cannot go to Joshua's time, but rather was "written long after Moses":

> That which we read in the third Chapter of *Deuteronomy* does manifest, that they are written long after *Moses*; Jair *the son of* Manasses *possessed all the Country of* Argob, *and it is call'd after his name,* Basan Hanoch Jair, *to this day* [usque in prafentem diem]. *Moses* could never have said *to this day*; For *Jair* scarcely had possession of his own Villages at that time, when *Moses* is brought in so speaking . . . .[42]

Continuing with the same trajectory as in the above example, La Peyrère adds his fifth argument:

> The like we read in the same *Deuteronomy*, in the same Chapter. *Only Og King of* Basan *was remaining of the race of the Giants. His iron bed is shown, which is at* Rabbath *of the children of* Ammon. For what needed *Moses* to have said to the Jews, that his bed was shown at *Rabbath* of the children of *Ammon*, that they might learn the bignesse of the Giant? Why, I say, needed he to send the Jews to another place to see the bed of the Giant, who had seen him in his own Land, and overcome him, and measur'd him as he lay along in the fields of *Basan*? It is a great deal more likely to think, that this Writer, to gain credit to what he wrote concerning the King and Giant *Og*, of whom he made mention, spake of his iron bed, as a testimony of the wonderfull spoils of that terrible Giant, which were not at that time to be seen at *Basan*, where *Og* lay, but in *Rabbath* of the children of *Ammon*, the succession of ages having changed the place.[43]

Finally, La Peyrère's sixth argument goes even farther in locating a date for the composition of the Pentateuch, at least for Deuteronomy. As with later scholars, La Peyrère dates the following portion of Deuteronomy to "long after David's time":

> We read also in the 2. of *Deuteronomy*, *The* Horræans *first dwelt in* Seir: *whom the children of* Esau *driving out, dwelt there, as* Israel *did in the Land of his possession, which the Lord gave him.* In these words it is said, That the *Idumeans*, who are the Sons of *Esau*, inhabited Mount *Seir*, driving out the Inhabitants of those Mountains, And that the Jews again inhabited this Mount *Seir*,

---

42. La Peyrère, *Systema Theologicum*, 4.1.199; and La Peyrère, *Theological Systeme*, 4.1.206.

43. La Peyrère, *Systema Theologicum*, 4.1.199–200; and La Peyrère, *Theological Systeme*, 4.1.206–7.

and gain'd Mount *Seir* as a possession, driving out and destroying those *Idumeans*. Yet it is most certain, that the *Idumeans*, according to *Moses* himself, were not thrown out in his time, as it is in *Deuteronomy* in the same Chapter. *And the Lord said to me*, saith *Moses*, *You shall pass through the confines of your brethren the sons of* Esau, *who dwell in* Seir, *and they shall be afraid of you; Therefore take heed you move not against them, for I will not give you of their Land one foot; for I have given Mount* Seir *in possession to* Esau. Therefore *Idumea* was not given to the Jews in the dayes of *Moses*, but long time after, as *David* Prophecies, Psalm 108. . . . And *David* made also good his prophecie, 1 *Chro.* chap. 18. . . . Therefore in the time of *David*, and not of *Moses*, *Edom* became a land of possession to *Israel*. . . . And hence it is gather'd, that these essayes of *Deuteronomie* were written long after *Davids* time, a great while after *Moses*.[44]

For La Peyrère, this is sufficient evidence to prove that the Pentateuch was not authored by Moses and actually dates from long after his time period. As he explains, "I need not trouble the Reader much further, to prove a thing in it self sufficiently evident, that the five first books of the Bible were not written by *Moses*, as is thought."[45] This is La Peyrère's explanation for all of the errors, contradictions, and other infelicities in the Pentateuch, as he writes, "Nor need any one wonder after this, when he reads many things confus'd and out of order, obscure, deficient, many things omitted and misplaced, when they shall consider with themselves that they are a heap of Copie confusedly taken."[46]

La Peyrère then proceeds to list some of the errors and defects in the Pentateuch.[47] For example, he notes that, "The 20 Chapter of *Genesis*, of *Abrahams* sojourning with *Abimelech*, King of *Gerar*, is misplaced: For it is not likely that the King would lust after *Sarah*, who was an old woman, and with whom it left off to be according to the manner of women, and who was not capable of pleasure."[48] His final conclusion is that the Pentateuch

---

44. La Peyrère, *Systema Theologicum*, 4.1.200; and La Peyrère, *Theological Systeme*, 4.1.207–8.

45. La Peyrère, *Systema Theologicum*, 4.1.200–201; and La Peyrère, *Theological Systeme*, 4.1.208.

46. La Peyrère, *Systema Theologicum*, 4.1.201; and La Peyrère, *Theological Systeme*, 4.1.208.

47. La Peyrère, *Systema Theologicum*, 4.1.201–2; and La Peyrère, *Theological Systeme*, 4.1.208–10.

48. La Peyrère, *Systema Theologicum*, 4.1.201; and La Peyrère, *Theological Systeme*, 4.1.208–9.

has multiple authors: "these things were diversly written, being taken out of several authors."[49]

Creation Accounts and Textual Difficulties

In addition to his denial of the Mosaic authorship of the Pentateuch, La Peyrère anticipated the conclusion of later biblical scholars with his claim that Genesis 1–2 represented two creation accounts.[50] This is now quite commonplace in contemporary biblical scholarship. Ever since Hermann Hupfeld isolated the Priestly (P) Source in the Pentateuch (1853), biblical scholars have understood Genesis 1–2 to represent two different creation accounts from two different sources, Genesis 1 representing the later P account, and Genesis 2 representing an earlier Yahwist (J) account. Jean Astruc was the first to distinguish these two accounts (1753) based on the different names for God, but unlike his source critical successors like Johann Gottfried Eichhorn and Hupfeld, Astruc actually believed that Moses put the two sources together. Even before Astruc, Henning Bernhard Witter had divided Genesis 1–2 into two different creation accounts (in 1711) on other stylistic grounds, but he apparently was not followed by anyone.

Unlike these later critics, La Peyrère did not focus on sources behind these two accounts, but he did divide Genesis 1–2 into two different accounts of creation or, more precisely, La Peyrère saw these as two different creations described by a single author. Of course, La Peyrère did not attribute that authorship to Moses, nor, as we have seen, did he attribute the Pentateuch as a whole to a single author. La Peyrère argued that the accounts were distinct not so much on stylistic grounds as in regards to theological content. Whereas Genesis 2 described Adam's creation, Genesis 1 depicted the creation of pre–Adamites. In other words, Genesis 1 detailed the original creation of Gentiles, whereas Genesis 2 represented the creation of Jews.[51]

According to La Peyrère, the Bible told the story of the Jewish people and primarily excluded the histories of the Gentiles, which could be found in other non–biblical historical sources. In the first part of his *Prae-Adamitae*, La Peyrère exposits Rom 5:12–14 (chapter 15 also brings Hosea into the

---

49. La Peyrère, *Systema Theologicum*, 4.1.202; and La Peyrère, *Theological Systeme*, 4.1.209.

50. Wetsel, "Isaac de La Peyrère," 379n20; Wetsel, "Histoire de la Chine," 205–6; Almond, "Adam," 166–68; Almond, *Adam & Eve*, 53; and Nahkola, *Double Narratives*, 87n31.

51 Especially La Peyrère, *Systema Theologicum*, 2.10.137–41; and La Peyrère, *Theological Systeme*, 2.10.112–17.

discussion), which he applies to Genesis 1-3 in order to describe human history in two distinct ways: Gentile history recounted in Genesis 1 and Jewish history recounted in Genesis 2-3. He begins by arguing that the sin Paul speaks of that came with the law was not referring to the law God gave Moses at Mount Sinai, but rather the law God gave to Adam.[52] At the same time, the sin was imputed to all of humanity, even to the pre-Adamites, those humans descended from those created before Adam, because "that Law which was given to *Adam*, was given to all men; and in that minute when God spake to *Adam*, in delivering to him his Law, he spake likewise to all men," since Adam was "then the Governour and Protector of all men."[53] The central point for La Peyrère was that there were humans before Adam and that these were the ancestors of Gentiles. According to La Peyrère, this pre-Adamite hypothesis best explained Genesis, St. Paul's Christian theology, and the ancient non-biblical records and histories of other peoples.[54]

La Peyrère was not the first to develop a pre-Adamite hypothesis as it existed for some time among both Muslim and renaissance thinkers.[55] For La Peyrère it was the errors, contradictions, inconsistencies, misattributions of authorship, etc., in the biblical texts, that helped him defend his pre-Adamite theory and bolster his messianic speculations.[56] His goal, which would carry over to modern biblical criticism, was to separate the

---

52. La Peyrère, *Præ-Adamitæ*, 1-3, 10.5-12 and 27-28; La Peyrère, *Men before Adam*, 1-3, 10.1-9, and 24-26; La Peyrère, *Systema Theologicum*, 1.1.66-67; and La Peyrère, *Theological Systeme*, 1.1.2-3.

53. La Peyrère, *Men before Adam*, 3.7-8. See ibid., 2-3, 7 and 19.3, 6-8, 16 and 46-47; La Peyrère, *Præ-Adamitæ*, 2-3, 7 and 19.7, 9-11, 20 and 45-46; La Peyrère, *Systema Theologicum*, 1.1.65-68; and La Peyrère, *Theological Systeme*, 1.1.2-5.

54. La Peyrère, *Præ-Adamitæ*, 8 and 26.21-25 and 58; La Peyrère, *Men before Adam*, 8 and 26.18-22 and 60-61; La Peyrère, *Systema Theologicum*, 61; and La Peyrère, *Theological Systeme*, F1. For comments on his overall theological scheme regarding sin, redemption and pre-Adamites, see Schnapp, "Pre-adamites," 399-412; Sheehan, "Sacred and Profane," 55-56; van Asselt, "Adam en Eva," 104-6; Starobinski-Safran, "Raison et conflits," 100; and Harrison, "Religion," 126-9. La Peyrère's pre-Adamite hypothesis was later used to justify slavery and racism. See Livingstone, "Cultural Politics," 208-9; Wetsel, "Isaac de La Peyrère," 376-77; and Popkin, *Isaac La Peyrère*, 2, 4, and 146-65.

55. Early Muslim versions of pre-Adamism existed, some apparently among Averroist sources. See Subrahmanyam, "Intertwined Histories," 143-44; Almond, "Adam," 164-66; Haarmann, "In Quest," 65; Harrison, "Religion," 222-23n168; Popkin, *Isaac La Peyrère*, 26, 30-31, 185n21; Popkin, "Pre-Adamite Theory," 52-53; and Borst, *Der Turmbau*, 338-39. For more precursors to La Peyrère's pre-Adamite thesis, see Almond, "Adam," 164-66; Harrison, "Religion," 222-23n168; and Popkin, "Pre-Adamite Theory," 50-69.

56. Nellen, "Growing Tension," 822; Wetsel, "Isaac de La Peyrère," 380-81; and Popkin, *Isaac La Peyrère*, 44 and 48.

errors from the original biblical text.[57] La Peyrère explains his hermeneutical purpose thus:

> The difficulty is, to know what are the words of the Copier, and which are the real words of the Original. And to speak the very truth, it is impossible to know all these things. Many things indeed there are, that if one take good heed, you shall find which are the Original, which the Copy. And if a hound who hunts after a wild beast where he sees most steps in the dust, according to his exquisite sent discerns them, and runs the track of the beast which he pursues.[58]

A Hermeneutical Revolution: The Use of Non-Biblical Historical Texts

One of La Peyrère's most important and yet most overlooked contributions is the use of other non-biblical historical texts to understand biblical history and human origins.[59] La Peyrère had precursors here, especially Joseph Scaliger, but it is especially after La Peyrère's use of non-biblical historical sources that such use became increasingly accepted in discussions of human origins and human history.[60] The chronologies and historical accounts of other cultures, from China, the Americas, Africa, northern Europe, etc., played an immensely important role in La Peyrère's scheme and are one

---

57. Popkin, *Isaac La Peyrère*, 49.

58. La Peyrère, *Systema Theologicum*, 4.2.203–4; and La Peyrère, *Theological Systeme*, 4.2.212.

59. Livingstone, *Adam's Ancestors*, 35, 44, and 48–49; Nellen, "Growing Tension," 820; Wetsel, "Isaac de La Peyrère," 376; van Asselt, "Adam en Eva," 108–9; Popkin, *History of Scepticism*, 223 and 230; Popkin, *Third Force*, 353; Popkin, *Isaac La Peyrère*, 48 and 69–70; Popkin, "Development of Religious Scepticism," 278–79; Quennehen, "Lapeyrère," 251–52; and Benítez, "La posterité," 183–202.

60. Shalev, "Measurer of All Things," 561. Isaac Vossius, Christina of Sweden's librarian, became famous for using the history of other peoples, especially in China, to call into question biblical authority, and he may have been influenced in this by La Peyrère whose work predates his own. See Weststeijn, "Spinoza sinicus," 537–61; and Åkerman, "Answer to the Scepticism," 92–101. On Scaliger's work on non-biblical chronologies, and his influence on La Peyrère, see Gibert, *L'invention critique*, 71–73 and 99; and Grafton, *Joseph Scaliger I*, especially 134–226; Grafton, *Joseph Scaliger II*; and Grafton, "Joseph Scaliger," 156–85. La Peyrère explicitly cites Scaliger in *Systema Theologicum*, 3.7.180, 3.8.181, 4.9.232, and 4.13.244; and La Peyrère, *Theological Systeme*, 3.7.177, 3.8.178, 4.9.256, and 4.13.275. But see Quennehen, "Lapeyrère," 243–55, on the challenges of assessing the accuracy of La Peyrère's use of Scaliger, and his sources in general, specifically regarding ancient non-biblical chronologies.

of the most enduring influences he had on the new biblical hermeneutic further developed by biblical scholars after him.[61] In his *Prae-Adamitae* La Peyrère writes that:

> Moreover, from this Tenet, which asserts Men to have been before *Adam*, the History of *Genesis* appears much clearer, and agrees with itself. And it is wonderfully reconciled with all prophane Records whether ancient or new, to wit, those of the *Chaldeans, Egyptians, Scythians,* and *Chinensiens*; that most ancient Creation which is set down in the first of *Genesis* is reconciled to those of *Mexico*, not long ago discovered by *Columbus*.[62]

By including the histories of other peoples from across the globe, La Peyrère was both minimizing the exclusivity of the Bible's claims concerning human origins, as well as challenging the traditional interpretive authorities within Christian traditions. It was not the Church's tradition extended through time, nor the official Magisterium, nor even Scripture alone, that held the key to understanding the history of the Bible, but rather other historical documents from other peoples.[63] Writing further La Peyrère explains the importance of using other historical texts:

> But whatsoever we have learned in the knowledge of things, we owe to the Greeks, and to Latine Authors, who have written after them. But says he, all things among the Greeks are very late, and you shall find that the building of Towns, and the inventions of Arts, was immediately found out, and but a day old. And they last of all began to write Historie. But the *Egyptians* and *Phœnicians* had a constant record of things past, the Greeks themselves confess. Those same Greeks, but very lately learned the use of Letters from the *Phœnicians*, being taught by *Cadmus*, who was himself a *Phœnician*. . . . But the Greeks, that could scarce assert their own affaires for truth from the first Olympiad, nor could be sure of any thing that was before the first Olympiad: yet by hearing and reading, knew such things as came to their ears concerning the *Chaldæans, Egyptians, Scythians*, and *Phœnicians*, the most noble of Nations.[64]

61. Titzmann, "Herausforderungen," 147–49 and 153–54.

62. La Peyrère, *Men before Adam*, 8.22; and La Peyrère, *Præ–Adamitæ*, 8.24–25. See also his comments in *Systema Theologicum*, 3.5.165–71, 3.6.171–76, and 3.7.176–80; and La Peyrère, *Theological Systeme*, 3.5.153–63, 3.6.164–70, and 3.7.171–77.

63. Livingstone, "Cultural Politics," 207; Gabriel, "Periegesis and Skepticism," 159–70; and Quennehen, "Lapeyrère," 251–52.

64. La Peyrère, *Systema Theologicum*, 3.6.172; and La Peyrère, *Theological Systeme*, 3.6.165.

It was through La Peyrère's pre-Adamite hypothesis and through his use of ancient non-biblical sources (especially chronologies) that La Peyrère became an important figure in the later discipline of anthropology, as it began to develop.[65] His geographical works on Iceland and Greenland are particularly important in this regard. The works of David Livingstone and Frédéric Gabriel have done much to shed light on how La Peyrère's geographical works fit into his larger hermeneutical framework.[66] Livingstone explains how, "by structuring the symbolic surface of map space, these cartographic images have the power to steer geographical imaginings into predetermined channels through naturalising, and thereby normalising, the identities they purport to represent."[67] This functions in a very specific way in La Peyrère's work on Iceland and Greenland, and in his discussion on the origin of the Vikings therein.[68] La Peyrère's friend François de La Mothe Le Vayer, who served as tutor to the young King Louis XIV, played a significant role in this context. La Mothe Le Vayer desired the fabrication of travel accounts, even by intellectuals who never embarked on such travels, to convince readers of the world's immense cultural diversity and use such diversity as a defense against traditional mores.[69] Both of La Peyrère's *Relations* (*du Groenland* and *d'Islande*) were penned as letters to La Mothe Le Vayer, and, indeed, both fulfillments of Le Vayer's political program.[70] As Gabriel explains:

> ... La Peyrère's *Relations* use the Book of the world as a reservoir of (potentially) skeptical signs. These signs are in opposition to, for example, legends as well as biblical books . . . through the simple act of putting topics in relation to one another from a

---

65. Livingstone, "Politics, Culture, and Human Origins," 180; Livingstone, "Preadamites," 41–66; and Gliozzi, *Adamo*, 535–66.

66. Livingstone, "Politics, Culture, and Human Origins"; Livingstone, "Cultural Politics"; Livingstone, *Adam's Ancestors*; Livingstone, "Geographical Inquiry"; Livingstone, "Preadamite Theory"; Livingstone, "Geography"; Livingstone, "Preadamites"; and Gabriel, "Periegesis and Skepticism." Harvey fleshes out the broader context of the "ongoing intellectual confrontation between Catholics and freethinkers in the France of Louis XIV" (173), in which these debates figure. Harvey uses the example of the Baron de Lahontan, who also challenged the origin of all humanity from Adam, and the biblical record, as a window into this broader context. See "Noble Savage," 161–91.

67. Livingstone, "Cultural Politics," 206.

68. Ibid., 207.

69. Gabriel, "Periegesis and Skepticism," 160–63. As with La Peyrère and Scaliger before him, La Mothe Le Vayer was a staunch defender of utilizing non-biblical sources to understand the Bible, and the history behind the Bible. He devoured the non-biblical literature, especially from missionaries to Asia and the Americas, in order to demonstrate that Christian rituals were not unique to Christianity. See Wetsel, "Biblicism and Historicity," 12.

70. Gabriel, "Periegesis and Skepticism," 162–4.

comparative perspective . . . La Peyrère goes in the direction of the *desiderata* of La Mothe le Vayer as well as in that of his own polygenic theses.[71]

Christian and Jewish Messiahs

All of La Peyrère's biblical exegesis, and even his entire hermeneutical program, served his unique messianic speculations, where he attempted to deconstruct the biblical text in order to reconstruct it to show what it "really means." In fact, it is precisely those features of his hermeneutic that had the most lasting effect upon modern biblical criticism that he used for the purpose of supporting his nationalistic messianic vision of the King of France and the Messiah bringing the Jewish people back to the Holy Land.[72] Jesus was the first messiah who came for the Gentiles, and a second messiah would return in the future, coming this time for Jews.[73]

La Peyrère's *Du Rappel des Juifs* is about Jews coming to France, which was regarded as a place of liberty because of the absence of slaves. The King of France would lead them with the messiah, and would return them to Holy Land.[74] Popkin does not think that La Peyrère's vision was apocalyptic nor that it involved any typically apocalyptic battle motifs, but rather Popkin sees it as completely peaceful. Popkin's comments notwithstanding, some of the language which La Peyrère employed elsewhere did indeed appear to imply some sort of apocalyptic battle, even if La Peyrère thought that such a battle might be close at hand. This is particularly evident in his letter, "To all the Synagogues to the Jews, dispersed over the face of the Earth," which was prefixed in English to the English translation of his *Prae-Adamitae*, and appended in Latin to the Latin text.[75] In it we read the following:

---

71. Ibid., 170.

72. Starobinski-Safran, "Raison et conflits," 97–98 and 101–3; Haran, *Le lys et le globe*, 173–76; Parente, "Isaac de La Peyrère," 171–78; Popkin, *Third Force*, 66 and 353; Popkin, *Isaac La Peyrère*, 3, 8, 44, 50, 52–54, 58–59 and 66; and Åkerman, *Queen Christina*, 203.

73. Parente, "Isaac de la Peyrère interprète de Paul," 169–86; Starobinski-Safran, "Raison et conflits," 97–98 and 101–2; Haran, *Le lys et le globe*, 173–76; and Popkin, *Isaac La Peyrère*, 8.

74. Nellen, "Growing Tension," 819; Wetsel, "Isaac de La Peyrère," 377; Popkin, "Jewish-Christian Relations," 165; Popkin, *Isaac La Peyrère*, 54; Popkin, "Development of Religious Scepticism," 275–77; and Yardeni, "La religion," 245–59.

75. "Synagogis Iudæorum Universis."

> Nor shall God onely restore to you [Jews] your Kingdom by the Spirit of his Christ, your *Messias*, but there shall likewise arise from your bones, or he is already risen, a King and an Avenger, and shall restore you with a strong Hand, and a stretched out Arm, to your Country and Holy Land. . . . My Bowels rejoyce as often as I call to minde this your King. . . . My Heart leaps as often as I call to minde the most warlike Prince, and first-born of Kings, girding his Sword to his Thigh, drawing his shining Blade, pressing earnestly upon his and your Enemies, dipping his foot-steps in blood, and drinking off the River, triumphing and ascending up to the Mountain *Sion*, and there of the Nations vanquished, erecting Trophies before the Lord.[76]

The language in this passage is far more apocalyptic than Popkin concedes in his earlier writings, and seems to envision a real battle in which an apocalyptic king is an "Avenger" who restores the Jews "with a strong Hand," and who draws his sword, presses his enemies, and dips his footsteps in "blood." La Peyrère gives indications that he thinks these events will happen very soon:

> I have spoken great things concerning you [Jews] in this Treatise; wherein I have handled your Election. Much greater are those which I shall speak in the next; where I shall handle your Restauration, which I certainly know shall be. And if God doth move here men's secret thoughts at all, I hope, and am confident, it shall be very shortly.[77]

THE THREE KINGS OF FRANCE AND THE MESSIAH: FRENCH NATIONALISM AND LA PEYRÈRE'S POLITICAL BIBLICAL INTERPRETATION

The hermeneutic at work in La Peyrère's work, as well as the many specific instances of his biblical exegesis, cannot be separated from his political program which they served. Throughout the various stages of his career, La Peyrère seemed to place different individuals in the position of King of France. At work in La Peyrère's oeuvre is a French nationalistic focus common to other French thinkers preceding and following him. Nor is his speculation over the role of the King of France a mere coincidence, but, as we shall see, is inextricably connected to his career as secretary and diplomat for the Prince

---

76. "To all the Synagogues."
77. Ibid., A4.

of Condé, one of the most politically active men in the France of the time. In the end, after his arrest and conversion, La Peyrère's vision was tailored to meet the needs of the time for his own protection, but the basic contours of his vision remained the same: the Jewish Messiah would return to rescue the Jews from their plight across the globe, and eventually restore the Holy Land where the Messiah would rule the world in a universal messianic age alongside his royal steward.

Gallican Politics

La Peyrère's initial vision of the messianic royal steward should be understood in relation to the role of Gallicanism and the church state conflict in Europe. The Conciliarist movement, which placed bishops and episcopal conferences above the authority of the pope, began with theological concerns regarding the relationship between papal authority and the authority of bishops. Conciliarism eventually transformed, especially in the modern period, into little more than a thin veil masking state politics. In states where secular rulers were responsible for the appointment of bishops, the call for a Council of bishops to trump the pope on theological matters was not far removed from the call for secular rulers to dominate the church.[78]

It was in the France of the seventeenth century, and particularly during the reign of King Louis XIV, that French Gallicanism became the paradigmatic form of Conciliarism and was solidified into a politically powerful opposition to papal claims of transnational authority.[79] In all its varied forms, however, Gallicanism represented a unique focus on the Catholic Church as it grew in French soil. French nationalism in its varied forms sprung in part from Gallican roots.

La Peyrère's French nationalistic messianic vision is firmly entrenched in this Gallican milieu. Cardinal Richelieu, and afterwards his successor Cardinal Mazarin, were the de facto rulers in military matters during the reigns of King Louis XIII and King Louis XIV's childhood reign, prior to his rise to the age of majority when Louis XIV became Europe's first absolute sovereign. La Peyrère initially tried to dedicate what became his *Du Rappel des Juifs* to Cardinal Richelieu. Richelieu was appalled and banned the

---

78. See comments in the first chapter of this volume; and Portier, "Church Unity," 27–37.

79. Ibid., 27–37. Gallicanism was an incredibly diverse phenomenon, and defies all attempts at homogenization. See Costigan, *Consensus*; Costigan, "Bossuet," 652–72; Costigan, "Consensus," 25–48; Portier, "Church Unity," 27–37; and Congar, "Gallicanisme," 1731–39.

text, barring it from publication. In 1643, the year after Richelieu died, La Peyrère promptly and anonymously published the work.[80]

It is possible that La Peyrère initially envisioned Louis XIV as the King of France. This of course is what most scholars have assumed, since, when La Peyrère wrote his work, Louis XIV was the King of France.[81] Furthermore, in La Peyrère's undated dedication for his work on Iceland, *Relation de l'Islande*, Louis XIV is named fulfilling a similar role.[82]

In La Peyrère's messianic vision, *Du Rappel des Juifs*, however, it does *not* appear to be Louis XIV who will be the universal King of France, rather someone else is wearing the French crown. In this *Du Rappel des Juifs*, the Messiah is envisioned returning to rule the world alongside the King of France, but the King of France for La Peyrère's work was someone with whom he was much more closely associated, namely Louis II de Bourbon, the Prince of Condé.[83] La Peyrère's universal role for the King of France in his messianic speculation would later resurface during time of the colonial and imperialistic period of Napoleon.[84]

The Man Who Would Be King

Richard Popkin and Susanna Åkerman appear to have uncovered a plot to overthrow the King of France, Louis XIV. This plot involved Oliver Cromwell, Queen Christina of Sweden and the Prince of Condé, all of whom were personal acquaintances of La Peyrère. The plot consisted in removing Louis XIV from the throne and placing the Prince of Condé in his stead, to rule as a Protestant monarch.[85] During a key portion of this time, immediately

---

80. La Peyrère, *Du Rappel*, Bks 1–5; Quennehen, "L'auteur des *Préadamites*," 349 and 360; Wetsel, "Isaac de La Peyrère," 378–79; and Popkin, *Isaac La Peyrère*, 6.

81. Schoeps, "Philosemitism," 141.

82. Popkin observes that, "In the dedication [to *Relation de l'Islande*], which is undated, a text from Isaiah 55 is cited to the effect that there will be a universal king who will spread God's message. Next it is said that this King is Louis XIV, who with the help of the Prince of Condé, will commence the conquest of the world" (*Isaac La Peyrère*, 10).

83. Nellen, "Growing Tension," 819; Wetsel, "Isaac de La Peyrère," 377; Yovel, *Spinoza and Other Heretics I*, 81; Åkerman, *Queen Christina*, 202; and Popkin, *Isaac La Peyrère*, 3, 8 and 58–60.

84. Starobinski-Safran, "Raison et conflits," 101–2; Popkin, "Millenarianism and Nationalism," 77–78, 81–82, and 84n32; Popkin, "Afterward," 184; Popkin, "Grégoire's American Involvements," 158–59; Popkin, *Isaac La Peyrère*, 3; and Åkerman, *Queen Christina*, 202.

85. Quennehen, "L'auteur des *Préadamites*," 364n81, 365–66, and 365n88; Popkin, "Millenarianism and Nationalism," 78, 80, and 82; Popkin, "Religious Background,"

following Christina's abdication of the throne of Sweden and her conversion to Catholicism, La Peyrère lived next to Christina as Condé's secretary.[86]

These political designs of Condé, Cromwell and Christina appear to be central to La Peyrère's biblical criticism. Popkin initially did not think there was sufficient evidence that La Peyrère was intent on political action, despite La Peyrère's clear political motivations. La Peyrère never seemed intent on the specific politics of the day, nor did he seem to incorporate them clearly into his vision. With regard to La Peyrère's arguments concerning the role of the French King, however, Yirmiyahu Yovel points out that, "in La Peyrère's thinking, these were outlines for an immediate political action, not visions of a distant future."[87] Furthermore, Popkin later conceded, "Thus what was being proposed in La Peyrère's first work was not a pipe dream but a program of political action."[88] Upon more careful inspection, like the work of both Popkin and his former student Åkerman, it becomes clear that in *Du Rappel des Juifs*, La Peyrère saw the Prince of Condé as the King of France.[89]

The plot apparently grew intense from 1654–1655, the years in which Christina left her position of royalty of her own free accord and chose to enter the Catholic Church. During this time La Peyrère continued serving Condé on his diplomatic missions, and he took up residence in Belgium living adjacent to Christina. In their plan, Cromwell would invade France with his military, and land at Bordeaux (former home of La Peyrère), which was heavily Calvinist. From Bordeaux, Cromwell's troops would incite the Huguenots into violent rebellion against the King. With an additional support of troops, Christina would lead the attack on France from the north. Personal letters have been discovered from one of the Prince's spies in London that discuss this plot.[90]

407; Popkin, "Jewish-Christian Relations," 168; Popkin, *Isaac La Peyrère*, 9, 40, and 180n49; Popkin, "Menasseh ben Israel II," 12–20; Åkerman, *Queen Christina*, 11, 200, 202, 204, 213–15, and 219; Åkerman, "Queen Christina," 148; and Katz, "Menasseh ben Israel's Mission," 57–72.

86. Åkerman, *Queen Christina*, 32 and 186; and Popkin, *Isaac La Peyrère*, 12.

87. Yovel, *Spinoza and Other Heretics I*, 82.

88. Popkin, "Millenarianism and Nationalism," 78. Indications exist that La Peyrère went to clandestine millenarian meetings, but it is precisely because the evidence was limited to such trivialities, and that he never apparently wrote or participated in other ways in the politics of his age, that Popkin initially thought his work was limited to hypothesis, prior to uncovering the plot to overthrow Louis XIV. See Popkin, *Isaac La Peyrère*, 9 and 179n30.

89. Popkin, "Jewish-Christian Relations," 165; and Åkerman, *Queen Christina*, 200 and 202–4.

90. Popkin, "Millenarianism and Nationalism," 78 and 80; Popkin, "Introduction," xxx; Popkin, "First Published Reaction," 6–12; Popkin, "Jewish-Christian Relations,"

The Prince of Condé sought an alliance with Christina and used La Peyrère as an intermediary. He likewise used La Peyrère on clandestine errands to England, the precise reasons for which are still unclear. It appears that a "marriage alliance" was being constructed between the Prince of Condé and Christina. Condé's family had been historically Protestant, but had only recently converted to Catholicism. Colonel Jean Baptiste Stouppe, a Calvinist spy, played an important and yet not completely understood role in this plot. Stouppe served as a close advisor and spy for Cromwell, and later, after the plot failed, he served as a military assistant for Condé. Stouppe was also a Protestant minister and the head of the French Reformed Church in London. One of Stouppe's main roles in this plot was through his delivery of secret messages between Cromwell to Condé. The plan failed because neither Cromwell nor Condé were willing to make the first move. Through his spy Stouppe, Cromwell informed Condé that if the Prince first declared himself King of France Cromwell would then invade Bordeaux to help Condé take over the nation. The Prince responded, again using Stouppe to relay the message, that if Cromwell would first launch his invasion in the south of France, the Prince would then declare himself King. Since neither was willing the make the first move the coup was never set in motion. Condé and Louis XIV made peace and Condé eventually became one of the King's military chieftains.[91]

Christina of Sweden's role in this entire affair was significant, especially considering the intellectual circles in which she was involved. Reviewing the complex contours of Christina's life in their historical, political and social context, Åkerman maintains:

> Thus, these activities amount to nothing less than a consistently pursued theologico-political conspiracy, which involved among other things, starting a Protestant revolution in France, putting Condé on the throne, or when that failed, creating an alliance

---

165, 168 and 175n26; Popkin, *Isaac La Peyrère*, 12, 40, and 180n49; and Åkerman, *Queen Christina*, 11, 213–15 and 219.

91. Quennehen, "L'auteur des *Préadamites*," 366; Popkin, "Millenarianism and Nationalism," 78 and 80; Popkin, "Introduction," xxx; Popkin, "First Published Reaction," 6–12; Popkin, "Jewish-Christian Relations," 165, 168, and 175n26; Popkin, *Isaac La Peyrère*, 12, 40, and 180n49; Popkin, "Menasseh ben Israel," 12–20; Åkerman, *Queen Christina*, 11, 213–15 and 219; and Katz, "Menasseh ben Israel's Mission," 57–72. Popkin writes that, "[Gilbert] Burnet spent quite a bit of time with Stouppe, who told him of his conversations with Cromwell in 1654–55. Letters of two of Cromwell's agents on the Continent, John Dury and John Pell, during this period, confirm various details in the scheming" ("Jewish-Christian Relations," 175n26).

between Mazarin's family and Cromwell's, and establishing a throne for Christina in Catholic lands.[92]

La Peyrère's post as Condé's secretary and diplomat required him to embark on missions throughout Europe: to Spain, the Dutch Republic, Scandinavia and England, from 1644–1655.[93] And thus he was enveloped in Condé's and Christina's political happenings. As an instance of his affection for Christina, La Peyrère dedicated his *La Bataille de Lents* (1649) to her, which painted Condé as a courageous leader, and Christina as of woman of good character.[94] Also noteworthy is that La Peyrère dedicated his *Relation de l'Islande* to Condé, which was published in 1663, but had already been completed as a letter to Le Vayer in 1644.[95]

Popkin suggests that part of the inspiration for such a plot was likely the fact, known both by La Peyrère and Condé, that a rabbi in Constantinople had proclaimed that 1588 marked the year that some unnamed future King of France was born. Although no one from the French royal family was born then, there was an important figure in French politics who was: Henry II de Bourbon, the first Prince of Condé, for whom La Peyrère and his family worked. Henry II de Bourbon was born in the precise year of the nativity of this rabbi's prophesied quasi messianic French King. Henry II de Bourbon was the father of Louis II de Bourbon, the very Prince of Condé involved in the plot.[96]

Christina's connection with La Peyrère was crucial for his scholarship. Her court had been a center of learning; Orientalist and Classical scholars came from all over Europe to see her collections of ancient documents from all over the globe. Significantly, La Peyrère acknowledged assistance on his book on Greenland from Gabriel Naudé, who had once been Christina's librarian. Naudé (1600–1653) studied Averroes at Padua and, after having spent a year as Christina's librarian, served as Cardinal Mazarin's librarian in Paris until 1651.[97] Through Christina and Naudé, La Peyrère likely had access to a wealth of ancient sources to use in his hermeneutical project.

---

92. Åkerman, *Queen Christina*, 219. On Christina's numerous other political machinations, see ibid., 6–7, 11–15, 21–23, and 134.

93. Popkin, "Millenarianism and Nationalism," 80.

94. La Peyrère, *La Bataille*; Quennehen, "L'auteur des *Préadamites*," 365n84; and Popkin, *Isaac La Peyrère*, 12 and 179n36.

95. Popkin, *Isaac La Peyrère*, 10.

96. Ibid., 9.

97. Åkerman, *Queen Christina*, 82 and 104–9; Popkin, *Isaac La Peyrère*, 179n43; and Oddos, "Recherches," 49.

Political Conversion and Royal Transformations

La Peyrère was arrested by thirty men in 1656, the year after he published *Prae-Adamitae* (and the year of its publication in English), the very year after the plot stalled, failing to put Condé on the French throne. La Peyrère was interrogated, informed that he must apologize to Pope Alexander VII, and was advised to convert to Catholicism.[98] La Peyrère followed through on the advice he was given. While still a prisoner in Belgium, he wrote his formal retraction of his views, and then, after he was freed from prison, he went to Rome to meet with Pope Alexander VII. His formal recantation was carefully written so as to appear to be an apology, and yet so as not really to contradict his views.[99] At the time, La Peyrère's conversion, so it was thought, would be the catalyst to numerous conversions throughout Europe, which did not in fact occur.[100]

After so much failure, La Peyrère presented himself before the Pope in Rome. Following this event, La Peyrère modified his messianic vision by placing Pope Alexander VII in the decisive role that previously La Peyrère had envisioned Condé playing as King of France (in his *Lettre à Philotime*), a role which La Peyrère re-contextualized in light of Alexander the Great.[101] This was an interesting political move, since Pope Alexander VII had a strong apocalyptic bent. In fact, some scholars think he chose his papal name in part because he saw himself as a new Alexander the Great. Alexander VII was certainly known as one of the greatest patrons of art and architecture, and he had a particular interest in antiquities and history related to his Tuscan home and heritage.[102] He was of course justly famous for his reconstructions of Rome.[103] Prior to becoming Pope Alexander VII, Cardinal Fabio Chigi had played a role at the peace treaties of Westphalia, as had Queen Christina, which put an end to the Thirty Years' War and the so-called European Wars of Religion of the sixteenth and seventeenth centuries. At the time, Chigi was suspected of being a crypto-Protestant, and upon becoming pope, he claimed he would be the final pope, and had hopes of bringing universal peace.

98. Popkin, *Isaac La Peyrère*, 14.

99. Ibid., 14–15.

100. Ibid., 16 and 181n60.

101. Wetsel, "Isaac de La Peyrère," 381; Popkin, "Jewish–Christian Relations," 165 and 167; Popkin, *Isaac La Peyrère*, 14–16 and 181n63; and Åkerman, *Queen Christina*, 205.

102. Payne, "Architectural Criticism," 156; Marder, "Bernini," 628–45; Rowland, "Etruscan Inscriptions," 423–28; and Krautheimer, *Rome of Alexander VII*.

103. Marder, "Bernini," 628.

Unsurprisingly, Pope Alexander VII was pleased with La Peyrère after his conversion and recantation, and offered to let him stay in Rome, which La Peyrère declined.[104] On the more clearly apocalyptic side of things, one of the first things he did as pope was to commission a Hebrew translation of St. Thomas Aquinas' works, although only one volume was ever actually produced. The project was intended for Jews who would eventually convert at the eschaton, which Alexander VII apparently thought he would witness. Thus, La Peyrère's role for the pope fit naturally with what were perceived to be his own predilections.

La Peyrère's most famous work, *Prae-Adamitae*, was widely read in the Dutch Republic after he visited there in 1655. Five different editions of his Pre-Adamite book were published in 1656.[105] His work had an enormous effect on others, even on entire disciplines like anthropology and geography.[106]

---

104. Popkin, "Jewish-Christian Relations," 167; Popkin, *Isaac La Peyrère*, 17 and 181n60; Åkerman, *Queen Christina*, 205; and Mac Curtain, "An Irish Agent," 399 and 403.

105. Nellen, "Growing Tension," 820 and 820n52; Jorink, "Horrible and Blasphemous," 430n6; Jorink, "Reading the Book," 63–64; Quennehen, "L'auteur des *Préadamites*," 366; and Popkin, *Isaac La Peyrère*, 14–15. Jorink explains the significance of La Peyrère's work in the Dutch Republic, in the context of the Dutch debates about Cartesianism and Copernicanism in "Horrible and Blasphemous," 429–550. He explains that, "the emergence of biblical criticism in the seventeenth century Dutch Republic was a result of many influences. Philosophy, in this case Cartesianism, was just one factor. There was also a rather disturbing tendency, from the orthodox viewpoint, *within* the group of intellectuals engaged in biblical scholarship, which included not only theologians but also philologists. These scholars were working in the tradition of humanism, and the object of their scholarship ranged from linguistics to chronology, and from ancient geography to biblical zoology" (432). The reception of La Peyrère's work in the Dutch Republic must be read in this broader context.

106. Livingstone, "Politics, Culture, and Human Origins," 180; Livingstone, "Preadamites," 41–66; Poole, "Francis Lodwick's Creation," 245–63; and Gliozzi, *Adamo*, 535–66. For the differing receptions of La Peyrère's work among his contemporaries and through the nineteenth and early twentieth century, especially in the context of anthropology, see Lewis, "William Petty's Anthropology," 277–79; Livingstone, "Politics, Culture, and Human Origins," 180–85; Livingstone, "Cultural Politics," 208–9; and McLoughlin and Conser, "First Man," 249. In the context of the nineteenth century, Livingstone explains that, "What readers in particular settings thought about whether La Peyrère should be vilified or valorized, about the proper governance of republics or the relations between the races, about whether polygenism saved or subverted the Hebrew Scriptures—all had a bearing on how reported findings of anthropological science were locally put to work" ("Politics, Culture, and Human Origins," 188). This is significant, Livinstone claims, because, "How scientific claims about human origins were made mobile during the nineteenth century was critically bound up with two intimately intertwined sets of historical geographies: the geographies of reputation and the geographies of reading. The circulation of Isaac La Peyrère's polygenetic account of human beginnings discloses this association. For how his reputation was staged

La Peyrère seems never to have given up on his pre-Adamite hypothesis despite his recanting, and that is apparently why he went to live with the Oratorians, to use their library and continue to search for evidence in support of his theories.[107]

His system of theology was partially a response to the Thirty Years' War, and thus as with his contemporaries Hobbes and Spinoza, La Peyrère's hermeneutical program can be read, in some way, as an attempt to bring peace.[108] The Thirty Years' War and the sixteenth and seventeenth century wars of religion in general loomed large in the seventeenth-century quest for a biblical interpretation to end all wars.[109]

La Peyrère's work in biblical exegesis was known to Spinoza, and became very important to Richard Simon, even where Simon disagreed strongly with his friend. Eighteenth-century biblical scholars like Jean Astruc still found themselves responding to what they saw as La Peyrère's corrosive biblical interpretation, and later nineteenth-century historical critics like Wellhausen looked back to La Peyrère as a pioneer in modern biblical scholarship. Thus, although little known today, La Peyrère's work helped set the course modern biblical criticism would travel for over three centuries.

---

had a critical bearing on how his theological anthropology was read. At the same time the value of his achievements was no less conditioned by how readers understood the cultural setting within which they themselves were located" ("Politics, Culture, and Human Origins," 197).

107. Wetsel, "Isaac de La Peyrère," 381; Popkin, *Isaac La Peyrère*, 16, 18–19, and 180n46; and McKee, "Isaac de La Peyrère," 459.

108. Popkin, "Millenarianism and Nationalism," 78. On La Peyrère's theology and his impact on emerging biblical criticism, see especially Gibert, *L'invention critique*, 85–88 and 112–13; Jorink, "Horrible and Blasphemous," 431; Räisänen, *Marcion*, 137–52; Popkin, *Isaac La Peyrère*, 42–59; Popkin, "Bible Criticism," 339–60; and Popkin, "Menasseh ben Israel," 59–63. Räisänen's essay entitled, "The Bible and the Traditions of the Nations: Isaac La Peyrère as a Precursor of Biblical Criticism" (*Marcion*, 137–52) and Grafton's essay entitled, "Isaac La Peyrère and the Old Testament" (*Defenders of the Text*, 204–13) are especially important and yet very neglected in the scholarly literature.

109. This is especially clear in the work of Hobbes, Spinoza, and Lodewijk Meyer (Frampton, *Spinoza and the Rise of Historical Criticism*, 21; and van Bunge, *From Stevin to Spinoza*, 95). The work of Cavanaugh has been especially important in calling into question the designation of such sixteenth and seventeenth century wars like the Thirty Years' War as "religious." See *Myth of Religious Violence*, 123–80; and Cavanaugh, "Fire Strong Enough," 397–420. See also the first chapter in this present volume.

3

The Biblical Criticism of Thomas Hobbes in Context

> That great Leviathan called a Common-wealth, or State . . . which is but an Artificiall Man; though of greater stature and strength than the Naturall, for whose protection and defence it was intended; and in which the *Soveraignty* is an Artificiall *Soul*, as giving life and motion to the whole body; The *Magistrates*, and other *Officers* of Judicature and Execution, artificiall *Joynts*; *Reward* and *Punishment* . . . are the *Nerves*. . . . Lastly, the *Pacts* and *Covenants*, by which the parts of this Body Politique were at first made, set together, and united, resemble that *Fiat*, or the *Let us make man*, pronounced by God in the Creation.[1]

In his controversial work, *Theology and Social Theory*, John Milbank explained "modern politics as biblical hermeneutics."[2] Indeed, as we have already seen in the first two chapters of this present volume, there are links between modern politics and modern biblical criticism. Biblical criticism, however, is typically seen as a scientific method for studying the Bible. Biblical criticism, and science in general, are often thought to be free from ideological influences. Joseph Fitzmyer, for example, comments that biblical criticism as a method is "neutral" and that it can "yield objective results."[3] Hobbes, the subject of this chapter, took a similar perspective and was one of the earliest modern biblical critics to argue that his method was scientific and that it follows the dictates of reason.[4]

1. Hobbes, *Leviathan* 2, 16.
2. Milbank, *Theology and Social Theory*, 17–20.
3. Fitzmyer, Review, 439.
4. Hobbes, *Leviathan* 2, 64–77, and 190–95; and Hobbes, *Leviathan* 3, 576, 656,

Thomas Hobbes is universally recognized as a political theorist. In addition to his role as a political theorist, however, Hobbes was also an early modern biblical critic. A number of scholars have noted Hobbes's foundational role in the rise of modern biblical criticism.[5] In this chapter, I will consider the manner in which modern politics informed and shaped Hobbes's criticism. First I will provide a cursory discussion of Hobbes's life, highlighting the political influences on Hobbes, wherein I will briefly discuss how the Thirty Years' War and the English Civil War provide the immediate context for Hobbes's biblical exegesis. Then I will examine Hobbes's biblical criticism in his *Leviathan*, pointing out the role politics played in his biblical hermeneutic. This chapter will focus on *Leviathan* not only because it is Hobbes's best-known work, but also because it is here that we find Hobbes's most extensive discussion on the Bible.[6] My overarching argument is that Hobbes' exegesis is a disingenuous mask for a covert political agenda which has subsequently influenced the entire discipline of biblical interpretation. In other words, Hobbes subverted the biblical text in order to make it support his political theory, but those Christians who adopted his hermeneutics were not always aware of this motivation in his exegesis. Hobbes's legacy continues today, not only in the realm of political theory, but also in the field of biblical interpretation.

Biblical criticism tends to limit the text to a single historical meaning, divorced from the Church and from theology. This is ironic because the stereotype of the Church during the patristic and medieval periods is that it was an oppressive institution which hindered biblical exegesis. As Milbank points out, however, the traditional exegesis fostered by the Church allowed for a plenitude of meaning by relying on multiple "senses" of Scripture. These interpretations included allegorical readings of Scripture which allowed for a fuller meaning in the biblical text. Hobbes, as well as the Protestant Reformers before him, desired to cut down on these allegorical interpretations, partly on account of how the Catholic Church benefited from allegorical interpretation.[7] Hobbes went further than the Reformers, however, in that he wished to separate biblical exegesis from the Church al-

---

and 1052–55.

5. Hahn and Wiker, *Politicizing the Bible*, 285–338; Bernier, *La critique du Pentateuque*, 25, 48, 127–32, 139, and 143–45; Hoffmeier, *Ancient Israel in Sinai*, 9; Preus, "Bible and Religion II," 22; Curley, "Notes on a Neglected," 70; Levenson, *Hebrew Bible*, 95 and 117; Barr, "Interpretation," 322; Blenkinsopp, *Pentateuch*, 2; Hayes, "History of the Study," 45; Popkin, "Bible Criticism and Social Science," 339; Harrison, *Introduction*, 9–10; and Sandmel, *Hebrew Scriptures*, 328.

6. Overhoff, "Theology of Thomas Hobbes's *Leviathan*," 527 and 534.

7. Springborg, "Hobbes's Biblical Beasts," 357–60 and 370n11.

together, relegating scriptural interpretation to the state sovereign. In effect, Hobbes replaces God with the state sovereign.[8] Hobbes's political philosophy determined the direction of his biblical philology.

In what follows, I will present how Hobbes's politics drove his biblical exegesis. This allows us to look anew at the modern biblical criticism that is heir to Hobbes's work. The benefit of this exposition is to recognize that the biblical criticism often taught today as "neutral," "objective," "scientific," and even "factual" is not any of these. While the historical critical method enables scholars to unearth valuable insights, we ought not allow the claim to neutrality or superiority passed down by Hobbes. Rather, as with all exegetical methods, scholars must ascertain the assumptions of the method and be aware of how this can influence their biblical interpretation.

THE POLITICAL SHAPE OF HOBBES'S LIFE: HOBBES'S EARLY YEARS

Thomas Hobbes was born in 1588 amidst a turbulent Europe. Hobbes's views on religion, evidenced in his publications, were tied to events in his own life, particularly to the Thirty Years' War.[9] Many contemporary thinkers from the time also influenced Hobbes's thought: Descartes, Machiavelli, Galileo, and Bacon. While in France, Hobbes and Descartes engaged in many debates, and the latter's distrust of tradition may be detected in Hobbes's writings. Machiavelli's writings, as well as the work of Galileo (with whom Hobbes met), had a profound influence on Hobbes's thought; and furthermore, Hobbes was Bacon's secretary.[10]

At the young age of nineteen, Hobbes began working for the elite Cavendish family, later becoming William Cavendish's personal secretary. Hobbes gained precious access to important political information due to the prestige the Cavendish family enjoyed. His own politics favored the Stuart Kings, especially James I. Some have even noted that Hobbes's first published work, a translation of Thucydides's *History of the Peloponnesian Wars*, evidences his political bent in which the sovereign has absolute authority. During this important time in his life, Hobbes became a voting member of the Virginia Company. Although this prominent position put him at political odds with James I, Hobbes was privy to important contacts and

---

8 Hobbes, *Leviathan 2*, 260–63; and Springborg, "Hobbes's Biblical Beasts," 353–54.

9. Milner, "Hobbes," 400.

10. MacIntyre, *Short History*, 130–40; Den Uyl and Warner, "Liberalism," 298; Skinner, "Thomas Hobbes," 153; Bowle, *Hobbes and His Critics*, 48; and Balz, *Idea and Essence*, 9.

resources which made the position worthwhile. It was also in this role that Hobbes was exposed to anti-Catholic currents in English culture, for which the Virginia Company is famous.[11]

LEVIATHAN

Hobbes wrote his *Leviathan* while in France, amidst his eleven-year exile during the English Civil War.[12] Hobbes's *Leviathan* itself is directed in part against the Catholic Church. Hobbes made a case in *Leviathan* for subordinating the Church to the State, thus maintaining the status quo in the England of the time.[13] In this text, Hobbes developed his theory of absolutism, and, as Emilia Giancotti remarks, "Although absolutism is not tied to a [specific] form of politics, monarchy is for Hobbes the perfect form [of politics for absolutism]."[14] Of course, "In Hobbes, [such] absolutism takes on the form of [sheer] power . . . ."[15] Hobbes argues, virtually, that all the rights of individuals are transferred to the sovereign.[16]

Scott Hahn and Benjamin Wiker have recently argued that *Leviathan* was structured on Marsilias' Averroist pattern, as Marsilius had constructed *Defensor Pacis*—and for a shared goal, earthly peace, via a common means, obedience to the temporal ruler—universal emperor for Marsilius, local state sovereign for Hobbes.[17] The work is divided roughly into two major parts, the first of which, as Hahn and Wiker explain, "is devoted to a thoroughgoing reductionist account of political life based upon Hobbes's entirely self-contained mechanistic-materialist physics."[18] The second of

    11 Martinich, *Hobbes*; Cooke, *Hobbes and Christianity*; Martinich, *Two Gods*; Johnston, *Rhetoric of Leviathan*; Malcolm, "Hobbes, Sandys," 297–321; Hamilton, "Radical Royalism"; MacGillivray, "Thomas Hobbes's History," 179–98; and Mintz, *Hunting of Leviathan*. For anti-Catholic currents in Hobbes and in the English background out of which he comes, see Hobbes, *Leviathan* 2, 184–187; Hobbes, *Leviathan* 3, 876 and 1106–9; Greenblatt, *Hamlet in Purgatory*; Tumbleson, *Catholicism in the English Protestant Imagination*; Duffy, *Stripping of the Altars*; and Grant, *Short History*, 105.

    12. Parker, *Class and State*, 155; and Skinner, "Ideological Context," 288.

    13 Eisenach, "Hobbes on Church," 217, 222–24, 226, and 236; and Springborg, "Leviathan and the Problem," 296. See Hobbes, *Leviathan* 3, 586–93, 604–9, 674–77, 694–97, 700, 708, 738, 742–51, 758, 852–55, 864–67, 906, 916, 920, 932, and 952–55.

    14 Giancotti, "La Teoria dell'Assolutismo," 236. See also Hobbes, *Leviathan* 2, 284–305.

    15 Giancotti, "La Teoria dell'Assolutismo," 231.

    16 Kavka, "Hobbes's War," 296. See Hobbes, *Leviathan* 3, 586–89, 604–9, 736–39, 852–55, 864–67, 906, 932, and 952–55.

    17. Hahn and Wiker, *Politicizing the Bible*, 299–300.

    18. Ibid., 299.

which is a biblical exegetical project used to bolster the conclusions set forth in the first part. *Leviathan* is set up in four parts in total, within the framework of the two major parts. The first part, which runs nearly 118 pages, deals with human nature—reason, religion, the imagination, etc. The second part of *Leviathan*, about 150 pages, concerns the nature of the modern state, or what Hobbes calls a "Common-wealth." It is in this section that Hobbes unpacks the basis for his political theory, discussing the importance of sovereignty, individual freedom, etc. *Leviathan's* third section is devoted to specifically Christian "Common-wealths," wherein Hobbes includes the majority of his discussion of religion and of biblical exegesis. This third and largest section takes up over 170 pages. Hobbes's final section, roughly sixty-five pages, deals with "the Kingdome of Darknesse," with the Catholic Church as its focus. It is here that Hobbes tackles the problems he finds in misinterpretations of Scripture.

Hahn and Wiker point out that Hobbes "unified the purely secular aim of Marsilian and Machiavellian political thought with a secular cosmology needed to support it, and did so through an explicitly nominalist (mathematical–mechanistic) philosophy that focuses on the complete mastery of nature, especially human nature—all of which he put forth in the context of the particularities of the English political scene."[19] As we saw in the first chapter with Descartes, the context for Hobbes was also one of strife, both that of the bloody Thirty Years' War, the last and bloodies of the so-called European "wars of religion," and also the English Civil Wars, and thus his goal, as with Marsilius and Descartes before him, was terrestrial peace.[20] The English Civil War and the Thirty Years' War are the proximate background to *Leviathan*, and they provide the key to understanding both Hobbes's political theory as well as his biblical hermeneutic.

The English Civil War and the Thirty Years' War

The English Civil War served to strengthen Hobbes's views on absolute sovereignty, which had already been developing for some time.[21] Hobbes spent this period in France where he moved among elite circles, putting him in contact with many of the most important contemporary French thinkers.[22]

19. Ibid., 285.
20. See also ibid., 285–86, 292, and 300.
21. Lopata, "Property Theory," 209–13.
22. Skinner, "Ideological Context," 288–89; and Skinner, "Thomas Hobbes," 153–54 and 159. One of these contacts later recommended Hobbes's work *De Cive* to King Louis XIV.

Hobbes's views on the necessity of an absolute sovereign were solidified on account of the violent anarchy witnessed in England when there was no sovereign to unite everyone. Hobbes returned from France after the Civil War and was greeted with a pension from the new King Charles II. More than the English Civil War, however, the general seventeenth century "Wars of Religion"—especially the Thirty Years' War—affected and shaped Hobbes's writing of *Leviathan*, and thereby his role in bringing to birth the Modern State and the privatization of religion.

The traditional story of the "Wars of Religion" has been shown to be overly simplistic, as we saw in the first chapter. Specifically, William Cavanaugh's article, "'A Fire Strong Enough to Consume the House': The Wars of Religion and the Rise of the State," and his more recent book length treatment, *The Myth of Religious Violence*, remain the most important criticism of this traditional story.[23] Rather than the *raison d'être* of the centralized modern state, the "Wars of Religion" were its violent birth pangs. These "Wars of Religion" were in fact preceded by the centralization of states and by the usurpation of Church authority by princes and nobles. Previously, states in a general sense were based on family bonds, feudal ties, etc., and were more personal in nature, involving complex space. With the modern state, however, we find the abstract notion of state involving simple space, based primarily on rigid lines of territory and on the sovereign's monopoly on the "legitimate" use of violence. In his Gifford Lectures, Owen Chadwick points out that as the State, "reached out to the furthest frontiers of the land, it trampled over the local customs and local rights on which men once relied for their freedom in a community."[24] Hobbes and his political theorist cohorts rooted their political theories of sovereignty on the need for individuals to be protected from each other on account of the newly defined religion, which consisted solely of private beliefs. These theorists looked at religion, i.e., Christianity, and saw a set of privately held beliefs rather than a whole, embodied, public way of life, as it had previously been viewed. Although in reality, as Cavanaugh and others have shown, Catholics and Protestants teamed up against their enemies in the so-called "Wars of Religion," Hobbes and his cohorts like Bodin and Rousseau chose to see in these wars Catholic versus Protestants. The "war of all against all" became Hobbes's *ad hoc* justification for a new biblical hermeneutic.[25]

23. Cavanaugh, "Fire Strong Enough," 397–420; and Cavanaugh, *Myth of Religious Violence*.

24. Chadwick, *Secularization*, 26.

25. Bray, "Science and Politics"; Burke, *Clash of Civilizations*; Collins, "State Building," 603–33; Cavanaugh. "Fire Strong Enough," 397–420; Asad, *Genealogies of Religion*; Toulmin, *Cosmopolis*; Brewer, *Sinews of Power*; Portier, "Church Unity," 25–54;

HOW HOBBES READS THE BIBLE: THE "WARS OF RELIGION" AND A NEW BIBLICAL HERMENEUTIC

Hobbes's politics and biblical hermeneutics were profoundly affected by his experience of living through the Thirty Years' War, the bloodiest of the so-called "Wars of Religion." Hobbes argues that, "during the time men live without a common Power to keep them all in awe, they are in that condition which is called Warre; and such a warre, as is of every man, against every man."[26] The solution for this state of war is the authority of the modern state. Only such a governing power can control and prevent the violence inherent in ungoverned human life. For Hobbes, religion is rooted in fear, especially the fear of death.[27] His thought was that if his blueprint was followed then there would no longer be any need to fear death on account of "Wars of Religion." One unified and scientific method of reading the Bible could potentially eliminate all religious conflict in a particular region. But ironically it was not simply the biblical hermeneutics that brought peace; it was their use by an absolute sovereign. Hence Hobbes's biblical hermeneutic was in the service of the state.

Hobbes proposed a new hermeneutic for Scripture, which he believed was scientific; for the Bible, he maintained, was easy to understand when one is aided by the proper use of reason.[28] In his own words, Hobbes explains:

> For it is not the bare Words, but the Scope of the writer that giveth the true light, by which any writing is to bee interpreted; and they that insist upon single Texts, without considering the main Designe, can derive nothing from them cleerly; but rather by casting atomes of Scripture, as dust before mens eyes, make every thing more obscure than it is; an ordinary artifice of those that seek not the truth, but their own advantage.[29]

Despite his contention that this new biblical hermeneutic is guided by natural reason in a scientific manner, Hobbes's biblical exegesis was driven by his politics. In fact, as shall be shown, all of Hobbes's examples of biblical

---

Gellner, *Nations and Nationalism*; and Springborg, "Leviathan," 289–303. See also all of the essays in Tilly, ed., *Formation of National States*, especially the chapters by Tilly, Finer, Ardant, and Braun.

26. Hobbes, *Leviathan* 2, 192. See also ibid. 2, 190; and Kavka, "Hobbes's War," 292.

27. Hobbes, *Leviathan* 2, 164–67.

28. Ibid. 2, 76; and Johnston, *Rhetoric of Leviathan*, 138.

29. Hobbes, *Leviathan* 3, 954.

exegesis, far from being the results of some formally neutral and objective exercise of "reason," simply support his political theories.[30]

The overarching conclusion of Hobbes's biblical exegesis as a whole is the necessity of a sovereign with absolute power. This conclusion is not accidental. In fact, it is not so much a conclusion but a starting point for Hobbes's interpretation.[31] In other words, Hobbes' political conviction is prior to and an assumption for his scriptural work. Linked with this presumption is Hobbes's materialism, which leads him to view the Bible as merely a work of humans, like any other historical text.[32] Hobbes criticized miracles throughout *Leviathan*, e.g., when he writes, "And thence it is, that ignorant, and superstitious men make great Wonders of those works which other men, knowing to proceed from Nature . . . admire not at all."[33] This materialism helps clear the way for the sovereign to wield absolute authority. Because there is no supernatural action in miracles, nor indeed, a supernatural authority, Hobbes can emphasize the necessity of an earthly authority.

Patricia Springborg, Arrigo Pacchi, and more recently, Hahn and Wiker, have brought Hobbes's Epicurean context to the fore.[34] As they show, Hobbes was an intimate friend of the famous early modern Epicurean Pierre Gassendi. Hobbes thus became an important player in the revival of the atomism associated with ancient materialists like the earlier figures Epicurus and Lucretius, for whom terrestrial existence was our only form of life; there is no afterlife on this assumption. Hobbes's Epicureanism and nominalism reduced all of reality to atomic motion and left little room, if any, to spirits; and even if there was room left for spirits, said spirits are material, as we shall see below. For Hobbes, as Hahn and Wiker underscore, "true science must be a nominalism modeled on Euclidean geometry."[35] As with Machiavelli before him, however, Hobbes understood the necessity of religion in

---

30 Pacchi, "Hobbes and Biblical Philology," 236–7. Pacchi argues that, " . . . Hobbes approached the Bible out of eminently political motives, in the belief that a thorough critical and philological revision of the text would provide support for his idea of State supremacy over the Church" (237).

31 Johnston, *Rhetoric of Leviathan*, 175–6. See Hobbes, *Leviathan 3*, 586–93, 604–9, 674, 694–97, 698–701, 708, 738, 742–51, 758, 852–55, 864–67, 906, 916, 920, 932, and 952–55.

32. Overhoff, "Theology of Thomas Hobbes's *Leviathan*," 527–29; and Clive, "Hobbes," 49.

33. Hobbes, *Leviathan 3*, 684.

34. Hahn and Wiker, *Politicizing the Bible*, 296–99; Springborg, "Hobbes and Epicurean Religion," 161–214; Springborg, "Hobbes's Theory," 61–98; and Pacchi, "Hobbes e l'epicureismo," 54–71.

35. Hahn and Wiker, *Politicizing the Bible*, 304.

order to maintain political power, thus he did not eliminate religion, but rather only the fear of consequences beyond physical life and death (such fear in which religion is rooted for Hobbes), beyond what a state sovereign can grant, and thus granting the sovereign full control over religion within the realm. This does not mean that Hobbes had no religion of his own. We can take him at his word that he had faith, but it was not what would have passed for the orthodoxy of the day.

For Hobbes, the sovereign is the head of the church as well as of the state, and thus has all authority in matters of religion.[36] The state's *telos* is peace, and the sovereign secures the peace through the violent imposition of will and through the social contract.[37] Thus, for Hobbes, "The imperative of the civil order drives, in effect, individuals to agree on the institution of one sovereign power capable of stating and imposing the law."[38] Obeying the sovereign is obeying God.[39] Hence it is crucial that there not be any rival authorities, such as a church that is distinct from government and making its own claims on the lives of citizens, perhaps even claiming that there is something more important than life as a citizen, such as the eternal life with God. The sovereign, as the chief religious authority, is the individual with the sole authority to interpret Scripture as well as to determine the exact canon of Scripture.[40] One might ask at this point, what role is left then for reason and science?

For Hobbes, reason and science play a role in biblical exegesis, but his notions concerning reason and science are intimately linked to his politics. Science and reason in this sense are political.[41] Hobbes sees some aspects of science as "infallible."[42] Hobbes even goes so far as to equate the word of God with "the Dictates of reason."[43] But despite the importance that Hobbes attaches to reason and science, he never elaborates on what exactly they are

---

36 Rudolph, "Thomas Hobbes," 472. See Hobbes, *Leviathan* 3, 586–89, 604–9, 674, 694–97, 698–701, 708, 738, 742–51, 758, 852, 864–67, 906, 916, 920, 932, and 952–55.

37 Tinland, "Droit a la vie," 154–56; and Glover, "God and Thomas Hobbes," 281. See also Hobbes, *Leviathan* 2, 254, 260–65, and 270.

38 Tinland, "Droit a la vie," 156.

39. Hobbes, *Leviathan* 3, 932; and Sutherland, "God and Religion," 377–78.

40. Hobbes, *Leviathan* 3, 586–89, 698–701, and 866.

41 Bray, "Science and Politics," 412n12. See, especially, Tumbleson, *Catholicism in the English Protestant Imagination*, 98–125, his fourth chapter, entitled, "'Reason and Religion': The Science of Anglicanism," for more detail on how "science" and "religion" were used in the seventeenth century as political tools, particularly in opposition to the Catholic Church.

42. Hobbes, *Leviathan* 2, 76.

43. Hobbes, *Leviathan* 3, 656.

or what role they play in biblical interpretation. In the end, the state ruled by a sovereign is in control of all political reasoning, and this includes biblical interpretation. When an individual is led by reason to disobey or contradict the sovereign, it is evident that she is in fact failing to use "right reason," especially if she thinks the Bible is permitting her to challenge the sovereign. This could never be the case; the Bible appears not as an authority in and of itself but only inasmuch as it is used and interpreted by the sovereign.

One noteworthy conclusion reached by Hobbes using his "scientific" method for biblical criticism was that Moses did not write the Pentateuch. While this is commonplace today, it was particularly significant at the time because Mosaic authorship of the Pentateuch during the seventeenth-century was an important symbol of Church authority as well as of the authority of Christian tradition and the Bible in general, as we saw in the previous chapter.[44]

Moses was a figure to be respected; his assumed authorship of the Pentateuch lent it both a credibility and a certain power. There was an authenticity assumed of the Bible because of its connection with one of its own key figures who had close personal interaction with God on Mt. Sinai. The Church's assumption of Mosaic authorship of the Pentateuch was a claim of the larger Jewish and Christian traditions, but it was also a way of asserting the Bible's authority in the face of those, like Hobbes, who would reassign ecclesial power to one absolute sovereign (per state). I should clarify that Hobbes never explicitly states that his challenge to Mosaic authorship is related to his assignment of ecclesial authority to the sovereign. Hobbes's arguments here, however, were a way of undermining Church power and asserting his politics, and his intentions in questioning Mosaic authorship would not have appeared as ambiguous then as they might to us today. Nevertheless, the trick was to make it seem as though his conclusions were merely the result of "science" and "reason," rather than motivated by his political commitments. Hahn and Wiker rightly emphasize that, "Hobbes's real goal was not to undermine completely the authority of Scripture and traditional authorship, but to shift the question of authority from the *text and authorship* to the *authority* of interpretation (and hence to the authority of the interpreter, the political sovereign)."[45]

---

44. Cooke, *Hobbes and Christianity*, 159 and 166; Pacchi, "Hobbes and Biblical Philology," 232; and Popkin, *History of Scepticism*, 217–18.

45. Hahn and Wiker, *Politicizing the Bible*, 322.

Moses and the Pentateuch

Hobbes's denial that Moses wrote the majority of the Pentateuch is the most commonly discussed link that connects Hobbes with contemporary biblical criticism, and undoubtedly, the idea that Moses did not write the Pentateuch does not strike us as surprising today. While he conceded that Moses may have written some of the Pentateuch, namely Deuteronomy 11–26, Hobbes maintained that the majority of it was from Ezra's time, and he uses several arguments to discredit Moses as author of the Pentateuch as a whole.[46]

The first argument Hobbes levels is the case of Deut 34:6, where it mentions that no one knew where Moses' tomb was to that day. Hobbes maintains that this passage could not reasonably be attributed to Moses, and hence Moses may not be the author of other passages as well.[47] The next major argument Hobbes employs is from Gen 12:6, where we find mention that, "the Canaanite was then in the land," which Hobbes infers means, "which must needs bee the words of one that wrote when the *Canaanite* was not in the land; and consequently, not of *Moses*, who dyed before he came into it."[48] Continuing in his assault, Hobbes maintains that because Numbers 21:14 mentions a non-biblical source that existed concerning Moses, there must be other sources behind the Pentateuch than Moses.[49]

From these three verses alone, Hobbes determines that, "It is therefore sufficiently evident, that the five Books of *Moses* were written after his time."[50] Undoubtedly others had had to consider these same passages; none used them to discount Mosaic authorship as a whole. While Hobbes's arguments against Mosaic authorship are coherent, his conclusions stemmed more from his political motivations than from the three verses he cited. By discrediting the Pentateuch in the seventeenth century, Hobbes was able to discredit the Genesis story and set up his own "in the beginning ... ," wherein the natural state of human beings is war. Again, Hobbes never explained his motivation for disproving Mosaic authorship, but by making this argument he moved toward delegitimizing the Church in honoring the

---

46 Hobbes, *Leviathan 3*, 590–93. Isaac La Peyrère, very likely a friend of Hobbes, denied the Mosaic authorship of the Pentateuch possibly a decade before Hobbes, and it is possible that Hobbes was influenced by La Peyrère's work. On La Peyrère, see Popkin, *Isaac La Peyrère*; Popkin, "Spinoza and La Peyrère," 182 and 190; Knight, *Rediscovering the Traditions of Israel*, 40 and 43; and Kraus, *Geschichte der historisch-kritischen*, 53–55, as well as the second chapter in this present volume. Popkin wants to argue that La Peyrère is the founder of modern biblical criticism (*History of Scepticism*, 215).

47. Hobbes, *Leviathan 3*, 590–93.

48 Ibid., 590.

49. Ibid., 590–93.

50. Ibid., 590.

conclusions of "reason." Challenging Mosaic authorship enabled Hobbes to question the rationality of Church interpreters and, likewise, to assert that biblical interpretation was better left in the hands of the sovereign, who held the highest authority.

Biblical Exegesis in the Service of the State

Although many scholars focus upon the important role Hobbes's denial of the Mosaic authorship of the Pentateuch played in his biblical hermeneutic, there are also other examples of his political exegesis at work, as evidenced by the structure of *Leviathan*'s passages containing biblical exegesis, which I will here briefly outline. First Hobbes denies the Mosaic authorship of the Pentateuch, then he proceeds through the rest of the Old Testament arguing that texts were written later than supposed by tradition. Hobbes continues by opposing the incorporeal nature of the Spirit and angels, as well as arguing for a "weak" view of biblical inspiration.[51] He follows this section by arguing that the Old Testament demonstrates the Israelites had a sovereign kingdom much like the sovereign state for which Hobbes argues; in other words, the biblical text supports his own political position of a sovereign with absolute authority.[52] Hobbes then includes an in-depth discussion of the "Word of God" and of prophecy.[53] Next comes Hobbes's discussion and discrediting of miracles.[54] After that, Hobbes logically explains the metaphorical nature of Christian eschatology in Scripture.[55] This is followed by a discussion of the biblical concept of "church."[56] He then elaborates at length upon the Kingdom of God, followed by overviews of Jesus' "office" and of ecclesiastical authority.[57]

The Catholic Church looms like a dark shadow behind these biblical discussions. In fact, in numerous places in *Leviathan* Hobbes shows the political issues he sees involved in Catholic doctrines, which, in light of his own exegesis, he believes to be unbiblical.[58] At root in these issues

---

51. Ibid., 610–33.

52. Ibid., 634–49. Compare with his comments on 672, 702, 742–51, 758, 816, and 984.

53. Ibid., 650–681.

54. Ibid., 682–97.

55. Ibid., 698–729.

56. Ibid., 730–33.

57. Ibid., 736–927.

58 Overhoff, "Theology of Thomas Hobbes's *Leviathan*," 545. See Hobbes, *Leviathan* 2, 184–87; and Hobbes, *Leviathan* 3, 732–35, 804–7, 880–83, 920, 966–77, 992–95,

is the problem of a transnational Church. The pope is seen as a foreign power, and therefore a threat to the absolute authority of the sovereign. For Hobbes, every individual in the state must have the territorial sovereign as their ultimate authority. A transnational Church like the Catholic Church endangers sovereignty, and therefore is seen as a threat to the state. Space does not permit me to delve into each issue Hobbes discusses, so I will limit the examination to four interrelated issues: the nature of the Kingdom of God in Scripture; the related concept of the privatization of "religion" in the Bible; Hobbes's philosophical materialism applied to the biblical notion of the Spirit; and the related concept of metaphorical eschatology.

Examples of Hobbes's Political Exegesis: The Kingdom of God as Terrestrial

Hobbes's exegesis of biblical passages concerning the Kingdom of God also tend to support his politics.[59] He remarks that, " . . . I find the Kingdome of God, to signifie in most places of Scripture, a *Kingdome properly so named*, constituted by the Votes of the People of Israel in peculiar manner."[60] Hobbes understands biblically, "that by the *Kingdome of God*, is properly meant a Common-wealth, instituted . . . for their Civill Government, and the regulating of their behaviour . . . ."[61] In his discussion of Luke 1:32–33, where the Angel Gabriel discusses Jesus' kingdom, Hobbes interprets the kingdom as "a Kingdome upon Earth."[62] This kingdom, for Hobbes, "is a Civill Kingdome."[63] It is terrestrial, and not otherworldly. The Kingdom of God is a human kingdom, and, since there are a variety of sovereign kingdoms in different regions of the world, so there must be multiple Kingdoms of God. What is crucial is for Hobbes is that the Kingdom of God can in no way signify anything *beyond* life on earth where an earthly sovereign would have no authority.

In this Kingdom of God that Hobbes finds in Scripture, "the Right of Regulating both the Policy, and the Religion, were inseparable."[64] Hobbes argues from this that it is natural that the sovereign in each Commonwealth must control all aspects of the Common-wealth, including what was

1002, 1098–1102, 1106–13, and 1122.
- 59. Hobbes, *Leviathan* 3, 634 and 638–45.
- 60. Ibid., 634.
- 61. Ibid., 640.
- 62. Ibid., 642.
- 63. Ibid., 644.
- 64. Ibid., 750.

considered the spiritual realm. Thus, the religion may differ from region to region, depending upon the will of the sovereign—*cuius regio, eius religio*.

In studying Numbers 27 and Deuteronomy 17, Hobbes concludes that in the High Priest, "the Civill and Ecclesiasticall Power were both joined together in one and the same person . . . "[65] Following along these lines Hobbes argues against any form of disobedience to the state on account of religion—or beliefs, which he considers to be mere opinion. Such "religious" disobedience is inconceivable in Hobbes' scheme; his biblical interpretation backs his claim that the state sovereign ought to have complete religious authority. Once more, this leaves no room for any kind of a transnational church or an authority that extends beyond life on earth. Hence we see the link between Hobbes's exegesis of particular passages and his larger project. In the case of considering the Kingdom of God, it is crucial for Hobbes that it not provide a rival kingdom to that of earthly citizenship.

In this same vein, Hobbes removes the sting from the Catholic Church's practice of excommunication. As he observes, "Nor is the Excommunication of a Christian Subject, that obeyeth the laws of his own Soveraign, whether Christian, or Heathen, of any effect."[66] Writing further, he explains, "Excommunication . . . when a Christian State, or Prince is Excommunicate by a forain Authority, is without effect. . . . *the Thunderbolt of Excommunication* . . . proceeded from an imagination of the Bishop of Rome. . . . "[67] Sovereigns have authority only within the confines of their own territory. Thus Hobbes is forced to concede that the pope is the sovereign of the Papal States.[68] Beyond that, however, the pope can have no authority; no one with another state sovereign can be censured by someone who does not govern her own state. Nor should any supposed chastisement by the Church be a subject of concern for citizens who belong solely to one, earthly kingdom.

Internal Convictions, External Obedience: The Privatization of Religion

In light of Hobbes's discussion of the absolute sovereignty held by a state's ruler, he has to account for the possibility of individuals being commanded to commit acts contrary to their faith. In this discussion, Hobbes shows how religion must be privatized. Accordingly, only what is in the silent recesses of one's heart truly matters. The only important external action, as regards

---

65. Ibid., 748.
66. Ibid., 804.
67. Ibid., 806.
68. Ibid., 862–67, 902, and 906.

faith, is the complete and absolute obedience to the sovereign. If a sovereign commands the individuals in the sovereign's territory to blaspheme God with their lips or commit some other external act of idolatry, the sovereign's will is to be done. Hobbes's logic is clear: the sovereign has no means to coerce a subject to change her heart, and since the only external actions which truly matter are obedience and fidelity to the sovereign, there is no harm in disobeying one's religious convictions in order to obey one's sovereign. In fact, only in obeying one's sovereign can one truly fulfill the dictates of one's religion, since the sovereign is the ruler of both the church and the state.

This view is stated most clearly in Hobbes's discussion of 2 Kings 5:17 where he argues that it is unwarranted to disobey the sovereign, even if the sovereign should command one to speak out against the Christian faith.[69] According to Hobbes, Naaman the Syrian was converted in his heart, but his outward actions were contrary to such a conversion. Hobbes maintains that, "by bowing before the Idol Rimmon, he denied the true God in effect, as much as if he had done it with his lips."[70] Naaman, nevertheless, was justified, according to Hobbes, because of the belief in his heart. Hobbes responds to this question as follows:

> And if it be further asked, What if wee bee commanded by our lawfull Prince, to say with our tongue, wee beleeve not; must we obey such command? Profession with the tongue is but an externall thing, and no more then any other gesture whereby we signifie our obedience; and wherein a Christian, holding firmely in his heart the Faith of Christ, hath the same liberty which the Prophet Elisha allowed Naaman the Syrian.[71]

In making this claim, Hobbes moves toward the privatization of religion, wherein belief is relegated to an unseen realm and external actions meanwhile remain in conformity with the wishes of the state sovereign. Such a division between interior and exterior would assure that citizens not dare to challenge the commands of their ruler in regard to external actions. It also assures that the individual can maintain personal views contrary to the ruler, so long as those beliefs remain internal.

In Hobbes's eyes, this is a safeguard to peace; for religious violence does not come from people *holding* various religious convictions, but rather it comes from people *acting* on religious convictions. By acting only in accordance with the direction of the state sovereign regardless of one's faith, the possibility of religious violence is eliminated. Hobbes's biblical

69. Ibid., 784–87.
70. Ibid., 784.
71. Ibid.

interpretation of the Naaman passage not unintentionally thus lends support to his overall project and indicates that it is Hobbes's political presumptions that drive his exegesis. For Hobbes, religion is best kept away from the public realm. What is most important in the life of a citizen is simply to follow the rule of his sovereign, who has the ultimate authority, as well as the ultimate responsibility in preventing war. Diverse religious beliefs will occur, but if these can be kept to the private sphere, they cannot cause any conflict or bloodshed. The Naaman passage provides Hobbes with scriptural support for a political position he already has reached. Once more, we see that it is not his exegesis that leads him to conclusions, but rather Hobbes interprets Scripture in such a way that it supports his political convictions.

Spirit as Wind

In preparing the ground for his naturalized eschatology, Hobbes naturalizes the notion of "Spirit" in Scripture, although not completely.[72] He posits that often when the Bible refers to the "Spirit of God" it is merely speaking about wind or breath. Thus, in Gen 1:2 where the Spirit of God hovers over the water, Hobbes interprets this Spirit as mere natural wind.[73] At other times, the Spirit may be a gift of understanding, as with Joseph's dream interpretations.[74] When Hobbes reads 1 Sam 19:20, where the Spirit of the Lord comes to Saul, he interprets the passage in another metaphorical way, evidencing his materialism: "by the *Spirit* of God, that came upon Saul, when hee was amongst the Prophets that praised God in Songs, and Musick . . . is to be understood, not a Ghost, but an unexpected and sudden *zeal* to join with them in their devotion."[75] In light of all of this, Hobbes maintains that "there be no Immateriall Spirit."[76] In his discussion of Luke 22:3, where Satan entered Judas Iscariot, Hobbes writes that:

> by the Entring of *Satan* (that is the *Enemy*) into him, is meant, the hostile and traiterous intention of selling his Lord and Master. For as by the Holy Ghost, is frequently in Scripture understood, the Graces and good Inclinations given by the Holy Ghost; so by the Entring of Satan, may bee understood the wicked Cogitations, and Designes of the Adversaries of Christ, and his Disciples.[77]

72. Ibid., 610–33.
73. Ibid., 614.
74. Ibid.
75. Ibid., 616.
76. Ibid., 1020.
77 Ibid. For more on "Spirit" in Scripture referring to wind, breath, gifts, life, etc.,

Thus Hobbes's views of the spiritual realms tend toward materialism which suits his political theory of absolute sovereignty. Belief in the supernatural implies that something exists beyond earthly kingdoms and that something transcends the world as seen by human eyes. For Hobbes, such a supernatural realm cannot exist because it would challenge the absolute authority of these earthly kingdoms. The importance of this naturalization can be further understood by examining Hobbes's understanding of what happens after death.

Political Eschatology: Purgatory as Lie, Heaven and Hell as Metaphor

One of the most important ways in which Hobbes's biblical exegesis is shaped politically is in his discussion of hell and purgatory.[78] In fact, as Jürgen Overhoff observes, "So important was the accurate interpretation of biblical eschatology for Hobbes that he dedicated almost a quarter of *Leviathan* to the task."[79] Significantly, Hobbes does not believe in an eternal hell, but rather argues that here the Bible speaks metaphorically—which is uncharacteristic of Hobbes, since he tends to prefer a "literal" interpretation over metaphorical or allegorical interpretations.[80] Purgatory thus becomes another doctrine against which Hobbes argues.

This is significant because of the political nature of contemporary debates concerning Purgatory. Eamon Duffy writes that, "the Reformation attack on the cult of the dead was more than a polemic against a 'false' metaphysical belief: it was an attempt to redefine the boundaries of human community, and, in an act of exorcism, to limit the claims of the past, and the people of the past, on the people of the present."[81] Of course, part of what was at stake with the doctrine of Purgatory was where money should go that was involved in the cult of the dead—to clergy or to the King. Hobbes and other political theorists of the time preferred that the money went to

---

see ibid., 610–23.

78 See Hobbes, *Leviathan* 2, 184–87; Hobbes, *Leviathan* 3, 972–77, 992–95, 1002, 1098–1100, and 1110. See also Overhoff, "Theology of Thomas Hobbes's *Leviathan*," 546, where he notes that Hobbes, "put his eschatological vision into the context of a thoroughgoing analysis of the 'Power Ecclesiastical.' . . . [Hobbes] himself suggested that eschatological issues were dealt with in *Leviathan* not least because of their political significance." Overhoff also notes the anti-Catholic focus in Hobbes's eschatological discourses (ibid., 545).

79. Overhoff, "Theology of Thomas Hobbes's *Leviathan*," 534.

80. Hobbes, *Leviathan* 3, 972–77 and 992–95.

81. Duffy, *Stripping of the Altars*, 8.

the state rather than to priests.[82] An example of this debate is Hugh Latimer, who thought that such money was squandered on Purgatory. The direction of these funds to the Church deprived the state of valuable income. Stephen Greenblatt recounts Latimer's belief that such a practice, "is rendering to God that which is Caesar's."[83] It is in this context that Hobbes writes his passages concerning Purgatory in *Leviathan*.

Hobbes explains that in order to maintain justice, the sovereign of the state must have the power over life and death of the state's subjects in the Common-wealth, and furthermore, there must not be any punishment worse than death, nor any reward greater than life, or else this possibility threatens the authority of the sovereign. Hobbes states that, "It is impossible a Common-wealth should stand, where any other than the Sovereign, hath a power of giving greater rewards than Life; and of inflicting greater punishments, than Death."[84] The Catholic doctrine of Purgatory—and even the traditional Christian teaching concerning heaven and hell—poses a threat to the sovereign's absolute authority, which, once again, is necessary for maintaining peace and avoiding religious violence.

Hobbes thus interprets the Bible in such a way that heaven and hell are seen to be more metaphorical than literal, which renders Purgatory inconceivable, although Hobbes leaves a little room for some sort of spiritual resurrection at an undetermined point in the future. As regards heaven, Hobbes makes it clear that heaven is terrestrial, like the Kingdom of God. He explains that, "By the Kingdome of Heaven, is meant the Kingdom of the King that dwelleth in Heaven; and his Kingdome was the people of Israel . . . the Kingdom of God is a Civil Common-wealth."[85] Hobbes's views on hell are similar; he claims, "that which is thus said concerning Hell Fire, is spoken metaphorically."[86] Furthermore, the fact that we are able to produce children "is an Immortality of the Kind."[87] He mentions later that by "soul" Scripture primarily means simply "life."[88] In short, Hobbes's eschatology is little more than a political tool. Here his biblical interpretation simply supports his argument that the state sovereign ought to be regarded as having ultimate authority. The people have nothing to anticipate beyond their

---

82. Ibid., 391.
83. Greenblatt, *Hamlet in Purgatory*, 34–35.
84. Hobbes, *Leviathan 3*, 698.
85. Ibid., 704 and 708.
86. Ibid., 714.
87. Ibid., 994.
88. Ibid., 972–77.

earthly kingdom, and they will find peace insomuch as they, and their fellow citizens, obey their ruler.

Thomas Hobbes's biblical hermeneutic was erected in order to serve his political ends, which necessitated creating a new biblical exegesis overturning the Church's traditional methods of interpretation. While Hobbes believed his hermeneutic the work of scientific and unbiased reason, Hobbes's biblical hermeneutic was in fact created to support the absolute authority of the Modern State's sovereign, which he called Leviathan, "that *Mortall God*."[89] The Modern State, epitomized in Hobbes's political theory, was forged in the carnage that was the Thirty Years' War, and the rest of the "Wars of Religion," which provided the immediate context for Hobbes's biblical hermeneutic. V. Philips Long explains that, "for thinkers such as ... Hobbes ... it was not so much the development of new critical methods that forced the abandonment of the older model of reality as it was the abandonment of the traditional, biblically derived model of reality, or worldview, that prompted the development of new methods."[90] Hobbes's exegesis was not neutral or objective as he maintained, but rather, like all methods, had its own motivations and ends, which in his case gave primacy to the state while undermining the Church and its transnational and otherworldly authority.

Although Hobbes is by no means the first biblical interpreter to separate the Bible from the Church's tradition of interpretation, nor to suppress the multiple senses of Scripture, he does appear to be one of the first to do all of this under the mantle of "science." Hobbes's biblical criticism is part of a modern development, and it is clearly related to modern politics. From an examination of his early political life, the impact of the English Civil War and the Thirty Years' War on his thought, and the actual biblical discussions woven into the very fabric of *Leviathan*, we can see how the modern politics which Hobbes created *ad hoc* shaped and gave texture to how he read the Bible. Hobbes thus laid the foundation upon which Spinoza and Richard Simon built, and these latter two figures came to exert a tremendous influence on biblical scholarship up to the present. Together these three figures are generally acknowledged as the founders of modern biblical criticism.

---

89. Hobbes, *Leviathan 2*, 260.
90. Long, "Historiography," 148–49.

4

The Biblical Criticism of Baruch Spinoza in Context

OVER THE PAST SEVERAL decades, it has become more commonplace to see Benedict de Spinoza, along with La Peyrère, Hobbes, and Richard Simon, listed among the pioneers of the modern historical critical method for interpreting the Bible.[1] Although studies of Spinoza and his background abound, I will attempt another look at Spinoza's methodological program by situating it within the social, historical, and political context of seventeenth century Europe.[2] Spinoza stands out as a key figure involved in the early debates about the quest for an objective method of biblical interpretation. He is one of the earliest figures to attempt to articulate a "scientific" method of biblical exegesis.[3] Jonathan Israel explains Spinoza's significance within the broader Enlightenment project as a whole:

    1. Hahn and Wiker, *Politicizing the Bible*, 339–93; Bernier, *La critique du Pentateuque*, 146–71, 174–76, and 188–92; Gibert, *L'invention critique*, 170–73; Kugel, *How to Read the Bible*, 29–31; Barr, "Interpretation," 322; Blenkinsopp, *Pentateuch*, 2; Hayes, "History of the Study," 45; and Sandmel, *Hebrew Scriptures*, 328.

    2. An exhaustive list of major studies on Spinoza would require a book in itself, but a sample of some important studies dealing with his biblical criticism, from which I have benefitted greatly, include the following: Polka, *Between Philosophy and Religion I*; Polka, *Between Philosophy and Religion II*; Frampton, *Spinoza and the Rise of Historical Criticism*; Preus, *Spinoza and the Irrelevance of Biblical Authority*; Zac, *Spinoza*; and Siegfried, *Spinoza*.

    3. Hahn and Wiker, *Politicizing the Bible*, 3, 5–7, 9, 14–15, 340–41, 357, 363, and 546; Averbeck, "Pentateuchal Criticism," 152–53; James, *Spinoza*, 148, 150, 168, 170–71; Nadler, *Book Forged in Hell*, 106–7 and 240; Gibert, *L'invention critique*, 10, 148–75, 178–79, 184, 186, 197–98, 265–68, 292, 297, 302, and 304; Sinai, "Spinoza and Beyond,"

it is impossible to name another philosopher whose impact on the entire range of intellectual debates of the Enlightenment was deeper or more far-reaching than Spinoza's or whose Bible criticism and theory of religion was more widely or obsessively wrestled with, philosophically, throughout Europe during the century after his death. If the great *Encyclopédie* of Diderot and d'Alembert allocates twenty-two columns of text to Spinoza, the longest entry for any modern philosopher, in its entry about him, as against the remarkably low figure of only four to Locke and three to Malebranche, in their corresponding entries, this was assuredly not because the editors of the *Encyclopédie* were so utterly unaware of what was relevant to their Enlightenment that they got their editorial priorities stupendously wrong or owing to some wholly inexplicable aberration that historians can in no way account for. The simple fact is—however much this runs counter to certain commonplace notions—that Spinoza was deemed by them to be of greater relevance to the core issues of the *Encyclopédie* not just than Locke and Malebrance but also Hobbes or Leibniz.[4]

193–213; Legaspi, *Death of Scripture*, 4, 7, and 23–24; Ska, *Exegesis*, XV–XVI and 257–59; Sæbø, "From the Renaissance," 41–42; Lemche, *Old Testament*, 259; Reventlow, *Epochen IV*, 92–113; Maier, "Wahrheit," 10–11; Sacchi, "Le pentateuque," 278; Alonso Schökel, "Arte narrativa," 149; Goshen-Gottstein, "Bible et judaïsm," 33–38; Frei, *Eclipse of Biblical Narrative*, 4, 17, 42, and 156; and Kraus, *Geschichte der historisch-kritischen*, 64. For a critical position regarding Spinoza's foundational role here, see Frampton, *Spinoza and the Rise of Historical Criticism*, entire book. Frampton has many good points, and especially his point about precursors to Spinoza should be heeded, as we have already mentioned quite a few in the first three chapters of this present volume. Spinoza's method, however, is unique in combining a hermeneutic of suspicion to the historical accounts contained in the Scriptures (which certainly predated him) with a disciplined secular methodological approach to the text. The reception and reaction to Spinoza in the centuries that followed underscore his influence. The fact that Julius Wellhausen explicitly mentions Spinoza as a key pioneering figure in the history of Pentateuchal source criticism should give one pause. See Wellhausen, *Prolegomena*, 6. To Frampton's credit he concedes that Spinoza "developed a biblical hermeneutic that anticipated modern historical-critical scholarship of the Bible" (1). Where Frampton is strongest is in his critique of especially Protestant scholars who give the Protestant Reformers a free pass, when in reality Spinoza et al. were building on top of the criticism of the Protestant Reformers, who themselves had precursors as well (e.g., Frampton, *Spinoza and the Rise of Historical Criticism*, 14; and the first chapter in this present volume).

4. Israel, "Early Dutch and German," 72–73. Elsewhere Israel claims that, ". . . Spinoza and Spinozism were in fact the intellectual backbone of the European Radical Enlightenment everywhere, not only in the Netherlands, Germany, France, Italy, and Scandinavia but also Britain and Iceland." See Israel, *Radical Enlightenment*, vi. In his sequel, he continues this sustained argument, contending that, "it was . . . the freethinkers, *esprits forts*, and *matérialistes*, particularly adherents of something called 'Spinozism' (which was not quite the same thing as Spinoza's philosophy), who set the

In this chapter I will proceed in four parts. First I will note Spinoza's rationale for his historical biblical hermeneutic, namely as an agent of peace in a turbulent society torn apart by religious strife. Then I will describe what I think are some of his personal reasons for his historical critique, partially as a form of revenge on the Jewish community that ostracized him. This second section will begin with an examination of Spinoza within his theological and political intellectual context. Next, I will describe Spinoza's program, and how he hoped to cripple traditional theological interpretations. I will do this in part by an examination of Spinoza's treatment of priesthood in the Old Testament. Finally, I will attempt to provide the broader social and political context of the time to show how Spinoza's method was at the service of modern centralized states over and against traditional theological communities. Ultimately, these parts illustrate that far from emerging as the result of some act of pure rationality, Spinoza's biblical criticism was from the beginning a political tool in the service of emerging European states.

A BIBLICAL HERMENEUTIC INTENDED FOR PEACE

The ideal of the historical critical method is an attempt to understand the real history behind the biblical texts; historical criticism is a hermeneutic whose goal is to discover "what really happened." Historical criticism uses a variety of modern methodologies, primarily literary, to serve this worthy goal. Christianity and Judaism are both historical religions and so an historical reading of Scripture would appear necessary, and even in the medieval period the idea of a *sensus literalis* was viewed as important for scriptural interpretation. In the early modern period, however, the emphasis on the *sensus literalis* shifted from an initial step to the end goal, where the exegete as historian went in search of so-called "objective history," a quest Peter Novick likens to "nailing jelly to the wall."[5]

Prior to the seventeenth century, precursors to such a method abound, as we saw in the first chapter. Travis Frampton emphasizes, more than most, how many of the Protestant Reformers themselves, particularly Martin Luther and John Calvin, are in fact important figures who helped pave the way for the modern historical critical method, especially in their attempt to prune allegorical interpretation.[6] Despite the many theological, philosophi-

---

pace and framed the agenda of scholarly and intellectual discussion not only during the Early Enlightenment but throughout the Enlightenment era." See Israel, *Enlightenment Contested*, 40.

5. Novick, *Noble Dream*, 7.
6. On the Reformers' varying roles here, see, e.g., Hahn and Wiker, *Politicizing*

cal, and historical precursors to historical criticism, it is in the seventeenth century that we find the first programmatic methods intended simply to investigate the history behind the biblical texts.[7] For Spinoza, the ostensible purpose in such an historical method was peace. He wanted to bring peace to Europe which had been so savagely ripped apart by what he believed to be religious violence.

Spinoza was born to Marrano parents in Amsterdam; as Marranos, his parents had converted to Catholicism in Portugal, and these Marranos in Amsterdam were newly returning to their Jewish roots. The violence of the Thirty Years' War (1618–1648) was still being waged during the first sixteen years of his life; this context of dismay and calamity is important to keep in mind, as it was for Descartes and Hobbes. The acknowledged disorder and hostility of this time contrasts with the older view that the seventeenth century Enlightenment was due to the greater objectivity of more "enlightened"[8] intellectuals, on account of their greater prosperity and security than before.[9] Indeed, the carnage and terror of the so-called

---

the Bible, 147–219; Frampton, *Spinoza and the Rise of Historical Criticism*, 2–3, 6n10, 12–14, and esp. 23–42; Zachman, "Gathering Meaning," 1–26; Hendrix, *Tradition and Authority*, esp. 236–7; and Kraus, "Calvins exegetische Prinzipien," 329–41.

7. The Renaissance is a particularly important period for the turn to history which Spinoza later epitomized. See, e.g., Reventlow, *Bibelautorität*, 16–36; Bently, *Humanists*; and Burke, *Renaissance Sense*. For how this turn to history plays out in the modern period, particularly under the influence of German universities, see, e.g., Fasolt, "History and Religion," 10–26; Fasolt, "Red Herrings," 17–26; Fasolt, *Limits of History*; and Novick, *Noble Dream*, his entire book.

8. Gillespie informs us that, "The crucial word here is enlightenment . . . . It was the recognition of this widespread and deeply held belief in the enlightening force of reason that led nineteenth-century scholars to characterize this earlier period as the age of Enlightenment. While the concept of the Enlightenment as a historical period only arose in the nineteenth century, the idea that reason could enlighten humanity had certainly been present in modern thought since at least the mid-seventeenth century . . . . The term 'enlighten' was actually first used in print in English in 1667 by Milton, whose God in *Paradise Lost* commands the archangel Michael to 'reveal to Adam what shall come. . . . As I shall thee enlighten.' Addison used the term obliquely in 1712 in referring to the time before 'the World was enlightened by Learning and Philosophy.' On this basis, Kant used the equivalent German term, 'Aufklärung,' in 'What is Enlightenment' in 1784. This usage almost certainly derives from the earlier theological and philosophical usage of the term 'light.'" See *Theological Origins*, 257. Gillespie proceeds to use the examples of Bacon, Descartes, and Hobbes as using "light" in this way. Then he points out how such "usage itself is clearly derived from the earlier distinction of the divine and natural light in scholastic thought, which in turn was indebted in different ways to the Augustinian notion of divine illumination and the Platonic analogy of the idea of the good to the sun" (257).

9. See, e.g., the comments in Toulmin, *Cosmopolis*, 16–18, where he writes, "The received view took it for granted that the political, economic, social, and intellectual

"wars of religion," which engulfed Europe in the sixteenth and into about the first half of the seventeenth centuries, is difficult for us to comprehend, since the warfare was not conducted with as devastating an arsenal as that of our own age.[10]

For seventeenth century biblical exegetes like Spinoza and his friend Lodewijk Meyer, the Thirty Years' War and other so-called religious wars demonstrated the inability of sectarian theological interpretations to serve any useful function to society.[11] These wars were of grave concern for Spinoza as he formed his political philosophy, which included his biblical hermeneutics; indeed, the very goal (at least ostensibly) of Spinoza's theo-political

---

condition of Western Europe radically improved from 1600 on, in ways that encouraged the development of new political institutions, and more rational methods of inquiry.... [However] In the 16th century, Europe enjoyed a largely unbroken economic expansion, building up its capital holdings from the silver in the holds of the treasure ships from Spain's South American colonies: in the 17th century, the prosperity came to a grinding halt.... from 1620 on the state of Europe was one of general crisis.... By 1600, the political dominance of Spain was ending, France was divided along religious lines, England was drifting into civil war. In Central Europe, the fragmented states of Germany were tearing one another apart.... Economic expansion was replaced by depression.... International trade fell away and unemployment was general, so creating a pool of mercenaries available for hire in the Thirty Years' War, and all these misfortunes were aggravated by a worldwide worsening of the climate, with unusually high levels of carbon in the atmosphere. (This was the time of the Little Ice Age... when the River Thames froze over at London, and whole oxen were roasted on the ice). As Spain lost its undisputed command of the South Atlantic, the inflow of silver became unreliable, and the growth of Europe's capital base was checked. There were recurrences of the plague: France was specially hard hit in 1630–32 and 1647–49, while the Great Plague of 1665 in England was only the last in a sequence of violent outbreaks. Meanwhile, a series of cool, wet summers had severe effects on food production. With 80 to 90 percent of the population dependent on farming, this led to widespread suffering and rural depopulation. In marginal upland areas above all... there was, from 1615 on, a steady fall in grain yields, and entire villages were abandoned, to swell the disease-ridden city slums." Significantly, Toulmin concedes that, "Amid these catastrophes, the United Provinces of the Netherlands... stands out as the sole exception, enjoying a Golden Age at a time when the rest of Europe went through a particularly bad patch" (18). Nevertheless, Spinoza was in contact with intellectuals (e.g., Menasseh ben Israel) who travelled throughout Europe and to the New World, and so was not completely enclosed within the Dutch Republic.

10. See the graphic description in Gillespie, *Theological Origins*, 129–30. For calling the allegedly religious motivations of these wars into question, see the first chapter of this present volume as well as the important studies, Cavanaugh, *Myth of Religious Violence*, 123–80, especially 142–78; and Cavanaugh, "Fire Strong Enough," 397–420.

11. So, Frampton's comment concerning Meyer, "The religious debates, culminating in the Thirty Years' War (1618–48), proved theology to be incapable of performing sound exegesis" (*Spinoza and the Rise of Historical Criticism*, 21). See also, van Bunge, *From Stevin to Spinoza*, 95.

work was to create a biblical method that would bring peace to Europe.¹² William Cavanaugh explicitly mentions Spinoza as a key figure in the nascent development of the mythology of the "wars of religion." Cavanaugh notes that, "Benedict de Spinoza's political writings were motivated largely by the divisions and wars that had plagued Spinoza's native Netherlands and the rest of Europe throughout his lifetime . . . . The preface to his *Tractatus Theologico-Politicus* sets up religious violence as the problem to be solved by the rest of the treatise."¹³ In Spinoza's own words we read:

> fear is the root from which superstition is born, maintained and nourished. . . . Since dread is the cause of superstition, it plainly follows that everyone is naturally prone to it. . . . It also follows that superstition must be just as variable and unstable as all absurd leaps of the mind and powerful emotions are, and can only be sustained by hope and hatred, anger and deception. This is because such instability does not spring from reason but from passion alone, in fact from the most powerful of the passions. Therefore it is easy for people to be captivated by a superstition . . . because common people everywhere live in the same wretched state, they never adhere to the same superstition for very long. . . . Such instability of mind has been the cause of many riots and ferocious wars. . . . It may indeed be the highest secret of monarchical government and utterly essential to it, to keep men deceived, and to disguise the fear that sways them with the specious name of religion, so that they will fight for their servitude as if they were fighting for their own deliverance and will not think it humiliating but supremely glorious to spill their blood and sacrifice their lives for the glorification of a single man.¹⁴

12. Hahn and Wiker, *Politicizing the Bible*, 363; Hammill, *Mosaic Constitution*, 67; Nadler, *Book Forged in Hell*, 52; Mack, *Spinoza*, 7; Leithart, *Deep Exegesis*, 18–19; Levering, *Participatory Biblical Exegesis*, 108, 113, 118, 131, and 137; Elazar, "Spinoza and the Bible," 7; and Levenson, *Hebrew Bible*, 94–96 and 117. As Israel writes, "The real causes driving Enlightenment toleration were certainly partly social and cultural: the devastation of the Thirty Years War and the complete stalemate resulting from the clash of Catholicism and Protestantism were the prime causes" (*Enlightenment Contested*, 144).

13. Cavanaugh, *Myth of Religious Violence*, 124.

14. Spinoza, *Tractatus Theologico-Politicus*, preface, no. 4–5 and 7; Israel, 4–6; Akkerman, 58–63; and Gebhardt, 6–7. All citations from Spinoza's *Tractatus Theological Politicus* in this chapter, since, unlike the previous chapters, it deals specifically with Spinoza, will be cited as follows. The first citation will be abbreviated as it is in this footnote, and will be to the chapter followed by the paragraph numbers used in Akkerman's edition of the *Tractatus Theologico-Politicus*. The second citation will be to the English edition, from which all English translation in this chapter will be taken, Spinoza, *Theological-Political Treatise*. The third citation will be to the pages of the current

Thus Spinoza and thinkers like him claimed they were formulating their rational methods for biblical exegesis in order to curb the violence they attributed to religion. Assuming that a normative systematic interpretation of the Bible may actually prevent religious warfare, Spinoza's alleged motivation would appear to be quite admirable, even if naïve. Spinoza's true motivations, however, were far more complex than a simple desire for peace.

ATTACKING THE SYNAGOGUE BY DECONSTRUCTING THE BIBLE

Spinoza's *Tractatus Theologico-Politicus* was not simply an attempt to bring peace to Europe, but also can be regarded as a tool for exacting revenge on the Synagogue; in other words, one of the purposes it served was attacking the Sephardic Jewish community of Amsterdam. Typically, scholars assume that Spinoza was kicked out of the Sephardic community in Amsterdam because of his heterodox views which he later published in his *Tractatus Theologico-Politicus*. On the contrary, as Jon Levenson points out, " . . . Spinoza turned against the Jewish tradition and even against the Jews themselves with fury. . . . History supplied Spinoza with the coffin into which he placed the Torah."[15]

I suggest that the image of Spinoza as the greatest Torah student from the Amsterdam community who became dissatisfied with traditional Jewish responses to theological difficulties he discovered through his erudition needs to be revised. In the apologetical defense of Spinoza's thought, *La vie de Monsieur Benoit de Spinosa*, which was previously thought to be a nearly objective or factual early attempt at biography, we encounter the

---

critical Latin edition established by Fokke Akkerman and corresponding French translation as found in Spinoza, *Tractatus Theologico–Politicus*, the first edition of which was originally published in 1999. This volume is the most thorough and up-to-date critical edition of the *Tractatus Theologico–Politicus*, with opposing pages of the Latin text with French translation. The fourth citation will be to the pages of the older 3rd volume of Gebhardt, ed., *Spinoza Opera*, since, although now obsolete, that remains the most accessible critical edition of the Latin text, a full text of which is available open access online. Silverthorne's and Israel's translation is taken from Akkerman's critical edition of *Tractatus Theologico–Politicus*, and follows the paragraph divisions in Akkerman, which are less cumbersome than Spinoza's original paragraph divisions.

15. Levenson, *Hebrew Bible*, 91 and 95. He explains further, "Today it is too easily forgotten that the context in which pioneers of biblical criticism like Spinoza and Thomas Hobbes presented their heterodox findings was one of political debate in which the authors' goal was to free the political order from subservience to religion. The easiest way to accomplish this goal was to attach the religious documents inextricably to a vanished political order" (ibid., 95).

mythic confrontation between Spinoza and the chief rabbi of his synagogue Saul Levi Morteira.[16] This dramatic battle of wits has imprinted itself in the imagination of a host of modern scholars, and yet, as Frampton points out, no reliable confirmation of such an epic duel exists.[17] In contrast, the archival evidence suggests that Spinoza stopped formal study in Judaism when he was about thirteen, bar mitzvah age, and hence, unlike his brother in law, he did not continue to advanced study.[18]

Despite this, Spinoza was clearly a gifted student who knew the Hebrew language, and was familiar with traditional rabbinic interpretation. The degree of his erudition within Judaism, however, is uncertain, and it now seems unlikely that he was as adept a scholar of Judaism as has previously been assumed. His skepticism was likely the result of a long process of study, which included a detailed immersion in Cartesian philosophy, as we shall see.[19] Spinoza's personal and educational background had him positioned in the right place to make a contribution to the development of modern biblical criticism within the seventeenth century.[20] Although never having been a convert to Christianity himself, Spinoza was raised among Marrano returnees to Judaism who were relearning how to live as Jews in the Dutch Republic which granted them a great deal of relative autonomy. Marrano patterns of thought and cultural habits almost certainly shaped Spinoza's thought as he grew up.[21]

16. *La vie*, ed. Wolf, 41–75. See Frampton's comments: "The image [in *La vie*] of a leisurely youth pursuing truth in the upper-level *medrassim* on the Hebrew Scriptures and the Talmud, discussing hermeneutical perplexities of biblical texts with friends, questioning the religious assumptions of his teachers and synagogue officials, and eventually confronting Talmud Torah's head rabbi, Morteira, in a final duel—however attractive this fictionalization may be, it distorts evidence from the Amsterdam archives" (*Spinoza and the Rise of Historical Criticism*, 132).

17. Frampton, *Spinoza and the Rise of Historical Criticism*, 94–120.

18. Ibid., 131–32 and 154; and de Mordechai Vaz Dias and van der Tak, "Spinoza Merchant," 103–71.

19. Frampton, *Spinoza and the Rise of Historical Criticism*, 154.

20. Two of the most accessible, insightful, and brief biographies of Spinoza are Popkin, *Spinoza*; and Nadler, *Spinoza*.

21. van Bunge, *Spinoza Past and Present*, 1–15; Yovel, *Other Within*, entire book, especially 334–36 which deals specifically with Spinoza; Popkin, *Spinoza*, 5–16; Yovel, *Spinoza and Other Heretics I*, entire book; and Albiac, *sinagoga vacía*, whole book. It should be noted that Albiac's otherwise fine and incredibly thorough book includes a vast array of uneven sources, and suffers in a few places from overreaching the evidence, especially regarding Spinoza's relationship with De Witt. It should be noted too that van Bunge's contribution to this discussion minimizes the Marrano background to understanding Spinoza. For a further critique of locating Spinoza in a Marrano context, see Frampton, *Spinoza and the Rise of Historical Criticism*, 18–22, which provides ample sources to consult.

After his ban, Spinoza clearly distanced himself from his Jewish heritage. Although never formally becoming a Christian, Spinoza depicted Jesus as superior to Moses in his *Tractatus Theologico-Politicus*. And, although he wrote a Hebrew grammar, which he never completed, he did so to assist his non-Jewish friends who desired to read the Old Testament in Hebrew, much as his first publication on Descartes was likewise for his friends. After his ban, Spinoza spent the rest of his days among Christians, albeit outside the bounds of Protestant orthodoxy, who had theological and political problems with Calvinists and Catholics. After his ban from the synagogue in Amsterdam, Spinoza had no positive interaction with the Jewish community again.[22]

In the past, scholars have put forth numerous theological reasons for Spinoza's ban from the Jewish community in Amsterdam. These range from heterodox views concerning God to the denial of the Mosaic authorship of the Pentateuch. The truth is that we do not know the exact reasons for his ban, and contrary to so much scholarly opinion, the evidence does *not* indicate that Spinoza's views concerning God, his denial of the Mosaic authorship of the Pentateuch, or any of his other later so-called "heresies," were already fully-formed while he was a member in good standing in his synagogue community, although any of these positions is possible. Rather, the evidence seems instead to support Levenson's supposition that Spinoza's heterodox views were at least a partial retaliation to the Jewish community that ostracized him.[23]

In fact, the archival and historical evidence seems to suggest that the reasons for Spinoza's ban were not explicitly theological at all, certainly not exclusively theological. Spinoza's merchant father was a well-respected member of the Jewish community in Amsterdam. After his father's death Spinoza publically defamed him, assigning responsibility to his father for withholding inheritance money, which Spinoza claimed contributed to his current debt. But Spinoza did not stop there. In an attempt to cancel his debt, Spinoza went (a second time) before the city of Amsterdam and formally requested to be adopted by a legal guardian appointed by the secular

---

22. In fact, Freedman maintains that, "Anti-Jewish sentiment is evident in every single chapter of the *Tractatus Theologico-Politicus*. In fact, it would be hard to imagine a modern anti-Semite leveling a more vicious attack at everything held dear by Jews." See "Father of Modern Biblical Scholarship," 37.

23. Indeed, Vlessing has surmised that, "Historians have approached this subject by stereotyping the Jews. Spinoza became the ideal Jew through his philosophical works and the Jewish leaders were pictured as evil. In fact both parties acted rationally. . . . Spinoza's philosophy was not a reaction to a bizarre collection of ideas within the Jewish community, but a sophisticated reaction to his own experiences. His first encounter with authority was not spiritual but legal." See "Jewish Community," 209–10.

authorities; he made this request at the age of twenty-three. His request was granted, and thereupon his debt was erased. Such events placed the Jewish community in Amsterdam in an uncomfortable position; Spinoza's turn to secular authority circumvented his Jewish community, and it was likely perceived by them as a threat to their accustomed relative autonomy as a community.[24]

What makes this case especially interesting is that when we examine many of Spinoza's later arguments in his *Tractatus Theologico-Politicus*, we find that they are not unique to him but rather predate his writing. Freedman isolates twenty foundational arguments highlighting what Spinoza believes to be historical problems with the Bible that he expands to make his case for justifying his historical method.[25] All twenty Freedman traces back to earlier sources, and, in fact, fourteen of them, a full two thirds, he traces back to sixteen pages of a single work by the Muslim Polemicist Ibn Ḥazm, who attacked Judaism and the Hebrew Bible after he was bypassed

---

24. Frampton, *Spinoza and the Rise of Historical Criticism*, 141–47 and 153; Vlessing, "Excommunication of Baruch Spinoza," 15–47; Vlessing, "Jewish Community," 195–211; and Kaplan, "Social Functions," 111–55. Based on archival research, Vlessing claims that Spinoza "had to be removed from the community because financial interests were at stake.... The Portuguese Jewish community tried ... to protect its international financial position by pronouncing this *herem*. It was in fact a conflict of interests between the individual and the group and between two legal systems" ("Jewish Community," 205 and 209). Frampton clarifies the situation when he explains, "the son of a former respected and prominent member of the *ma'amad*, *parnassim*, and *deputados* took matters into his own hands by openly criticizing his father before the city court and by sidestepping Jewish law, going outside the jurisdiction of the Portuguese neighborhood.... The religious officials of the Talmud Torah could not afford to ignore the public image of the Jewish community. They did not want to jeopardize the religious and economic freedom they had in Holland, not experienced by Marranos, who had lived in Spain or Portugal beforehand. To maintain the relatively amicable relationship they had with the public, they had to appear as a cohesive, peaceful, and restrained subpopulation by keeping the status quo religiously, politically, and economically. Consequently, the *ma'amad* could not tolerate anyone in their midst who might endanger the welfare of the larger whole by bringing the Talmud Torah under further public scrutiny" (*Spinoza and the Rise of Historical Criticism*, 143–44). The Dutch Jewish community in the seventeenth century played an important role in the Dutch economy, particularly regarding international trade, and this was partly the reason for such relative autonomy. The Jewish community in Amsterdam was therefore accorded certain rights, like dealing with issues of financial debt from within set community structures in the synagogue, etc. On all of the above, see Vlessing, "New Light," 43–75; Popkin, *Third Force*, 149–71; Israel, "Dutch Sephardi Jewry," 76–97; Kaplan, "Portuguese Community," 23–45; Michman, "Historiography," 7–29; Israel, "Changing Role," 31–51; Kaplan, "On the Relation," 82–94; Israel, "Economic Contribution," 505–35; Kaplan, "Portuguese Jews," 37–51; Swetschinski, "Kinship and Commerce," 52–74; Israel, "Some Further Data," 7–19; and Koen, "Earliest Sources," 25–42.

25. Freedman, "Father of Modern Biblical Scholarship," 31–32.

for a governmental office which was given instead to the Jewish Shmuel Ibn Nagrela, also known as Shmuel Ha Naggid.[26] Among Spinoza's many arguments are his claims against the Mosaic authorship of the Pentateuch.

Medieval Muslim biblical criticism, such as Ibn Ḥazm's, was extremely sophisticated and was transmitted all the way into the nineteenth century, as Hava Lazarus-Yafeh's work has demonstrated.[27] Such a borrowing of argumentation from a Muslim polemicist indicates that, like Ibn Ḥazm, Spinoza probably developed his biblical criticism, at least in part, as a weapon of revenge on the Jewish community rather than out of disinterested scholarship. Not only do Spinoza and Ibn Ḥazm employ many of the same arguments, but they shared anti-Jewish sentiments, although, arguably Ibn Ḥazm's were harsher and more explicit.[28]

Spinoza is quick to criticize what Enlightenment thinkers will denounce as priestcraft,[29] the subtle manipulation of the laity by Machiavellian priestly rulers and clerical aristocracy.[30] Reminiscent of Machiavelli, Spinoza identifies one of the chief problems when he writes:

> In searching out the reason for this deplorable situation, I never doubted that it arose because, in the religion of the common people, serving the church has been regarded as a worldly career, what should be its unpretentious offices being seen as lucrative positions and its pastors considered great dignitaries. As soon as this abuse began in the church, the worst kind of people came

---

26. Ibid., 32–33. See Freedman's entire article (31–38) for his complete arguments. On Ibn Ḥazm, his biblical criticism, and particularly his critique of the Torah, see, e.g., Pulcini, *Exegesis as Polemical Discourse*; Adang, *Muslim writers on Judaism*; Adang, *Islam frente a Judaísmo*; Martinez-Gros, "Ibn Hazm contre les Juifs," 123–34; Fierro, "Ibn Hazm," 81–89; Rif'at, "Ibn Hazm on Jews"; Adang, "Schriftvervalsing," 190–202; Roth, "Forgery and Abrogation," 203–36; Powers, "Reading/Misreading," 109–21; Aasi, "Muslim understanding"; Adang, "Ibn Hazm on Jews"; and the other sources referenced on Ibn Ḥazm in the first two chapters of this present volume.

27. Lazarus-Yafeh, *Intertwined Worlds*.

28. Freedman, "Father of Modern Biblical Scholarship," 33.

29. Lucci, *Scripture and Deism*, especially 41, 55, and 127; Lucci, "Judaism and the Jews," 182, 187, and 197; Barnett, *Enlightenment and Religion*, 45–67; Barnett, *Idol Temples*; and Champion, *Pillars of Priestcraft*.

30. In this context, with regard to Machiavelli, Hahn and Wiker explain that, "The gap between the appearance of holiness and the underlying reality of corruption in the Curia became, for Machiavelli, the paradigmatic form of princely deception. . . . Machiavelli inferred that the same gap exists in the Biblical text itself. His discovery of the "key" to the underlying motives of biblical figures created a new mode of exegesis, and Machiavelli therefore can rightly be considered as one of the earliest, and certainly the most influential, sources of the hermeneutics of suspicion." See *Politicizing the Bible*, 144.

forward to fill the sacred offices and the impulse to spread God's religion degenerated into sordid greed and ambition.[31]

Spinoza had a number of important influences on his thought and his main theo-political work dealing with biblical exegesis, his *Tractatus Theologico-Politicus*, beyond the possibility of Ibn Ḥazm. One of the most significant influences on Spinoza was his English contemporary Thomas Hobbes, who we discussed in the previous chapter, and whose *De Cive* belonged to Spinoza's personal library. Although not certain, it is likely that Spinoza utilized the 1668 Latin translation of Hobbes' theo-political work *Leviathan* of 1651 in the final revisions of his 1670 *Tractatus Theologico-Politicus*.[32] As we saw in the last chapter, Hobbes' *Leviathan*, completed during his self-imposed French exile to avoid the carnage of the English Civil War, helped pave the way for modern biblical criticism through its critique of the traditionally held Mosaic authorship of the Pentateuch and naturalization of spiritual realities in Scripture.

Another likely influence was the French Calvinist-turned-Catholic—perhaps of Marrano background—Isaac La Peyrère, who was the focus of our second chapter.[33] La Peyrère's infamous work of biblical exegesis, *Pre-Adamites* (1655), which we covered in the second chapter, was also on Spinoza's shelf, and a number of scholars, following the work of Richard Popkin, believe the two may have met each other when La Peyrère visited the Dutch Republic in 1655.[34] La Peyrère's work, which he completed by 1648,[35] represented a wholesale critique of Scripture, more thorough than

31. Spinoza, *Tractatus Theologico-Politicus*, preface, no. 9; Israel, 7; Akkerman, 64–65; and Gebhardt, 8.

32. Hahn and Wiker, *Politicizing the Bible*, 370, 376n182, 381–83, 385, 388–90; Hammill, *Mosaic Constitution*, 76, 81, 89, and 93–95; James, *Spinoza*, 84, 95–96, 119, 236, 241–51, 259, 272–73; Nadler, *Book Forged in Hell*, 30–31, 34, 92, 94–96, 119, 188, 190, 193; Nelson, *Hebrew Republic*, 132–3, 151n84; Curley, "Spinoza's Exchange," 13n6; Harvey, "Spinoza on Ibn Ezra's," 54; Lorberbaum, "Spinoza's Theological-Political," 170, 172–73, 178–79, 183n11, and 184n28; Parkin, "Reception of Hobbes's *Leviathan*," 450–1; Verbeek, *Spinoza's Theologico-Political Treatise*, especially 8–10; Verbeek, "Spinoza on Theocracy," 336; Curley, "I Durst Not," 497–593; Schumann, "Methodenfragen," 47–86; Boss, "Les principles," 87–123; Osier, "L'herméneutique," 319–47; and Sacksteder, "How Much of Hobbes," 25–39.

33. Hahn and Wiker, *Politicizing the Bible*, 345–50; Nellen, "Growing Tension," 822–3; Malcolm, "*Leviathan*," 242–43, 243n4, 247–48; Albiac, *sinagoga vacía*, 124–29; Popkin, "Spinoza's Earliest," 37–54; Popkin, *Isaac La Peyrère*, especially, 26–59 and 80–93; and Popkin, "Some New Light," 171.

34. La Peyrère's book created quite a stir just before Spinoza's excommunication. On the reception of his work in the Dutch Republic of 1655-659, see Jorink, "Reading the Book of Nature," 63–65.

35. As discussed in chapter two, the final form of the text was published in 1655.

that of Hobbes, although both were subjugating Scripture for the purposes of redeploying it in their respective theo-political controversies: Hobbes in defense of the English monarchy and La Peyrère in defense of the political aspirations of his employer, the Prince of Condé.[36]

Spinoza's friend and in many ways disciple, Lodewijk Meyer (1629–1681), is another important figure in this discussion, since his 1666 *Philosophy as the Interpreter of Holy Scripture* was one of the most significant unnamed works against which Spinoza was arguing in his *Tractatus Theologico-Politicus*.[37] Meyer sought to interpret Scripture via the lens of Carte-

---

La Peyrère apparently commenced drafting the text as early as 1635, the first portion of which was being circulated in unpublished form in 1643. Gabriel Naudé mentions the work in a 1642 letter. Drafts exist already from 1644. La Peyrère's *Pre-Adamites* was published bound together with his larger work *Theological System*. They were likely completed and bound together no later than 1648. Quennehen, "Lapeyrère," 244.

36. See the discussions in Pietsch, *Isaac La Peyrère*, 124–39 and 196–228; Popkin, "Millenarianism and Nationalism," 74–84; Pacchi, "Hobbes and Biblical Philology," 231–9; and Reventlow, *Bibelautorität*, 328–70.

37. Hahn and Wiker, *Politicizing the Bible*, 353–6; Gibert, *L'invention critique*, 131–49 and 166; Leithart, *Deep Exegesis*, 7–11 and 15–17; Frampton, *Spinoza and the Rise of Historical Criticism*, 175–95; Israel, *Radical Enlightenment*, 197–217; Preus, *Spinoza and the Irrelevance of Biblical Authority*, xi, 8, 8n22, 11–12, 34–67; Klever, "Spinoza's Life," 29–31; Walther, "Biblische Hermeneutik," 227–300; Preus, "Hidden Opponent," 361–88; Macherey, "Louis Meyer," 168–172; Lagrée, "Sens et vérité," 75–92; Lagrée, "Louis Meyer," 31–44; and Zac, *Spinoza*, 27–29. Preus has done a lot to help us see that Spinoza's criticisms of Maimonides in his *TTP* is also a veiled critique of Spinoza's friend and contemporary Meyer. However, it is also clear that Spinoza is in fact taking on Maimonides himself, and specifically his *Guide of the Perplexed*, as Diamond has recently demonstrated by examining carefully Spinoza's discussion of the word spirit. See Diamond, "Maimonides, Spinoza," 321–36. Diamond explains that, " . . . Spinoza's treatment of the biblical God as a 'consuming fire' directly challenges its Maimonidean philosophical, juridical, and political constructions . . . . Spinoza devoted so much attention to the term *ruach* and subjected it to his lexicographical microscope far more than any other. Spinoza's initial exhaustive survey of the biblical term *ruach* can be better appreciated as an opening salvo in the attack on Maimonides' lexicographical edifice. Consistent with Spinoza's assault on this critical dimension of the *Guide of the Perplexed*, his *Theologico-Political Treatise* launches almost immediately into an extended philological analysis of the term *ruach*, also specifically dealt with in the *Guide*, which . . . implicitly targets virtually every facet of Maimonides' hermeneutic of the Bible" (321). As Preus et al. have shown, Meyer would have appeared to Spinoza as guilty of similar hermeneutical problems involved in a philosophical exegesis that Spinoza was attempting to overcome. The literature on Maimonides' influence on Spinoza has been rapidly growing for some time. As one very important example, see Chalier, *Spinoza Lecteur*, entire book. On the relationship between Spinoza's work and his friend and disciple Adriaan Koerbagh, see Hahn and Wiker, *Politicizing the Bible*, 350–3; Nadler, *Book Forged in Hell*, 38–44; Wielema, "Adriaan Koerbagh," 61–80; and Jongeneelen, "La philosophie politique," 247–67. On Spinoza's relationship and possible influence from and on Quaker exegetes like Samuel Fisher, see Popkin, "Spinoza and

sian philosophy, but he did so on fairly standard theological foundations, including the doctrine of Scripture's divine inspiration.

Spinoza's indebtedness to Descartes is overwhelming, even though Spinoza parts ways from standard Cartesian philosophy.[38] For Spinoza, "Descartes was his ticket to modernity."[39] Hahn and Wiker explain that, "Meyer's *Philosophia* and Spinoza's *Tractatus* often travelled together as one book, a marriage that made perfect sense. Meyer provided the framework as a prolegomenon, and Spinoza . . . spelled out the full consequences, consequences all the more radical precisely because of Spinoza's radicalizing of Descartes."[40] I think this is generally correct, even though Meyer's work is almost certainly one of the main implied targets of Spinoza's criticism in his *Tractatus Theologico-Politicus*, and although Spinoza disagrees with Descartes. Descartes' methodic doubt was an important underlying tool for Spinoza's biblical criticism. Moreover, although Spinoza took issue with Meyer's particular application of Cartesian philosophy to biblical interpretation, it likely had more to do with the traditional theological views concerning inspiration that Meyer retained than rationalism. As Preus makes clear, Meyer was "attempting to show how scripture's divine truths might be recovered through a philosophical method."[41] To drive the point home, Hahn and Wiker correctly identify Spinoza's debt to Descartes when clarify that, "Spinoza's entire philosophical approach, which undergirds his exegetical method, is based upon a radicalization of Descartes's project, one that

---

Bible Scholarship," 391–92; Popkin, "Spinoza's Earliest," 37–54; Popkin, "Some New Light," 171–77; Popkin, "Spinoza and Samuel Fisher," 219–36; Popkin, "Spinoza's Relations," 14–28; and Popkin, "Spinoza, the Quakers," 113–33.

38. See Hahn and Wiker, *Politicizing the Bible*, 259, 281, 342–3, 388, 546; James, *Spinoza*, 9–11, 92, 144–7, 150, 155, 218; Gregory, *Unintended Reformation*, 48, 60, 116; Mack, *Spinoza*, 7 and 11n1; Beyssade, "Deux latinistes," 55–68; van Bunge, *From Stevin to Spinoza*, entire book, especially 34–121, for situating Spinoza within his Dutch Cartesian context; Wilson, "Spinoza's Theory," 89–90; Garrett, "Spinoza's Ethical Theory," 267; Della Rocca, "Mental Content," 19–42; Curley, *Behind the Geometrical Method*, entire book; and Curley, "Spinoza's Geometric Method," 151–69. James writes that, "Just as Descartes urges us to shed our prejudices about the natural world and only to accept ideas that we cannot doubt, Spinoza extends this project to theology by setting out to shake off his preconceptions about what Scripture says, and only accept claims that he is absolutely sure it asserts" (*Spinoza*, 144–45).

39. Yovel, *Spinoza and Other Heretics I*, 206.

40. Hahn and Wiker, *Politicizing the Bible*, 355. On the following page, Hahn and Wiker explain, "Clearly, Spinoza's philosophy and hence his treatment of Scripture were part of a larger, more general philosophical movement rooted in the new mechanist-materialist worldview as interpreted according to a mathematical-mechanical approach, and which had direct implications for a radically new approach to Scripture. Spinoza would go on to provide one" (356).

41. Preus, *Spinoza and the Irrelevance of Biblical Authority*, 38n14.

itself rests on a presumed identity of being (nature) and the mathematical mode of human knowing."[42] Descartes' universe was Spinoza's universe.[43]

As important as Descartes was for Spinoza's initial philosophy and for applying Cartesian methodic doubt to Scripture, Francis Bacon was probably even more significant for Spinoza's purposes of developing a historical method, patterned on the then burgeoning hard sciences.[44] The hidden influence here is that of nominalism (and also Averroism).[45] Michael Waldstein sums up the history by explaining how William of Ockham took Scotus' voluntarism further, transforming it into nominalism. Luther was completely indebted to nominalism and passed it on to Protestants. Both Descartes and Bacon learned nominalist philosophy and bequeathed it to

---

42. Hahn and Wiker, *Politicizing the Bible*, 546.

43. Moreover, as Spinoza begins his *Tractatus Theologico-Politicus* by lamenting wars that have come about on account of religious strife, so too Descartes situates his own *Discourse on Method* within the milieu of the Thirty Years' War. See the comments on this in Gillespie, *Theological Origins*, 185.

44. See, e.g., Manrique Charry, "La herencia de Bacon," 121–30; Preus, *Spinoza and the Irrelevance of Biblical Authority*, 7n19, 24n73, 26n80, 38, 158n9, 159, 159n12, 161–68, 163nn20–21, 181, and 195; Gabbey, "Spinoza's Natural Science," 170–2; Curley, "Kissinger," 341n35, where he also notes Bacon's fondness for Machiavelli; Donagan, "Spinoza's Theology," 343; Donagan, *Spinoza*, 16–17; and Zac, *Spinoza*, 29–32. Gabbey explains that, "the first-order fact-gathering business of natural philosophy was viewed by Spinoza in a Baconian way.... The compilation of 'natural and experimental histories' was the first step in Bacon's method, and Spinoza's inference of definitions (i.e., of essences or natures) parallels Bacon's inductive extraction of forms and natures" ("Spinoza's Natural Science," 170). Donagan lucidly explains the parallel between Bacon's method and what Spinoza is attempting: "Just as a Baconian 'history of the mechanical arts' would be a collection of experimental data about the various kinds of mechanism there are, so a Spinozist 'history' of the Jewish Scriptures would be a collection of information of whatever sorts are pertinent to its interpretation" (*Spinoza*, 17). Preus illuminates the matter further: "Bacon believed that natural histories would get at things as they really were, in contrast to reason's imaginative and sometimes distorted constructions when unchecked by facts.... Natural histories... rendered the *sensus literalis* of the book of nature, which would yield new knowledge of God's works, just as the literal sense of scripture, brought out by the reformers, had yielded new understanding of God's Word.... Like Bacon, Spinoza takes a bottoms-up approach that begins with the data, in this case all relevant factual information needed as a foundation for understanding the Bible..." (*Spinoza*, 164).

45. See Hahn and Wiker's chapter, "The First Cracks of Secularism: Marsilius of Padua and William of Ockham," in *Politicizing the Bible*, 17–59, which lays the groundwork for both how Averroist (via Marsilius) and nominalist (via Ockham) philosophy will undergird later biblical criticism as it develops, especially in the Reformation and its aftermath leading up through the Enlightenment. Their later chapters do a good job of integrating this material, showing how it plays out throughout history as biblical scholarship becomes critical. See also Gillespie's chapter, "The Nominalist Revolution and the Origin of Modernity," in *Theological Origins*, 19–43.

modernity through their reconceptualization of the world.⁴⁶ What is missing from this brief summary is the role of Francisco Suárez mediating the scholastic tradition filtered through nominalism to both Bacon and Descartes.⁴⁷ Michael Allen Gillespie situates Bacon firmly within his nominalist

46. Waldstein, "*Analogia Verbi*," 99–101, where he writes, "Duns Scotus's student, William of Ockham, radicalizes his teacher's emphasis on divine free will to the point of nominalism, that is, 'name-ism.' He argues that God could command us to hate him, in which case hatred rather than love would be good. 'Good' is thereby reduced to a mere *name imposed at will*. Ockham's nominalism cuts the bonds of analogy and participation that unite God and creatures and thus obscures the interior goodness of creatures. It sees this order as an order God happens to have imposed on them from the outside, one among many orders he could have imposed. It regards natural beings as artifacts, not as natural beings, not as having an interior principle of order toward the good. They reflect the free divine power, not the divine being, goodness and wisdom. They have no inner participation in the being and goodness of God. . . . Luther was strongly influenced by Ockham, mainly by way of the Ockhamist Gabriel Biel (1420–1495). Bacon inherited the same philosophical premises in his Calvinist theological training. . . . One of the main philosophical forces at the very origin of natural science is the ambition for power over nature as articulated by Bacon and Descartes. According to Bacon, 'Human knowledge and power coincide in the same. . . . For nature is not conquered except by obeying.' On this point, Bacon's secretary, Thomas Hobbes, agrees with his employer. 'Knowledge is for the sake of power.' The extent of the power sought by Bacon is vast: 'the power and empire of the human race itself over the universe of things.' Bacon's choice of mechanics as the master-science of nature follows from his choice of power as the end. . . . Descartes studied Bacon before he began his first major work in natural philosophy. In his Discourse on Method (1637), he lays down the goal of his philosophy in agreement with Bacon." See Waldstein's earlier comments, "All who reflect about their Christian faith in the modern age experience the pressure of the scientific picture of the world or, more exactly, of the choices and philosophical premises implicit in that scientific picture. These premises, which lie in the voluntaristic nominalism of William of Ockham and the choice of mathematical mechanics as the master science of nature by Bacon and Descartes, destroy the metaphysics of analogy and participation . . . " (97). See also Gregory, *Unintended Reformation*, 36–38 and 49; Matthews, *Theology and Science*; and Gillespie, *Theological Origins*, 37–41.

47. E.g., Gregory, *Unintended Reformation*, 53; Ariew, *Descartes*, entire book for the late medieval scholastic context for Descartes' thought, but especially 3–4, 49–54, 71–72 for Suárez's influence; Gillespie, *Theological Origins*, 174 and 190; Faye, "Dieu trompeur," 61–72; Marion, "A propos," 109–31; and Wells, "Objective Reality," 33–61. Reviewing some of the reference material in Gilson, *Index* is instructive here. Gilson's introduction mentions how neither Bacon, Descartes, nor Spinoza, thought in a complete vacuum, but were in fact all three indebted to prior philosophical work within late medieval scholasticism. On Suárez's influence on Hobbes see especially Forteza, "La influencia," 40–79. On the influence of nominalism on Hobbes see Hahn and Wiker, *Politicizing the Bible*, 301–7; Gillespie, *Theological Origins*, 215, 228–34, and 248–53; and Callaghan, "Nominalism," 37–55. At one point Ariew insightfully hints that Suárez "seems to have been as much a Scotist as a Thomist (or perhaps may be better understood as neither Thomist nor Scotist)" (*Descartes*, 87). Indeed, it seems that although St. Thomas is certainly one of Suárez's primary masters, he filters St. Thomas through his other masters, Scotus and Ockham, as well as the general Jesuit reading of

context and details the "extent of the power sought by Bacon" (in Waldstein's words).[48] This picture lifts the veil which Spinoza carefully placed over his hermeneutic. As we shall see below, as Bacon called for the torture of nature for the sake of power, so Spinoza sounds the call to eviscerate Scripture, with a specific political power in mind.[49] His use of history as the sharpened instrument will be the tool he will use.

SPINOZA'S BLUEPRINT FOR MODERN BIBLICAL CRITICISM

Spinoza's new historical method for interpreting the Bible functioned as a weapon for him, a weapon whereby he attempted to demolish the very foundations of Scripture as revelation. For Spinoza, history did not so much have to do with development over time, rather, for Spinoza, "history," was much closer to the Greek notion, having to do with the study of "facts," and thus the natural realm was an analogue for history.[50] More than Herodo-

---

the Dominican Scholastic tradition. It should be noted that a critique of the growing tendency to trace modernity to Suárez is found in Miner, "Suarez," 17–36. Miner is cautious about making Suárez the first modern, and for good reason. I would only point out that, whereas Suárez may not be the first modern, the so-called early moderns must be understood in the terms of their relationship to, and influence from, late medieval scholasticism. Since so many of these thinkers read and or formally studied Suárez, they imbibed his metaphysics even when and where they disagreed with it. Significantly, Freudenthal's very important but apparently all-but completely forgotten 1887 essay on Spinoza provided important background information highlighting the influence of medieval (including Suárez) and so-called Protestant scholasticism on Spinoza. See "Spinoza und die Scholastik," 84–138.

48. Gillespie, *Theological Origins*, 38–39, who writes, "While *humility* gains us entrance to the study of nature, *cruelty* is the means by which we reach our end. Mere experience will take us only into nature's outer courts. To come to nature's inner chambers, we must tear it to pieces, constraining, vexing, dissecting, and torturing nature in order to force it to reveal the secret entrances to its treasure chambers. Only as merciless servants who bind and torture their master to learn the source of his power can we win from nature the knowledge of its hidden forces and operation."

49. Whether or not Bacon actually envisioned "torturing" nature through experimentation can be questioned. Peter Pesic challenges this notion, arguing instead that Bacon envisioned experimentation with nature to be a mutual difficult "trial" between the scientist and nature. See Pesic, "Wrestling with Proteus," 81–94. Nevertheless, the fact remains that the description of the experimentation of nature in Bacon's method is that of being physically ripped apart, dissected. No such physical dissection and thus destruction is envisioned on behalf of the scientist.

50 Reventlow, *Epochen IV*, 104. See also Yovel's comments that, "Spinoza's rationalism—the view that everything in the universe, down to its minutest details, is inscribed and structured by reason (which expresses the immanent essence of God)—is fundamentally atemporal and ahistorical, construed *sub specia aeternitatis*" (*Spinoza and*

tus or Thucydides, however, Spinoza was adapting a Baconian method to redeploy in the study of the history of the text of the Bible, or, more appropriately, he was using a Baconian method applied to the history *behind* the biblical texts.

What Spinoza presents us with in his *Tractatus Theologico-Politicus* is a sort of Magna Carta of modern biblical criticism. He presents a fundamental shift in how the study of the Bible is to proceed. James Kugel claims that, "In a few pages of his remarkable little book the *Tractatus Theologico-Politicus* (1670), Spinoza outlined a new proposal for *how* the Bible was to be read, and this program became the marching orders of biblical scholars for the next three centuries."[51] Indeed, modern biblical critics would follow the rough outlines of Spinoza's method even when they departed from his conclusions and from his philosophical starting points. It should be made clear, however, that far from merely attempting to construct an objective method for the scientific study of the Bible, Spinoza intended his method to serve his politics, as Shlomo Pines so clearly states, "The exegesis and the critical historiography of Spinoza aided him well in his polemic and political propaganda. And in fact, this was without a doubt the principal intention for which he invented his exegetical and historical method."[52]

This is the danger in any attempt to distance oneself from the biblical narratives in order to secure a neutral or objective stance towards Scripture; to be neutral is to pick a side, it is to have a specific secular commitment. It is impossible to be completely free of theological and philosophical commitments when approaching Scripture. Spinoza's method, despite the ostensible intent to be of use to common people over and against the ruling theological political elite, requires a tremendous amount of education and effort. Israel comments that:

> Perhaps the most formidable aspect of the *TTP*, viewed from a historical perspective, however, was precisely that it set out a new critical methodology and expertise in Hebrew philology resulting in a set of extremely challenging propositions designed to curtail theology's sway which are then pressed into the service of a general system and a body of moral philosophy

---

Other Heretics II, 23).

51. Kugel, *How to Read the Bible*, 31. See also Barthélemy's comments that, "Spinoza . . . presents a sort of 'discourse on method' for biblical criticism in chapters seven to ten of his *Tractatus*" (*Studies in the Text*, 53). And later, in the same introductory essay, " . . . Spinoza clearly formulated for the first time the agenda of what would later be called 'higher criticism'" (ibid., 54).

52. Pines, "Spinoza's *Tractatus Theologico-Politicus*," 17.

that is in turn integrally linked to a particular kind of republican political thought.[53]

The political motivations are ever present in Spinoza's *theo-political* work, as Menachem Lorberbaum clarifies, unmasking Spinoza's hidden purpose: "The agenda of the *TTP* is hence twofold: it seeks to destroy, to the extent possible, the theological foundations of institutionalized religion, and concomitantly to salvage a significant kernel that would enable the channeling of the elements of existing historical religions for the purposes of the sovereign."[54]

Spinoza did not invent wholesale the technical principles of the criticism Spinoza wielded in his theo-political battle rather they had already existed for some time. He inherited (in some cases directly in other cases indirectly) specific arguments against traditional attributions of authorship from much earlier traditions—Gnostic sources, Porphyry, Ibn Ḥazm, Ibn Ezra, et al.[55] Further textual and source critical issues had already emerged in the work of Peter Abelard, Lorenzo Valla, Erasmus, et al., as well as from Spinoza's contemporaries Louis Cappel, Isaac Vossius, et al.[56] Even his lengthy comments concerning the introduction of vowel pointing in the Hebrew text of the OT shows his awareness of the more recent debates from

---

53. Israel, "Early Dutch and German," 85. See also Sæbø's comment that, "The critical philosophy of Spinoza—and of the subsequent Spinozism—not only encouraged rationalization and secularization but promoted even a shift of authority, from theology to philosophy, from biblical revelation-based faith and ecclesiastical tradition to the scepticism of critical minds" ("From the Renaissance," 41).

54. Lorberbaum, "Spinoza's Theological-Political," 169. See Yovel's comments on how Spinoza's "biblical hermeneutics is not only an independent science in itself; it is also—and primarily—a weapon in combating historical religion and a vehicle in constructing a purified substitute for it" (*Spinoza and Other Heretics II*, 3).

55. Barthélemy, *Studies in the Text*, 3–5; Gibert, *L'invention critique*, 230–36; Reventlow, *Epochen II*, 246–58; Simon, "Abraham ibn Ezra," 377–87; Sela, *Abraham Ibn Ezra*; Sáenz-Badillos, "Abraham ibn Ezra," 85–94; and Freedman, "Father of Modern Biblical Scholarship," 31–38.

56. Jorink and van Miert, "Introduction," 1–14; Nativel, "Isaac Vossius," 243–54; Barthélemy, *Studies in the Text*, 16–24, 27–30, 33–35, and 51–52; Mews and Perry, "Peter Abelard," 3–19; Linde, "Lorenzo Valla," 35–63; Visser, "Thirtieth Annual," 7–31; Gibert, *L'invention critique*, 39–63, 94–101; Legaspi, *Death of Scripture*, 12–17 and 19–22; Reventlow, *Epochen IV*, 80–82; Shuger, *Renaissance Bible*, 14–15, 17–22, and 47–49; Jorink, "Horrible and Blasphemous," 433 and 441–47; Rummel, "Textual and Hermeneutic," 215–30; Burnett, "Later Christian Hebraists," 789–92; Reventlow, *Epochen II*, 155–61; Preus, *Spinoza and the Irrelevance of Biblical Authority*, 32nn100–101, 97nn90–91, and 181; Köpf, "Institutional Framework," 160; Delph, "Valla Grammaticus," 55–77; Popkin, "Spinoza and Bible Scholarship," 390; Goshen-Gottstein, "Textual Criticism," 372–76 and 374n34; and Bentley, "Biblical Philology," 8–28.

Elias Levita to the Buxtorf brothers.[57] Unfortunately, insufficient attention has been paid to the influence medieval Muslim philosophy and biblical criticism on Spinoza, although some wonderful studies in this regard do exist.[58] Spinoza's knowledge of both Maimonides and Ibn Ezra would be one clear means of having such thought mediated to him, but he likely was aware of segments of medieval Muslim thought more directly.[59]

57. Barthélemy, *Studies in the Test*, 13-20, 28-29, 34, and 36; Gibert, *L'invention critique*, 27, 237-45, 281-3; Legaspi, *Death of Scripture*, 19-20; Reventlow, *Epochen IV*, 79-82; Aranoff, "Elijah Levita," 17-40; Burnett, "Later Christian Hebraists," 787-89; Kugel, *How to Read the Bible*, 697-98n60; Newman, "Elye Levita," 90-109; Preus, *Spinoza and the Irrelevance of Biblical Authority*, 32n100, 97nn90-91, 181; Burnett, *From Christian Hebraism*; Goshen-Gottstein, "Textual Criticism," 371-72, 375, and 375n38; and Muller, "Debate Over," 53-72.

58. Hahn and Wiker, *Politicizing the Bible*, 343 and 358-62; Fraenkel, "Reconsidering the Case," 213-36; Djedi, "Spinoza et l'islam," 275-98; Fraenkel, "Spinoza on Philosophy," 58-81; Fraenkel, "Could Spinoza," 1-50; Martin, "Rethinking Renaissance Averroism," 3-28; Israel, *Enlightenment Contested*, 615-39; Ramón Guerrero, "Filósofos hispano-musulmanes," 125-32; Pacheco, "El 'Mahâsim al-mayâlis,'" 671-87; Arnaldez, "Spinoza et la pensée arabe," 151-74; Horowitz, "Averroism," 698-727; Tornay, "Averroes' Doctrine," 270-88; and Wolfson, *Philosophy of Spinoza I*, 8-13, 30, 125-26, 157, 189-90, 190n3, 197-99, 284. Djedi concludes, "A modern philosopher, Spinoza nevertheless is an heir of Judeo-Islamic thought" ("Spinoza et l'islam," 298). Arabic learning in seventeenth century England was immensely popular among English scholars, including those associated with the Royal Society, members with which Spinoza corresponded. Russell notes that, "there was a remarkably widespread interest in Arabic. In England it led to Arabic professorships in universities, first at Cambridge (1632), then at Oxford (1634), with Arabic as a requirement for the Arts degree. Arabic was taught at such schools as Westminster. Immense collections became established in private hands and in libraries. . . . Bi-lingual editions of Arabic texts were printed; grammars and dictionaries were prepared . . . . 'forward-looking' natural philosophers pursued Arabic manuscripts, particularly in astronomy and mathematics. After the founding of the Royal Society (1660), Arabic subjects featured substantially in the correspondence and queries of the Fellows . . . . Arabic interest permeated English society at all levels . . . . This was not an isolated phenomenon, unique to England, but emerged against the background of similar developments on the Continent, particularly in the Netherlands . . . . " See Russell, "Introduction," 1. Gillespie opines that, "the nominalist alternative that arose in reaction to scholasticism was probably also indebted to Islamic thought" (*Theological Origins*, 299n3). See also Shuger, *Renaissance Bible*, 13-16.

59. Hahn and Wiker, *Politicizing the Bible*, 343, 358-62; Fraenkel, "Reconsidering," 213-36; Martin, "Rethinking Renaissance," 3-28; Mack, *Spinoza*, 32; Djedi, "Spinoza et l'islam," 277-78 and 280-81; Fraenkel, "Spinoza ," 58-81; Arnaldez, "Spinoza et la pensée arabe," 152-3; Horowitz, "Averroism," 698-727; Tornay, "Averroes' Doctrine," 270-88; Wolfson, *Philosophy of Spinoza I*, 9-10, 13, 30, 157, 189-90, 190n3, 284. Israel points out that, "via bilingual Toledo, northern Spain, Provence, and Naples, Averroes' doctrines powerfully penetrated thirteenth-century Latin Christendom (and western Jewry), as part of the wider Aristotelian revolution of the thirteenth century . . . . Spanish clandestine academic Averroism became in fact the prime source of the underground Deism rife among the crypto-Jews in the Iberian world from at least as far back

One key move Spinoza makes in his criticism is a more developed criticism of the sources. Spinoza employed his Cartesian doubt to the traditional attributions of authorship in the Old Testament. The purpose was not to ascertain who actually was responsible for writing the books—for which he tentatively credits Ezra—although this was one central quest for which his method explicitly calls. Rather, Spinoza's source criticism served a different purpose. Dominique Barthélemy clarifies how, "Spinoza, as La Peyrère before him, thought, therefore, that if it could be shown that the books of the Old Testament had not been written by Moses and the Prophets but by much later compilers, one would be obliged to question the sacred nature of this collection of books."[60]

In his *Tractatus Theologico-Politicus* Spinoza outlines the contours of his method of biblical interpretation, on what he argues must be followed in order to arrive at the true meaning of the text.[61] At the outset of his work, Spinoza explains how he came about writing the *Tractatus Theologico-Politicus*. He was upset with religious strife and the dearth of recourse to "the natural light of reason" around him. Thus, he writes, "I resolved in all seriousness to make a fresh examination of Scripture with a free and unprejudiced mind, and to assert nothing about it, and to accept nothing as its teaching, which I did not quite clearly derive from it. With this proviso in mind, I devised a method for interpreting the sacred volumes."[62] One of the key moves Spinoza makes—indeed, many scholars see this as the main purpose in writing his *Tractatus Theologico-Politicus*—is the radical and absolute separation of

---

as the fifteenth century, a current of thought which persisted uninterrupted through the sixteenth and seventeenth centuries" (*Enlightenment Contested*, 624–5).

60. Barthélemy, *Studies in the Text*, 63.

61. On Spinoza's method, see Spinoza, *Tractatus Theologico-Politicus*, preface no. 10, Ch. 7 no. 2–18; Israel, 8–9, 98–111; Akkerman, 68–71 and 278–311; Gebhardt, 9, 98–112; Hahn and Wiker, *Politicizing the Bible*, 375–77; James, *Spinoza*, 150–54; Nadler, *Book Forged in Hell*, 134–42; Barthélemy, *Studies in the Text*, 53–57; Gibert, *L'invention critique*, 161–5; Sinai, "Spinoza and Beyond," 196–203; Nadler, "Bible Hermeneutics," 831–4; Bagley, *Philosophy*, 16; Kugel, *How to Read the Bible*, 31–32; Reventlow, *Epochen IV*, 105–6; Walther, "Biblische Hermeneutik," 227–99; Walther, "Biblische Hermeneutik und/oder theologische," 623–69; Yovel, *Spinoza and Other Heretics II*, 14–19; Moreau, "Le méthode d'interprétation," 109–14; Garrido, "El método," 269–81; Zac, "Spinoza et le langage," 612–33; Zac, "Spinoza et l'état," 201–32; and Malet, *Le traité*. James explains that, for Spinoza, "constructing a history of the Bible is in effect a matter of borrowing the method of analysis integral to Descartes' natural philosophy and applying it to theology. Scripture, Spinoza proposes, can be subjected to the same form of enquiry that Cartesian philosophers use to investigate nature. Furthermore, since Cartesianism proceeds entirely on the basis of natural reasoning, it follows that interpreting the Bible in this fashion does not require a supernatural light" (*Spinoza*, 150).

62. Spinoza, *Tractatus Theologico-Politicus*, preface, no. 10; Israel, 8–9; Akkerman, 68–69; and Gebhardt, 9.

faith from reason, and of theology from philosophy.⁶³ Spinoza claims that he has no intent on making faith and theology subordinate to reason and philosophy. Indeed, his fifteenth chapter is entitled, "Where it is shown that theology is not subordinate to reason nor reason to theology, and why it is we are persuaded of the authority of Holy Scripture."⁶⁴ Nevertheless, since, for Spinoza, theology and faith tend to deal solely with interior matters, often with matters of the imagination, and reason deals with objective reality, for those who do not share his mechanistic worldview, who resist the privatization of their faith, Spinoza's program takes theology and faith into exile.

The weapon of Spinoza's method is the acid of his historical enquiry. Scripture is to be studied historically, using "no other light than that of natural reason," as with any other ancient book.⁶⁵ Spinoza's method required an exhaustive account of the history and philological points of each text, after

63. Ibid., ch. 14 no. 1–14, ch. 15 no. 1–10; Israel, 178–94; Akkerman, 464–503; Gebhardt, 173–188; Hahn and Wiker, *Politicizing the Bible*, 380–81; James, *Spinoza*, 57, 94, 134–35, 142, 218; Nadler, *Book Forged in Hell*, 20, 65; Bagley, *Philosophy*, 10, 12; Polka, *Between Philosophy and Religion I*, 3 and 25; Popkin, *History of Scepticism*, 244; Preus, *Spinoza and the Irrelevance of Biblical Authority*, 15n45, 74, 81, 194, and 207; Gross, "Reading the Bible," 29; Shulman, "Use and Abuse," 44 and 46; and Zac, "Philosophie," 81–95. James notices how Spinoza is in effect attempting to subjugate theology to philosophy; no longer is philosophy the *ancilla* [handmaid] of theology, but rather philosophy is transformed into theology's master (*Spinoza*, 134).

64. Spinoza, *Tractatus Theologico-Politicus*, ch. 15 title; Israel, 186; Akkerman, 482–83; and Gebhardt, 180.

65. Ibid., ch. 7, no. 18; Israel, 111; Akkerman, 310–11; and Gebhardt, 112. Levering comments astutely, "Spinoza's key principle corresponds, in a certain way, to the parallel that the medieval (and some patristic) theologians had drawn between 'the book of Nature' and 'the book of Scripture.' He argues that one must interpret nature and Scripture by using the same methods. . . . The difference with patristic-medieval interpretation thus begins with a different understanding of 'nature': for the patristic-medieval tradition, nature is a created participatory reality that signifies its Creator and possesses a teleological order; for Spinoza nature simply yields empirical data within the linear time–space continuum. It is not that the medieval rejected empirical study of nature; rather the difference is that Spinoza's 'nature' is metaphysically thin" (*Participatory Biblical Exegesis*, 115). Likewise, Dungan emphasizes, "Nothing is rightly understood about the rise of modern biblical criticism if close attention is not paid to the shifting meanings given to the term 'nature' throughout this period" (*History of the Synoptic Problem*, 149). See also Hahn and Wiker, *Politicizing the Bible*, 280–81, 361–62, 364–68, 385, 391–92, 544; James, *Spinoza*, 54, 142, 145, 148, 161, and 178; Nadler, *Book Forged in Hell*, 32, 66, 76–103, 132–35, 137, and 139; Leithart, *Deep Exegesis*, 17; Hippler, "Spinoza et l'histoire," 155–76; Preus, *Spinoza and the Irrelevance of Biblical Authority*, ix, 2, 16–17, 22, 54, 98, 100, 156, and 158; Boss, "L'histoire," 179–200; Popkin, "Philosophy and the History," 626–27; and Zac, "Durée," 29–36. Preus observes that, "Under Spinoza's relentless critique, the Bible would become one ancient book among and comparable to others, irrelevant as an authority" (*Spinoza and the Irrelevance of Biblical Authority*, 2).

which discussion Spinoza proceeds basically to tell his readers that such an attempt is impossible.⁶⁶ The main points of his method may be outlined as follows:

1. The construction of a "natural history" of the Bible: "The [correct] method of interpreting nature consists above all in constructing a natural history, from which we derive the definitions of natural things, as from certain data. Likewise, to interpret Scripture, we need to assemble a genuine history of it and to deduce the thinking of the Bible's authors by valid inferences from this history, as from certain data and principles."⁶⁷
2. To construct this history, from Scripture alone.⁶⁸
3. Constructing a history of Scripture will proceed via several steps:
4. it "must include the nature and properties of the language in which the biblical books were composed and in which their authors were accustomed to speak."⁶⁹ This step will further involve:
5. to "investigate *all* the possible meanings that *every* single phrase in common usage can admit."⁷⁰
6. it "must gather together the opinions expressed in each individual book and organize them by subject so that we may have available by this means *all* the statements that are found on each topic."⁷¹

---

66. Hahn and Wiker, *Politicizing the Bible*, 375–7; Barthélemy, *Studies in the Text*, 56–58; Bagley, *Philosophy*, 16; and Dungan, *History of the Synoptic Problem*, 172. Bagley explains Spinoza's point thus, "If one recognizes that there are numerous difficulties that cannot be resolved even by appealing to the methodical interpretation of Scripture that is propounded by Spinoza in the treatise and if one acknowledges the modest feasibility of resolving many of the problems that will be encountered in the process of interpreting the Scriptures then it becomes increasingly clear that it is preferable and more sensible to adopt a minimalist approach to understanding or interpreting the doctrines and meanings of Scripture rather than to become embroiled in endless wrangling about the significances of difficult, obscure, or corrupted passages of Scripture, a procedure which Spinoza believed to be characteristic of the prevailing tradition of theology or religion" (*Philosophy*, 17).

67. Spinoza, *Tractatus Theologico-Politicus*, ch. 7, no. 2; Israel, 98; Akkerman, 278–281; Gebhardt, 98.

68. Ibid., ch. 7, no. 2–5; Israel, 98–100; Akkerman, 280–83; Gebhardt, 98–99.

69. Ibid., ch. 7, no. 5; Israel, 100; Akkerman, 282–83; Gebhardt, 99–100.

70. Ibid.; Israel, 100; Akkerman, 282–83; Gebhardt, 100. Emphasis added. Here Spinoza sees Hebrew as being the most important language, including for the New Testament.

71. Ibid.; Israel, 100; Akkerman, 282–85; Gebhardt, 100. Emphasis added.

7. then the exegete must "make note of any that are ambiguous or obscure or seem to contradict others."[72]
8. the exegete "must explain the circumstance of *all* the books of the prophets."[73] This final step will involve:
9. investigating all aspects of "the life . . . of the author of each individual book."[74]
10. investigating all aspects of the "character . . . of the author of each individual book."[75]
11. investigating all aspects of the "particular interests of the author of each individual book."[76] These include:
12. "who exactly" was "the author of each individual book."[77]
13. "on what occasion . . . the author of each individual book" wrote their book.[78]
14. "for whom . . . the author of each individual book" wrote their book.[79]
15. "in what language . . . the author of each individual book" wrote their book.[80]
16. the exegete must investigate "the fate of ach book."[81] This includes:
17. "how it was first received."[82]
18. "whose hands it came into."[83]
19. "how many variant readings there have been of its text."[84]
20. "by whose decision it was received among the sacred books."[85]

72. Ibid.; Israel, 100; Akkerman, 284–85; Gebhardt, 100.
73. Ibid.; Israel, 101; Akkerman, 286–87; Gebhardt, 101. Emphasis added.
74. Ibid.
75. Ibid.
76. Ibid.
77. Ibid.
78. Ibid.
79. Ibid.
80. Ibid.
81. Ibid.
82. Ibid.
83. Ibid.
84. Ibid.
85. Ibid.

21. "how all the books which are now accepted as sacred came to form a single corpus."[86]

22. "*All* this, I contend, has to be dealt with in a history of the Bible."[87]

This method has much to recommend itself, and the modern historical critical method continues to be indebted to these admirable pursuits. The limitation of Spinoza's method, however, was that nothing more could be done with the text. Only after such an impossibly thorough historical investigation is complete can the exegete begin to examine the theological significance of the biblical texts. Spinoza emphasizes that, "Only when we have this history of Scripture before us and have made up our minds not to accept anything as a teaching of the prophets which does not follow from this history or may be very clearly derived from it, will it be time to begin investigating the minds of the prophets and the Holy Spirit."[88] Immediately after this, Spinoza emphasizes that this too "requires a method."[89]

Spinoza proceeds to enumerate the steps involved in this method, after which he examines how to study philosophical questions in Scripture (again with a proper method in hand). He then concedes some serious obstacles involved that make his method prohibitively difficult: (1) "it requires a *perfect* knowledge of the Hebrew language";[90] (2) there is also "our inability fully to reconstruct the history of Hebrew";[91] (3) moreover, "the very nature and structure of the [Hebrew] language create so many uncertainties that it is impossible to devise a method which will show us how to uncover the true sense of all the statements of Scripture with assurance";[92] (4) "numerous ambiguities [in Hebrew] are inevitable, and . . . not method will resolve them all";[93] and finally, (5) the method "requires a history of the vicissitudes of all the biblical books, and most of this is unknown to us."[94] One of the purposes of all of this tedium is to narrow down the point of Scripture to a few general moral principles (love of neighbor and obedience to the state) which in turn served both his religious and political ideals.[95]

---

86. Ibid.
87. Ibid. Emphasis added.
88. Ibid., ch. 7, no. 6; Israel, 102; Akkerman, 288–89; Gebhardt, 102.
89. Ibid.; Israel, 102; Akkerman, 288–89; Gebhardt, 102.
90. Ibid., ch. 7, no. 11; Israel, 106; Akkerman, 296–99; Gebhardt, 106. Emphasis added.
91. Ibid., ch. 7, no. 12; Israel, 106; Akkerman, 298–99; Gebhardt, 106.
92. Ibid.; Israel, 106; Akkerman, 298–99; Gebhardt, 106–7.
93. Ibid., ch. 7, no. 14; Israel, 108; Akkerman, 302–3; Gebhardt, 109.
94. Ibid., ch. 7, no. 15; Israel, 109; Akkerman, 304–5; Gebhardt, 109.
95. James, *Spinoza*, 188, 189n9, 194, 196, 203, and 205; Nadler, *Book Forged in Hell*,

THE BIBLICAL CRITICISM OF BARUCH SPINOZA IN CONTEXT   129

The assumption undergirding his method was based on Cartesian skepticism applied to biblical interpretation.[96] Spinoza relied upon Cartesian methodic doubt in that disembodied reason became the ultimate judge of Scripture. So-called biblical truths could not rest on any other authority, not even prophetic or divine authority. The following examples illustrate Spinoza's skeptical stance toward the biblical texts. For Spinoza, no God exists apart from nature itself. Hence Old Testament prophets were not inspired by God in any traditional understanding, but rather they simply had

---

141–42 and 154–56; Gatens, "Spinoza's Disturbing Thesis," 455–68; Dungan, *History of the Synoptic Problem*, 174, 216, 238, and 253; Fix, "Bekker and Spinoza," 30; and Brown, "Philosophy and Prophecy," 199. Dungan explains that, "Spinoza is following a carefully devised strategy. Having insisted that the necessary place to begin is by answering a long list of questions regarding the physical history of the Bible, the ostensible goal of which is to prepare the researcher to infer clear and distinct and (morally) certain generalizations about the intentions of the authors, Spinoza suddenly leaps forward and says, well, actually, everyone already knows the basic doctrines of Scripture, and he lists them. The immediate effect of this move is to create an impulse in the interpreter to dispense with the theological synthesis step promised at the conclusion of the historical research. But he is not finished. He proceeds to isolate this list and set it apart from any potentially damaging theological speculation if anyone is foolhardy enough to hazard that step after some research" (*History of the Synoptic Problem*, 236).

96. Preus, *Spinoza and the Irrelevance of Biblical Authority*, 195. A number of scholars have argued that Spinoza's skeptical views were cryptic, that Spinoza employed a sort of "dual language" in typical Marrano style. See, e.g., the arguments of Strauss, *Spinoza's Critique*, esp. 35–52, 107–46, and 215–68; Yovel, *Spinoza and Other Heretics 1*, esp. 15–39 and 128–52; Strauss, *Persecution*, 142–201; Yovel, "Marrano Patterns," esp. 475–77; Yovel, "Spinoza," 305–33; and Strauss, "On a Forgotten," 27–31. This view has been heavily criticized, e.g., in Frampton, *Spinoza and the Rise of Historical Criticism*, esp. 20 and 20n49; van Bunge, "Spinoza and the Idea," 105–26; Levene, "Ethics and Interpretation," 57–110; van Bunge, "Spinoza's Jewish Identity," 100–118, esp. 102–3; Donagan, "Spinoza's Theology," 345 and 369–71; Harris, *Is There an Esoteric Doctrine*; and Harris, *Salvation*, esp. 206–10. Frampton provides the main argument against Strauss and Yovel's modification of Strauss's argument: "If Spinoza were trying to cancel his true thoughts and intentions, using dual language, why publish the *TT-P* anonymously?" (*Spinoza and the Rise of Historical Criticism*, 20n49). And furthermore, on the same page, Spinoza was not himself a Marrano, a Sephardic Jewish convert to Catholicism. In response to Frampton's question (and implied argument) here, I would suggest that the *Tractatus Theologico-Politicus* includes arguments that were too controversial at that time, like the denial of the Mosaic authorship of the Pentateuch, which would explain Spinoza's anonymity; dual language was insufficient to protect the author. The point of such dual language, however, was to help soften the blow so as to convince the reader that not every methodological suggestion within the book was necessarily bad. Spinoza wanted to convince his readers to actually employ his method and this was the reason for dual language, as Dungan makes clear in *History of the Synoptic Problem*, esp. 214, where he underscores that Spinoza "realized he had to accommodate to some extent to the views of his audience." Also, although Spinoza was not himself a true Marrano, he spent over the first twenty years of his life in a prominent Marrano community, so he would be well accustomed to numerous aspects of Marrano culture.

brilliant imaginations. Spinoza likewise denied the existence of miracles and views the Holy Spirit simply as peace of mind from doing what one ought to do. Finally, Spinoza reduced all the moral precepts of the Bible to loving God and loving one's neighbor, but unlike the way in which this Jesus-like idea has been traditionally understood by Christians, for Spinoza it held a threefold significance: to tolerate differences in private beliefs, to help those in need, and to obey the state. Any other moral laws from the Bible had no relevance, since they were intended only for earlier states, like the Hebrew Nation of the Old Testament.

David Dungan points out how Spinoza believed there were certain platitudes that could be known and universally accepted—like love of neighbor—and how Spinoza used the assumption of such platitudes, combined with his historical method, to eviscerate Scripture of more complex theological meaning.[97] Spinoza's study of the Bible led him to conclude that we do not know enough about the original meaning of the words in their original languages, nor can we arrive at sufficiently complete historical biographies of the authors, etc. In effect, after laying out the details of his new historical method, Spinoza proceeded to show how there was no realistic way to answer the questions he multiplied; all the exegete is left with are the numerous historical questions and the fruitless investigations to try and answer them. Spinoza did not believe anything more should be done with the biblical texts until the complete histories were discovered. Dungan makes clear, "Spinoza and his followers multiplied questions about the physical history of the text to the point that the traditional theological task could never get off the ground."[98] In short, his method of investigating Scripture did more to paralyze the exegete than to further theological biblical understanding.

Within his method, Spinoza appears to adopt the Protestant notion of *sola Scriptura*; he claims to interpret Scripture by recourse to Scripture alone.[99] His advocacy of a sola scriptura like position is aimed against

---

97. Dungan, *History of the Synoptic Problem*, 236–40. Frampton is very critical of Dungan here, but he does not fully engage Dungan's arguments (*Spinoza and the Rise of Historical Criticism*, 14–17).

98. Dungan, *History of the Synoptic Problem*, 172.

99. James makes clear, however, "When Spinoza claims to be interpreting Scripture by Scripture, he means that he is interpreting Scripture by Scripture as opposed to interpreting it against the standard of clarity and distinctness used by Cartesian philosophers. His method does not prevent him from appealing to non–biblical historical and philological sources; on the contrary, it demands that he do so whenever these can help him to work out, for instance, what a word means or when a book was written" (*Spinoza*, 158). See also Nadler, *Book Forged in Hell*, 133–34.

ecclesiastical authorities.[100] To adapt Jaroslav Pelikan's witticism, Spinoza's adherence to *sola Scriptura* notwithstanding, he "showed that the 'Scriptura' has never been 'sola.'"[101] This brings us to another key interpretive move by Spinoza, and that is his exaltation of literal exegesis.[102] Indeed, Yirmiyahu Yovel labels Spinoza "the enemy of allegorization,"[103] and his biblical hermeneutic as "an anti-allegorical method of interpretation."[104] And yet, Spinoza's literal exegesis smacks of secular allegorism.[105] Spinoza rapidly turns shades of Machiavelli when we examine his "literal" exegesis in *TTP*. His literal exegesis, or rather his secular allegorization—ostensibly an attempt to unmask the powerful politics at play barely discernible between the lines of the Hebrew text—is a façade for his political machinations.

MODERN POLITICS, MODERN BIBLICAL INTERPRETATION, AND THE FATE OF THEOLOGICAL EXEGESIS

Historical biblical methodologies like Spinoza's became tools of state used to flatten out perceived religious threats to citizens' physical safety stemming from rival biblical interpretations. It is no coincidence that Spinoza saw the state as the necessary controller of religion in the public square. Nor should it seem a coincidence that state-run universities would replace religious

---

100. Preus, *Spinoza and the Irrelevance of Biblical Authority*, 12, 12–13n38, 134, and 134n91; and Greschat, "Bibelkritik und Politik," esp. 331–32 which shows the differences between the Reformers' understanding of *sola Scriptura* and Spinoza's.

101. Pelikan, *Reformation of Church and Dogma*, vii, where he writes, "Despite their protestations of 'sola Scriptura,' the Reformers showed that the 'Scriptura' has never been 'sola.'"

102. E.g., Spinoza, *Tractatus Theologico-Politicus*, ch. 7, no. 5; Israel, 100–101; Akkerman, 284–85; Gebhardt, 100–101; Nadler, *Book Forged in Hell*, 131; Lasker, "Reflections of the Medieval," 69; Kreisel, "Philosophical Interpretations," 114; Yovel, *Spinoza and Other Heretics I*, 29,144, 151, and 231n5; Yovel, *Spinoza and Other Heretics II*, 17; and Zac, "Spinoza et le langage," 612–33.

103. Yovel, *Spinoza and Other Heretics I*, 144. In context, Yovel is showing how Spinoza uses allegory despite the fact that he opposes allegorical interpretation in general.

104. Ibid., 231n5.

105. Levenson demonstrates this basic point when he unmasks Spinoza's hermeneutic of suspicion and discontinuity: "The Bible in Spinoza's naturalistic theology becomes another political text, and its real meaning lies not in its textuality, but in its historical message, of which its own authors may have been unaware. The *meaning* of the Bible belongs to the contemporary moralizing historian. And when the message is derived from the underlying history and not from the manifest text that it often contradicts, then we are very much in the world of modern historical criticism and far indeed from the world of traditional religion . . . " (*Hebrew Bible*, 96).

magisteria as the loci of biblical interpretation, much as Spinoza's contemporary Thomas Hobbes envisioned the state sovereign, or the officials she appointed, as *the* authority on all matters of biblical interpretation. In short, Spinoza's program, which survived into the eighteenth and nineteenth centuries, through German and English translations, removed Scripture from its home in the synagogue and church, in Jewish and Christian liturgical life, and placed it instead as a political tool in the hands of emerging modern states.[106] In the eighteenth and nineteenth centuries, states would use such academic programs to domesticate further both Judaism and Christianity, which was Spinoza's true motivation in the first place.

In order to understand Spinoza's theo-political project, we must understand that he is writing in the midst of his contemporary Dutch political situation.[107] As Susan James explains, "in seventeenth-century Holland the interpretation of Scripture was . . . a subject of tense theologico–political conflict."[108] Steven Nadler likewise explains Spinoza's goal for inserting his newly refined method into this ongoing theo-political debate; namely, by deconstructing Scripture's supernatural and divine status Spinoza renders the Bible a dead letter, a natural literary work from which some moral profit may be derived, but one which will be unusable for state politics.[109]

106. Spinoza's work was particularly preserved through Richard Simon's appropriation of his methods. Johann Salomo Semler brought Simon's works into the German speaking world. Semler represented cutting edge philological analysis severed from any theological moorings. See, e.g., Sheehan, *Enlightenment Bible*, 95 and 114–15; and Hornig, *Johann Salomo Semler*. Johann Lorenz Schmidt translated Spinoza's *Ethics* into German in 1744, bringing Spinoza into German scholarly circles in the eighteenth century. Sheehan explains that, ". . . Schmidt wanted to tear the Bible out of the hands of traditional Christian theology" (*Enlightenment Bible*, 126).

107. James, *Spinoza*, entire book, especially 2, 4, 13, 30, 40, 52, and 141; Nadler, *Book Forged in Hell*, 21–25, 33, 110–11, 130; Steinberg, "Spinoza's Curious Defense," 222; Preus, *Spinoza and the Irrelevance of Biblical Authority*, 2, 5, 24, and 108; Krop, "Spinoza," 107–36; Smith, *Spinoza*, entire book; Van der Wall, "*Tractatus Theologico-Politicus*," 201–26; Feuer, *Spinoza*, 70 and 119–35; and Zac, "Le chapitre XVI," 137–50. Preus explains that, " . . . Spinoza's thorough critique of scripture in the *TTP* was intended to undermine theocratic ambitions in the Dutch Republic" (*Spinoza*, 2).

108. James, *Spinoza*, 141. Thus, as Preus notes, "Spinoza's assault on scripture would undercut the theocratic pretentions of the divines" (*Spinoza*, 4n10).

109. Nadler, *Book Forged in Hell*, 111, where he pens the following: "By showing that the Bible is not, in fact, the work of a supernatural God—'a message for mankind sent down by God from heaven,' as Spinoza mockingly puts it—but a perfectly natural human document; that the author of the Pentateuch is not Moses; that Hebrew Scripture as a whole is but a compilation of writings composed by fallible and not particularly learned individuals under various historical and political circumstances; that most of these writings were transmitted over generations, to be finally redacted by a latter-day political and religious leader—in short, by naturalizing the Torah and the other books of the Bible and reducing them to ordinary (though morally valuable)

Through his *Tractatus Theologico-Politicus*, which he shrewdly published anonymously, Spinoza was able to attack several battlefronts at the same time. His evisceration of the Torah and his exaltation of the New Testament and of Jesus in place of Moses, as well as his stringent critique of Maimonides, the Pharisees (a slightly less-than-veiled reference to Spinoza's Jewish contemporaries), Spinoza was able to exact revenge on the Jewish community that excommunicated him. His evisceration of the Torah, and his more heavily veiled critique of Christian dogma and New Testament history, as well as his overt dismissals of Roman Catholic papal authority, struck out both against the Catholic Church and Catholic lands who had threatened to control the Netherlands in the not-so-distant past, as well as against the Calvinist orthodoxy which threatened to take tyrannical control of the Dutch Republic and perhaps convert it into a new Geneva. Finally, his more subtle critique of Maimonides and his comments on philosophy could be taken as pedagogical or collegial jabs at his intellectual sparring partners and comrades in philosophical arms, the Collegiants, Quakers, and other heterodox Protestants with whom he exchanged ideas, especially Meyer.

Spinoza's discussion of the change in the OT priesthood from firstborn sons within the tribes of Israel to the sons of Aaron within the priestly tribe of Levi provides a useful examination of Spinoza's method. Here we see clearly the influence of Machiavelli, among others. Machiavelli exerted a great influence on Spinoza who read him assiduously.[110] Graham Hammill has recently argued that, "Machiavelli enables—and Spinoza develops—a critical assessment of absolutism based on its attempt to manipulate and control the theological imaginary upon which political community

---

works of literature, Spinoza hopes to undercut ecclesiastic influence in politics and other domains and weaken the sectarian dangers facing his beloved Republic."

110. Hahn and Wiker, *Politicizing the Bible*, 342–43 and 388; Hammill, *Mosaic Constitution*, 1, 21–22, 32, 66–68, 72, 78, 85–87, and 99; Viroli, *Machiavelli's God*, 17–18; Del Lucchese, *Conflict*, whole book; Lorberbaum, "Spinoza's Theological-Political," 170–71, 173, 177, and 183n19; Morfino, *Il tempo*, entire book; Nadler, *Spinoza*, 111 and 270; Den Uyl, "Power, Politics," 83; Balibar, "Spinoza," 3–36; Smith, *Spinoza*, 34–38; Curley, "Kissinger," 315–17, 327–29, 332–33, and 341n35; Preus, "Spinoza, Vico," 91n89; Septimus, "Biblical Religion," 399–433; Albiac, *sinagoga vacía*, 103 and 105; Mulier, *Myth of Venice*, 170–81; and Calvetti, *Spinoza lettore*, entire book. Curley maintains that, "Spinoza is arguably the most Machiavellian of the great modern political philosophers" ("Kissinger," 315).

depends."¹¹¹ Moreoever, Machiavelli championed secular allegorization like that found in Spinoza.¹¹²

Spinoza demystifies the Bible, naturalizing the supernatural.¹¹³ He argues forcefully for the impossibility of miracles, and demonstrates with sustained argument (spanning an entire chapter) that the prophets, rather than receiving divine oracles from God as a matter of public revelation, were simply possessed of vivid imaginations.¹¹⁴ As Scott Hahn and Benjamin Wiker put the matter, "Here, Spinoza revealed the key to his method of interpreting Scripture, even while concealing the ultimate reasons. . . . *Since miracles are impossible, therefore* the scientific exegete must look for another explanation of their common occurrence in Scripture."¹¹⁵ Unsurprisingly, that explanation was political. In the style of Machiavelli, Spinoza argued that so-called miracles, which in reality must simply have been nothing more than natural phenomena, were described as miracles, not only on account of the piety of the people, but at root on account of the sheer political

---

111. Hammill, *Mosaic Constitution*, 99. Hammill's third chapter, "Spinoza and the Theological Imaginary" (67–99) shows how Spinoza, "one of Machiavelli's most perceptive readers" (22), developed, honed, and took further Machiavelli's work, following the theo–political trajectory Machiavelli initiated.

112. Indeed, Hahn and Wiker insightfully underscore how, "In future exegesis, Machiavelli's mode of procedure is repeated, but in the service of other philosophies. . . . The pattern set is one in which the philosophy, no matter how far removed it is from the assumptions of the biblical text, becomes the secret knowledge that allows the exegete to wield the exegetical threshing tool. Passages that fit become the key to illumination; passages that do not must either be reinterpreted against the apparent meaning, or inferred to have some less than noble source. . . . The task of the enlightened exegete, then, is to ferret out all the 'real' passages—the ones that fit the philosophy—and reinterpret the rest, giving some *other* explanation for their appearance in the text" (*Politicizing the Bible*, 145). Spinoza would explicitly disagree with this caricature of what he is attempting to do, since he argues against reading the text in line with one's philosophy, *pace* Meyer. This is not a caricature of Spinoza's exegesis, however, but a description of Machiavelli's implicit principle. Spinoza's likely protestations notwithstanding, this is precisely what he actually does, *de facto*, in his exegesis, even if it is not *de jure* an official dictum within his explicit method.

113. Ibid., 364–68; Hammill, *Mosaic Constitution*, 87; James, *Spinoza*, 139–84; Gregory, *Unintended Reformation*, 60; Nadler, *Book Forged in Hell*, 76–103; Rosenthal, "Miracles," 231; Garrido Zaragoza, "La desmitificación," 3–45; Popkin, "Hume and Spinoza," 87–89; and Zac, "Spinoza et le langage," 612–33.

114. Hammill, *Mosaic Constitution*, 13–14 and 72–81; James, *Spinoza*, 51, 94, and 130–3; Nadler, *Book Forged in Hell*, 76–103; Rosenthal, "Miracles," 231; Gross, "Reading the Bible," 22–36; Preus, "Spinoza, Vico," 79–81 and 84–85; Popkin, "Hume and Spinoza," 87–89, where he shows that Spinoza's demonstration of the impossibility of miracles is even more forceful than Hume's; Malet, *Le traité théologico-politique*, 118; and Zac, *Spinoza*, 69–82.

115. Hahn and Wiker, *Politicizing the Bible*, 365.

power of their rulers. Michael Rosenthal explains that, in Spinoza's mind, "Miracles are especially useful not only in producing veneration but also in consolidating and maintaining political power."[116]

Spinoza shared with many of his contemporaries a disdain for the priesthood and any priestly class.[117] This should not simply be read as a criticism of the synagogue officials (although this is certainly true in part), but rather, shares much in common with later eighteenth- and nineteenth-century criticisms of OT priesthood as a guise for attacks on the Catholic priesthood—only for Spinoza, all Christian clergy are in sight. Yovel writes that, "When Spinoza describes the political rule of God through his priestly representatives, he thinks more of the rabbis in the Diaspora than of Moses and the Levites. But his chief targets lie in the Christian world. He aims at the political claims of the pope and the Catholic establishment; at the demands of the Dutch Calvinist *predikanten*" (among others).[118]

Likewise, Spinoza's views on prophecy are "clearly derived from Spinoza's own scientific account of the nature of prophecy; and although he attempts to find support for it in the Bible itself, in fact this is a general rationalistic presupposition derived from his philosophy and then superimposed on the text."[119] Again, this serves his political program even as it violates his own methodological principles. Just as it is impossible to have the Scripture alone without a tradition to identify what constitutes Scripture and how Scripture should be interpreted, so it is impossible to have a biblical interpretation without philosophical and theological assumptions. As with many later practitioners of historical criticism, Spinoza does not articulate his philosophical assumptions.

Spinoza's political views, like Hobbes's, fit broadly in the Erastian camp—what would be Gallicanism and other forms of Conciliarism in the Catholic world—a theo-political view that ultimately placed power in the hands of the state sovereign. Spinoza emphasized this using his discussion of the Hebrew state to bolster this claim, which included official biblical interpretation (as well as all public expression of religion) to rest in the hands of the head of state.[120] Yovel explains that, "By making the political authori-

---

116. Rosenthal, "Miracles," 241.

117. James, *Spinoza*, 202. Israel explains, "Freethinkers, in short, followed Spinoza in depicting priesthood as professional agents of prejudice, uncritical thinking, and ignorance" (*Enlightenment Contested*, 102).

118. Yovel, *Spinoza and Other Heretics I*, 196. See also Preus, *Spinoza*, 4–5; and Feuer, *Spinoza*, 69.

119. Yovel, *Spinoza and Other Heretics II*, 195n21.

120. Steinberg, "Spinoza's Curious Defense," 219; Nelson, *Hebrew Republic*, 130–34; Legaspi, *Death of Scripture*, 132; Levering, *Participatory Biblical Exegesis*, 112 and 137;

ties the sole interpreters of what is considered the word of God, Spinoza grants the secular government a monopoly over the normative domain as a whole—that is, over right and wrong, justice and injustice in all their valid applications."[121]

Starting with the biblical Hebrew state, the "Hebrew Republic," was familiar territory in early modern European political discourse.[122] In the *Tractatus Theologico-Politicus*, Spinoza understands the Israelite theocracy instituted by Moses in the wilderness after the exodus from Egypt as an attempt by Moses to bring civil order to their newly formed nation. The golden calf episode reduced Israel to a wretched servitude. The angry God of the wilderness unleashed his wrath against Israel. The Levites thus replaced the firstborn priests. Priestly rule proved a disaster in the history of Israel, instigating rebellion and virtual anarchy. After the monarchy takes over, to bring peace to Israelite society, a new strife ensues, that of throne vs. altar, state ruler vs. priest.[123] Michael Legaspi explains the upshot, that, "Spinoza's Moses harnessed powerful religious impulses and kept dangerous social forces in check by creating a free and equal society held together

---

Sermoneta, "Biblical Anthropology," 245–46; and Zac, "Le chapitre XVI," 137–50.

121. Yovel, *Spinoza and Other Heretics I*, 134. In his second volume, Yovel clarifies how for Spinoza, "The state, the political government, is to become the sole and true 'interpreter' of the nuclear moral-religion, to which the message of Scripture has been reduced by biblical hermeneutics" (*Spinoza and Other Heretics II*, 15).

122. James, *Spinoza*, 120, 265–69, and 271–73; Nelson, *Hebrew Republic*, entire volume; and all of the essays in Schochet, Oz-Salzberger, and Jones, ed., *Political Hebraism*.

123. Spinoza, *Tractatus Theologico-Politicus*, ch. 17, no. 7–15 and 26–29; Israel, 213–20 and 225–29; Akkerman, 544–63 and 574–83; Gebhardt, 205–212 and 217–20; James, *Spinoza*, 269–76 and 278; Nadler, *Book Forged in Hell*, 144–46; Legaspi, *Death of Scripture*, 133–34; Bagley, *Philosophy*, 37; Balibar, "*Jus-Pactum-Lex*," 171–206; Yaffe, "Histories and Successes," 62–63 and 65–68; and Zac, "Spinoza et l'état," 213. Legaspi summarizes: "The installation of a priestly class had disastrous results. The Levites became living reminders to the Israelites of their 'defilement' and 'rejection' by the biblical god. Spinoza characterizes the Levites as fault-finding nuisances and self-righteous, censorious 'would-be theologians.' The people, for their part, resented and rebelled against the priests, throwing the whole society into chaos and disorder. When a monarchy was introduced to stabilize the state, power struggles only took new forms: between king and Levite, for example, and between king and prophet" (*Death of Scripture*, 133). Yaffe suggests, "Perhaps it is not too far-fetched for us to describe Spinoza's history (as opposed to Ezra's) as falling somewhere between a modern account of an old-country saga and a statesmanship manual for future citizens of liberal democracies. Like the former, it recalls the deeds and misdeeds of authoritative figures dead and gone but more or less vivid in popular and pious memory. Like the latter, however, it is meant to have current practical application. Its chief application crystallizes as its old-fashioned authoritativeness melts" ("Histories and Successes," 67–68).

by piety and common morality. He demonstrated how religion could serve noble political ends."[124]

Spinoza's discussion here provides a useful example of secular allegory. The text seems to say one thing, but for Spinoza it "really" means something else. His literal exegesis amounts to little more than a secular theo-political allegory; what the text "really" means is *Realpolitik*. Levenson notes that, "Now any student of the Hebrew Bible knows that priests, prophets, and kings all take it on the chin quite a bit in that book, and the very worth of all three institutions was questioned at times. But what Spinoza does not respect is the claim of the text itself that each of them was divinely ordained and the fact that, on balance, the Bible is positive about them all."[125]

Spinoza's method is far too restrictive; so much so that it fails miserably on the grounds of explanatory power. This is unsurprising, of course, since Spinoza constructed his method to restrict the range of possible conclusions to support his theo-political project.[126] Part and parcel of this project was to keep Scripture in the past; indeed to distance the exegete from the world of the text as much as possible. As Robert Barron, following Levenson, rightly notes, "this hyperconcentration on the intention of the historical author within his historical period, and in abstraction from the wider literary, theological, and metaphysical context, has led effectively to the relegation of the Bible to the past."[127] For Spinoza, biblical exegesis is "an offensive weapon."[128] In his mind, "biblical hermeneutics is an aggressive activity, offering the philosopher a mode of involvement in the social and cultural processes of his time."[129] His method has been fairly left intact throughout the centuries since his death. Scholars in the Enlightenment and, later in the midst or wake of the *Kulturkampf*, built upon Spinoza's hermeneutic, honing various aspects while standing on his Machiavellian shoulders to construct theo–political tools of their own to denigrate the Judaism of the

---

124. Legaspi, *Death of Scripture*, 134.

125. Levenson, *Hebrew Bible*, 96.

126. Israel writes, "The key feature of the tradition of Bible interpretation instituted by Spinoza, and elaborated by Meyer, Koerbagh, Isaac Vossius, Goeree, and later Toland, Collins, Wachter, Giannone, and Edelmann, was precisely its strictly philosophical character, its use of philosophy not just to uncover discrepancies in the Biblical text or elucidate perplexing passages in the light of historical context, but to assess its significance, thereby completely detaching our view of Scripture from any theological grounding and ecclesiastical authority" (*Radical Enlightenment*, 449).

127. Barron, "Biblical Interpretation," 182.

128. Yovel, *Spinoza and Other Heretics II*, 11.

129. Ibid.

other in their midst, and utterly stomp out the Catholic bogeyman they feared might cause harm to the State.

Spinoza contributed to turning Bible into a material book, like any other.[130] Spinoza launched biblical criticism in the direction which it has followed. Regarding the titles of the *Tractatus Theologico-Politicus* chapters 7–10, Pierre Gibert notes that they "mark a significant change of paradigm in the critical approach of the biblical corpus."[131] Levenson too emphasizes Spinoza's significance when he clarifies that what Spinoza pioneered "was the systematic transference of the normativity of the Bible from its *manifest text* to its *underlying history* (at least as he reconstructed it)."[132] For Spinoza, such a method was not sought for the sake of better understanding the text, but, as Yovel reminds us, Spinoza's point was to create a hermeneutic that would have a concrete effect in the politics of his day and for future generations. Spinoza was attempting to make an effective intervention in the course of the social and political events in the Dutch Republic.[133]

Rather than the general assumption that Spinoza's construction of a historical method of biblical interpretation arose out of his desire to end violent religious conflict, I argue that the evidence from his socio–political background indicates that the method emerged from more personal and political desires. Spinoza had personal motivations in creating a method that would attack the biblical and Talmudic foundation of the Jewish society which ostracized him. More importantly, such a method served the political goal of furthering the secularization of nascent European states. The end result of the program, as it advanced through the centuries, was the removal of the Bible from tradition-specific religious contexts into its exile in modern universities, often at the service of modern states.

---

130. Hammill, *Mosaic Constitution*, 81; and James, *Spinoza*, 128.

131. Gibert, *L'invention critique*, 170. Ska similarly notes that: "Spinoza is undoubtedly the father of the historical–critical method and of modern exegesis although he is more a philosopher than a real exegete. To be sure, there is a great distance between the *Treatise* and, say, the *Prolegomena zur Geschichte Israels* or *Die Composition des Hexateuchs und der historischen Bücher des Alten Testaments* by Julius Wellhausen. But, to appreciate the novelty of Spinoza's 'natural' interpretation of Scripture (*interpretation naturae*), we should not look first of all for precise exegetical methods and even less for hypotheses about the formation of single biblical books. Spinoza's main contribution to modern exegesis is to be found in his systematic *secular* approach to the Holy Scripture. He brought the Bible down to earth and made it possible to hear the different, sometimes discordant, voices which resonate within this literary work" (*Exegesis*, 259).

132. Levenson, *Hebrew Bible*, 96.

133. Yovel, *Spinoza and Other Heretics I*, 136.

5

Biblical Hermeneutics and the Creation of Religion

THE TERM "RELIGION" IS so commonplace these days that one rarely questions that a simple definition exists. Each day our periodicals demonstrate the ease of using this word. The seemingly facile usage of "religion," however, obscures its original political-historical context. In this final chapter, I will complement the work of various scholars who argue that the emergence of religion as a modern category denoting private beliefs was primarily a political construct that facilitated the removal of the newly redefined religious from the public sphere. In addition to other historical accounts that describe this process, I will add the consideration of biblical interpretation, arguing that the *raison d'être* of the historical-critical method for studying the Bible in the seventeenth century, as we have seen in the previous chapters with Isaac La Peyrère, Thomas Hobbes, and Baruch Spinoza, was precisely to assist in the political task of transforming the public sphere.

The work of William Cavanaugh is particularly helpful in considering the argument at hand. In his 2009 volume entitled *The Myth of Religious Violence*, his 2002 work entitled *Theopolitical Imagination*, and his now classic 1995 article, "'A Fire Strong Enough to Consume the House': The Wars of Religion and the Rise of the State," Cavanaugh persuasively argues that the word "religion" has a complex past and that the traditional story of the "Wars of Religion" is problematic.[1] Following Talal Asad's description

---

1. Cavanaugh, *Myth of Religious Violence*, especially chapters 2 and 3; Cavanaugh, *Theopolitical Imagination*, 31–42; and Cavanaugh, "Fire Strong Enough," 397–420. Also invaluable are Nongbri, *Before Religion*; and Asad, *Genealogies of Religion*, 37–45.

in his now famous 1993 book entitled *Genealogies of Religion*, Cavanaugh notes that in the medieval period, religion had to do with the practice of the virtues within the church's liturgical life, or with religious orders, monastic discipline, or the worship of God; in fact was often used primarily of monastic life and discipline.[2] In the fifteenth through eighteenth centuries political theorists such as Jean Bodin, Hobbes, Spinoza, John Locke, and Jean-Jacques Rousseau redefined religion as pertaining to private beliefs, matters that did not belong in the public sphere: in other words, the newly defined secular realm.[3]

Cavanaugh finds an early example of the redefinition of religion in the very idea that the wars of sixteenth- and seventeenth-century Europe were religious, as we covered in detail in the first chapter. As we saw, the standard story is that after the Reformation doctrinal disputes broke out all over Europe's divided Christendom and these religious disputes turned into bloody battles; modern centralized states then emerged in order to use their justified monopoly on the legitimate use of violence to bring peace to these sectarian conflicts.[4] Cavanaugh objects to this on the three counts we covered in the first chapter. First, state centralization was a much longer process that reached back into history at least six hundred years, well before the Reformation itself; the wars were the final stages of state centralization.[5]

I also benefited greatly from Pickstock, *After Writing*, 146–54; and Harrison, "Religion."

2. Cavanaugh, *Myth of Religious Violence*, 64–68; Cavanaugh, "Fire Strong Enough," 403–4; Asad, *Genealogies of Religion*, 37–45; and Southern, *Western Society*, 214. Asad explains, "During the period [early Middle Ages] the very term *religious* was therefore reserved for those living in monastic communities; with the later emergence of nonmonastic orders, the term came to be used for all who had taken lifelong vows by which they were set apart from ordinary members of the Church" (39n22). Writing further, he mentions, "For medieval Christians, religion was not a universal phenomenon: religion was a site on which universal truth was produced, and it was clear to them that truth was not produced universally" (45n29). St. Thomas Aquinas used *religio* in his *Summa Theologiae* in I–II.49–55 and II–II.81.7–8 to refer to the reverence for God habitually developed within the church's communal liturgical practice.

3. Morrow, "Secularization," 14–32; Cavanaugh, "Fire Strong Enough," 403–8; Smith, *Meaning*, 31–44; and Figgis, *From Gerson to Grotius*, 124. In his more recent work, Cavanaugh links the beginnings of this transformation with the fifteenth-century works of Nicholas of Cusa and Marsilio Ficino. See Cavanaugh, *Myth of Religious Violence*, 69–85 for a more complete history of this change.

4. If by religious such stories included thick descriptions of religion as ways of life, including politics and not merely doctrinal beliefs, such stories would be less problematic, although with adherents of the same "religions" fighting each other, these narratives would still remain difficult to maintain. The stories as they are told, however, expressly deny the public and political implications of religion as a complete way of life, and instead view these conflicts as over differing beliefs.

5. Cavanaugh made the following observation, in the specific context of the

BIBLICAL HERMENEUTICS AND THE CREATION OF RELIGION 141

Second, these "religious" battles were not primarily between Catholics and Protestants, but, as we saw in the first chapter, between Catholics and Catholics, and thus clearly were not over religious matters of doctrine and private beliefs. Protestants fought on either side, teaming up with Catholics, in these battles.[6] Third, to describe the wars as religious is not only inaccurate, but anachronistic, since the definition of religion as private beliefs was being redefined as such at precisely this time. The purpose of such a

---

emergence of religion as a category denoting private beliefs and the use of the adjective "religious" to modify these wars: "the principal promoters of the wars in France and Germany were in fact not pastors and peasants, but kings and nobles with a stake in the outcome of the movement toward the centralized, hegemonic state" (*Theopolitical Imagination*, 31).

6. E.g.: (1) in 1618, Protestant Bohemians fought against the Holy Roman Empire, which was Catholic, enlisting the aid of Frederick V, a founder of the Protestant Union, but the Protestant Union refused to enter the fray; (2) in 1626 the Lutheran John George, the Elector of Saxony, joined forces with the Catholic Holy Roman Empire to retake Protestant Bohemia, but later the Lutheran George attacked the Catholic Holy Roman Empire; (3) Catholic France came to the aid of the Protestant Grisons in Switzerland in their battle against the Catholic Habsburgs; (4) in 1628 Dutch Calvinists came to the aid of Catholic France in order to fight Huguenots in La Rochelle; (5) in his battles the Calvinist Elector of Brandenburg George William used the Catholic Count Adam of Schwarzenberg as his main advisor; (6) the Catholic Albrecht von Wallenstein, leader of the Catholic soldiers of the Holy Roman Empire used the Lutheran Hans Georg von Arnim as one of his main commanders, and his soldiers were composed of both Catholics and Protestants; (7) from 1634-1635, Catholic France under Cardinal Richelieu's authority, sent soldiers to aid the Protestant Swedes in their battle against the Catholic Holy Roman Empire; and (8) the bulk of the final half of the Thirty Years' War was primarily fought between the Catholic Habsburgs and the Catholic Bourbons. See, Cavanaugh, *Myth of Religious Violence*, 142-77; and Cavanaugh, "Fire Strong Enough," 399-403. No one has made this case as strongly as Cavanaugh. Cavanaugh pointed out that the regions which already had concordats with the pope, limiting papal authority within their realms, remained Catholic through the Reformation, and the Protestant Reformation was only successful in regions that had not been able to secure any other means of limiting the pope's authority. Both Catholic and Protestant state rulers wanted to restrict foreign (i.e., papal) authority in their realms. Confessional conflicts were incidental when they occurred: E.g., (1) in 1547 the Catholic Holy Roman Emperor Charles V attacked Lutheran states, but for the purposes of consolidating authority; (2) in 1572 the Catholic Queen Mother Catherine de Medici launched the St. Bartholomew's Day massacre slaughtering Huguenots, but this had to do with the threat French Calvinism posed to the ecclesiastical system in France, which, because of earlier concordats, was viewed as a threat to French royal authority. To recognize the complexity involved, and see how in most cases these wars involved Catholics fighting Catholics and Protestants fighting Protestants, simply look at the tally Cavanaugh provides, a brief example of which I began this footnote. In what sense can these be called religious wars? Cavanaugh includes over forty examples of this in his *Myth of Religious Violence*. See also Skinner, *Foundations of Modern Political Thought*, 15, 59-60, and 254-59; Salmon, *Society in Crisis*, 189-90; Figgis, *From Gerson to Grotius*, 6; and Palm, *Calvinism*, 51-55.

redefinition was to declaw the church's authority on political matters and to exorcise the public realm of the newly defined religious.

In this final chapter, I now hope to expand upon Cavanaugh's work, in light of the chapters which have come before, by describing one way in which political theorists aimed to undermine the church's authority, namely, by using the Bible for their own ends in competition with the church. For the remainder of this chapter I will proceed in two parts. First, I will briefly describe how the Bible went from being both a material and visual artifact encountered primarily in communal liturgical life to being held captive by emerging modern European states where it increasingly became thought of principally as a book.

In the second part, which constitutes the bulk of my claim, I will argue that the political theorists like Hobbes and Spinoza whom we have already discussed helped create a new method for interpreting the Bible that facilitated its transformation into a book. While the Reformation had already played a large role in pruning away the complex allegorical interpretations of Scripture, Hobbes and Spinoza, following La Peyrère, took the Reformation focus on the *sensus literalis* of Scripture to a new level by turning the focus to the merely historical. By making such a hermeneutical shift, La Peyrère, Hobbes, and Spinoza effectively limited the formerly multifaceted Scripture experience, changing it from a theological wellspring, encountered in a multitude of diverse material and visual locations and situations, into a particular kind of book that is a primarily historical text—a book in the most limited sense of a collection of printed words on a page. The purpose of La Peyrère, Hobbes, and Spinoza in approaching Scripture in this manner was primarily political, as we have already seen, and their biblical exegesis always served their political convictions. In the wake of the seventeenth-century "wars of religion," Hobbes and Spinoza wanted to demonstrate why their political programs were the solution to the problems of the time.

Cavanaugh's account of this time period has brought to our attention the flaws in the standard telling of this history, and it has done much to help us understand how religion became regarded as a private affair. The standard account of the history of biblical interpretation also has its flaws. Chief among these is that we have failed to see the political motivations of those who are regarded as the founders of modern biblical criticism. This present book is my modest attempt at helping to correct this state of affairs within the history of biblical scholarship. My attention to these flaws stems both from a desire for a more accurate understanding of the history and from a desire that the vestiges of this Bible battle be recognized and their origin properly attributed to the politics of the time. In many cases, scholars continue to reproduce the biblical arguments and conclusions of Hobbes and Spinoza, among others, without recognizing that their exegetical work was constructed in order to provide a biblical support for their political convictions. In their hands, the Bible became a book and a tool to be used by those who held the ultimate authority over life and death, namely, the rulers of modern states.

LIVING WATERS FLOWING THROUGH DIVERSE TRIBUTARIES: SCRIPTURE'S MANIFOLD FORMS IN MATERIAL, VISUAL, AND AUDITORY CULTURE

Our contemporary experience of the Bible is that of a book, which can be purchased in a multitude of locations with various covers, in various translations and print sizes, according to the preferences of the reader. Prior to the end of the fifteenth century, however, only the wealthy elites and monks, scribes, and others who spent their time in libraries and scriptoria had easy access to actual textual copies of the Bible. Before we can ascertain the change that occurred regarding the way the Bible was understood, we must first consider how it was encountered prior to this alteration. For those who sought to assert the power of the state over the transnational church, concretizing the Bible and limiting its multifaceted influence was of utmost importance. Political theorists recognized that in order for a state to have authority over its people who were believing Christians, the state would have to demonstrate that the Bible supported the state's claims to authority contra the church. One way this was done was by privatizing the Bible and relegating it to the realm of "religion." In other words, La Peyrère, Hobbes, Spinoza, and others sought to extract the Bible from the liturgical world of common worship and common, manifold interpretations.

Even those like monks, rabbis, bishops, and others who had access to the Bible as a text had in the forefront of their thoughts and habits of reading the liturgical cycle, rather than the order of the canon bound as a book and serving as a historical artifact. Often their reading of the sacred page served an explicit liturgical purpose geared toward worship. At other times, when they studied the texts on their own, they made associations between scriptural passages based upon the liturgical juxtaposition of texts in the liturgical cycles of readings, not to mention the fact that many of these manuscripts were artistically illuminated and the written text itself was often artistically calligraphic.[7] The Bible as a book was not simply let-

---

7. Candler notes, "Even when sufficient literacy is achieved by the medieval monk so as to permit reading privately in one's cell, this form of engagement with the text is never abstracted from a rigorous daily routine of matins, masses, vespers, and so on.

ters to be read, but rather an entry into the sublime. Hence the beauty of the writing and the meticulousness of the accompanying images were as much a part of the Bible as the words contained therein. "Illumination" meant precisely what it claimed; the pictures brought to light the message of the text. Scripture was used for meditation—for *lectio divina*—and it became a living text to those who were immersed in it.[8] Both the professed religious and laity relied on Scripture as a way to interpret and make meaning in their world.

For the vast majority of Jews and Christians the primary encounter with Scripture was not at all textual in the sense of reading books. The Bible was embedded in material and visual culture, but not primarily in book form. Rather, the most common way in which Scripture was encountered was in liturgical worship. In buildings architecturally indebted to images of the Bible, with mosaic and painted images reflecting biblical scenes, reciting and singing prayers that were biblically based, listening to Scripture proclaimed, engaging in gestures inspired by biblical texts: this constituted the Mass's visual, material, and auditory encounter with the Bible.[9]

The Bible was hence not primarily viewed as a book, and certainly not a personal belonging that could be carried around at leisure and read in private. Books are tangible, they are bound together, and their contents are typically arranged in a fixed order, moving from front to back, left to right, or, in the case of Jewish Hebrew Scriptures, right to left. But, in the liturgy, different texts from various parts of the book are read "out of book order" together at various times. So, in the liturgy of the synagogue, a text from the front of the book, in the Torah, might be read alongside a text from the middle of the book, in the Prophets. At the Mass, a Gospel reading from the New Testament, proportionately near the end of the Bible, might be read after a reading from the Old Testament, closer to the beginning or middle of

---

Lectio divina is, however 'private' reading might be, always a matter of reading and interpreting not just communally but liturgically. . . . It is not a possibility for such religious to abstract their reading from the liturgical cycle of daily masses and annual feasts, the use of the entire body, hands, knees, lips, tongue, ears, not to mention the eyes, all of which the reading of such texts requires." See *Theology, Rhetoric, Manuduction*, 7; and also Illich, *In the Vineyard*, 82.

8. For an excellent discussion of the ways in which even those medieval Christians who had access to printed Bibles in the monasteries and universities still encountered Scripture in these polyvalent ways, see Turner, *Eros and Allegory*, 162; and Leclercq, *L'Amour des lettres*.

9. Candler, *Theology, Rhetoric, Manuduction*, 7, 9, 15, 18, 27, 38–39, 50, 66, 74, 77–82, 151–60, and 162; D'Costa, *Theology in the Public Square*, 112–13, 119–22, 132–33, and 138; Illich, *In the Vineyard*, 69 and 82; and Ong, *Presence of the Word*, 269. So also today, the Bible is primarily encountered in this liturgical form by both Christians and Jews alike.

the Bible. During certain liturgical seasons, like the end of Ordinary Time, the first reading might come from a New Testament book found even closer than the Gospels to the back of the Bible, and so the "order" might seem even more disorderly, at least as far as how one typically reads books.

In such a liturgical context, it is easy to see how Scripture functioned polymorphically for the majority of people. It was not taken home and read at any time. Rather, certain portions were listened to in community and were juxtaposed with other portions. In Christian contexts, Old Testament passages were read in light of New Testament passages, and vice versa. Certain passages were further meditated upon in other prayerful contexts, such as the rosary and stations of the cross. Other senses than hearing were also involved in experiencing Scripture. In Christian contexts there was the smell of incense, while in Jewish Havdalah liturgies there was the smell of spices. For both religious traditions the taste of wine and bread was sometimes involved. Music, artwork, and gestures like kneeling, sitting, standing, beating the breast, bending the knee, bowing at the waist, and others—all of these affected how Scripture was understood and experienced.[10]

This multifaceted experience of Scripture extended beyond the normal form of the liturgy as well. Whether in the shape of passion plays, Corpus Christi processions, recited prayers, artwork displayed in the home, jewelry, clothing, Passover Seders at home, or similar other instances, Scripture was brought to life and made a part of the everyday world and imagination of both Jews and Christians.[11] This was a world where there was no secular hermetically sealed off from divine work; "religion" had not yet come to denote a privatized set of beliefs.[12] There were diverse ways of encountering and responding to Scripture, and there were always issues to debate, but the debate that would develop which envisioned the church and state vying for power had not yet reached its most vigorous phase.

---

10. Candler, *Theology, Rhetoric, Manuduction*, 152–55 and 162.

11. For an excellent discussion of the Bible's multifaceted presence in material, visual, and auditory culture, see Jansen, *Making of the Magdalen*. Here Jansen uses the images of Mary Magdalen found in sermons, artwork, naming practices, journal entries, and so on to demonstrate the creative interaction of Christians with the Mary Magdalen of both the biblical text and popular legend.

12. See, e.g., Morrow, "Secularization," 14–32.

HOW THE BIBLE BECAME A BOOK: THE ROLE OF HOBBES AND SPINOZA

In contrast to this manifold experience of Scripture, the Bible began to be encountered as a book—primarily an object of print culture—with the advent of the printing press.[13] Common people were now able to own and read their own personal or family copies of the Bible in printed form.[14] In Reformation England, parishioners supported the Reformation by bringing their personal copies of printed Bibles in English to Mass and reading aloud from them in order to interrupt the community's liturgical celebration.[15]

The Reformation also brought with it a certain level of distrust in creative allegorical interpretations of Scripture. When the full panoply of patristic, rabbinic, and medieval biblical interpretation is surveyed, it quickly becomes apparent that not every interpreter was a strict adherent of what has come to be called the *quadruplex sensus* of Scripture. Much more was occurring in allegorical or spiritual biblical interpretation than typology, tropology, and anagogy.[16] In the Christian world, great interpreters such as Pope St. Gregory the Great and St. Thomas Aquinas set out guidelines for how one was to engage in spiritual interpretation, and there always appeared some cautions about using any and every allegorical reading. Protestant Reformers, however, were nonetheless uneasy with the liberties of such interpretation. In this move, as we saw in the first chapter, they joined thinkers such as William of Ockham, who also readily attacked allegorical interpretations.[17]

It is important to note, however, that, despite this distrust of the allegorical, the Protestant Reformers were quite clear about the centrality of

---

13. Candler, *Theology, Rhetoric, Manuduction*, 10, 13, 15, 30, 33, 74, 76–77, 79, 119, and 160; Duffy, *Stripping of the Altars*, 420 and 450; Pickstock, *After Writing*, 161n139; Bossy, *Christianity in the West*, 97, 99–101, and 103; and de Certeau, *Practice of Everyday Life*, 134 and 137.

14. Of course, even in printed form, and precisely as a book, the Bible as book could function as an important part of material and visual culture, and, in fact, could do so in new ways, as McDannell's discussion of the Bible in American homes primarily in the nineteenth century makes clear in her *Material Christianity*, 67–102. My primary point is that Scripture's content was experienced more frequently by more people in more diverse ways prior to the printing press and prior to the modern focus on the Bible's historical aspects. It is important to point out, however, that even with the printing press, in the sixteenth century Bibles were still too prohibitively expensive for most families to own. See van der Coelen, "Pictures for the People," 185–205.

15. Duffy, *Stripping of the Altars*, 420.

16. See, e.g., the comments in Bucur, "Sinai, Zion, and Tabor," 33–52; and Bucur, "Exegesis," 92–112.

17. Minnis, "Material Swords," 292–308; and Harrison, *Bible*.

reading the Bible theologically; they saw it as pertaining to God and how to relate with God. Their concerns were for Christian souls, and they saw the Bible's literal interpretation as furthering this theological goal. Hence the Reformers may have attempted to read the Bible more literally than allegorically, but the focus was still primarily theological. On the other hand, it was not long before this supposed literal interpretation came to provide the theological underpinnings for political theories in opposition to the transnational church. Luther's "two kingdoms" is perhaps the most noteworthy application, for it was out of concern for people's souls that Luther proposed this sharp dichotomy. As such it provides the precursor to Cavanaugh's description of the modern understanding of religion: "The concept of religion being born here is one of domesticated belief systems which are, insofar as it is possible, to be manipulated by the sovereign for the benefit of the State. Religion is no longer a matter of certain bodily practices within the Body of Christ, but is limited to the realm of the 'soul,' and the body is handed over to the State."[18]

With political theorists the focus narrowed from the theological to the historical. While it may be argued that Hobbes and Spinoza retained their own theological concerns, their arguments regarding the Bible did not stem primarily from anxiety for salvation. They were concerned with state control of people's bodies more so than the good of souls, now relegated to the private realm, thanks in part to the trajectory set by the Protestant Reformers. Biblical interpretation turned away from primordially unified supernatural and natural concerns to focus on the natural and historical alone. There had already been a precedent for this, particularly among Renaissance thinkers and even earlier, including the medieval figures William of Ockham and Marsilius of Padua, the Renaissance luminary Niccolò Machiavelli, the Protestant Reformers Martin Luther and John Calvin, as well as La Peyrère's, Hobbes's, and Spinoza's seventeenth-century contemporary Richard Simon, as we saw in the first chapter.[19] Hobbes and especially Spinoza went much further than their predecessors however, as we have already seen, and in their works we may see the beginning stages of what came to be called the historical-critical method of biblical studies.

18. Cavanaugh, "Fire Strong Enough," 405.

19. E.g., Pietsch, *Isaac La Peyrère*; and Müller, *Richard Simon*. Indeed, an important work that has made a significant contribution to the field demonstrating that there were many precursors to La Peyrère, Hobbes, and Spinoza, particularly in the Reformation, is Frampton, *Spinoza and the Rise of Historical Criticism*, 23–42. More recently, see Hahn and Wiker, *Politicizing the Bible*. See also Zachman, "Gathering Meaning," 1–26; Hendrix, *Tradition and Authority*, 236–37; and Popkin, "Some New Light," 171–88.

We have already seen how Hobbes and Spinoza began to focus on the historical background to the Bible to a degree that had never before been attempted with such forcefulness, even as they relied upon the works of others (like La Peyrère and Machiavelli for Hobbes and, in addition to all three of these individuals, Ibn Ḥazm for Spinoza).[20] Although both ostensibly allowed for theological readings of Scripture, the very methodological guidelines of their programs, as we have seen, indicate that a theological reading of the Bible is virtually impossible. Hobbes's naturalistic and historical reading of the Bible necessitated the understanding of Scripture the understanding of Scripture as a text similar to other historical texts. While he continued to acknowledge the importance of the Bible as an authority to Christians, his methodological approach to reading the Bible represents a fundamentally different way of encountering Scripture than in the past. Hobbes claimed that he was using "science" and "reason" in examining the Bible, yet all of his exegesis merely supported his already existing political convictions, especially the conviction that the state sovereign had absolute authority over all his citizens. By employing biblical interpretation in this way Hobbes furthered the concept of the Bible as a book to be examined as a historical artifact.

Spinoza, as we have seen, went even further than Hobbes in detailing a methodological program for biblical interpretation, many points of which survived into contemporary historical-critical methodologies. Like Hobbes, Spinoza argued that the state needed to have absolute control over any expressions of religion in the public sphere. Moreover, as with Hobbes, Spinoza removed supernatural elements from the Bible, with his denial of the existence of miracles, etc. The ostensible goal of both Hobbes's and Spinoza's methods was to reduce violence on behalf of religion, since they thought their methods would lead to accord instead of discord. Thus, for Spinoza, the Bible was a book, a historical text, that, if regarded primarily as an objective text, could bring peace. The readers needed only to apply reason in their approach to this book, and they would all reach the same conclusions, as if it were basic geometry or algebra.

Violence allegedly in the name of religion was the primary factor motivating the turn to history in the work of these early modern political philosophers and biblical interpreters. These theorists blamed the contemporary conflicts on differing religious standpoints. A historical method for reading the Bible—one which was ostensibly neutral and objective—promised to

---

20. Malcolm, *Aspects of Hobbes*, 383–431; Preus, *Spinoza and the Irrelevance of Biblical Authority*; Overhoff, "Theology of Thomas Hobbes's *Leviathan*," 527–55; Cooke, *Hobbes and Christianity*; Martinich, *Two Gods of Leviathan*; Johnston, *Rhetoric of Leviathan*; Combs, "Spinoza's Method," 7–28; and Zac, *Spinoza*.

them the opportunity for all people to agree on the meaning of biblical passages. While many came to the conclusion that the state ought to have the ultimate authority vis-à-vis the church, the very phrase *cuius regio, eius religio* indicates that these supposedly unbiased methods for interpreting the Bible ironically rendered a multiplicity of religious denominations rather than common religious convictions leading to peace.

In the minds of Hobbes and Spinoza, the reason for fearing religious violence was to be found in the religious wars of the previous decades. Now we have come full circle. These allegedly religious wars provided Spinoza with the justification for the privatization of religion, newly redefined, as well as for a biblical hermeneutic that matched such political aims. This involved a new definition of religion, private beliefs, and the transformation of Scripture. No longer was Scripture theological, about God and human relationships with God, nor was it experienced in diverse forms of auditory, material, and visual culture. The Bible was now simply a written text like any other, dealing with people from long ago, and it was to be read historically by trying to get behind the text in search of "objective" history. This is not to say that individuals and communities no longer experienced Scripture in such polymorphic ways; they did and they continue to do so. The Bible, however, became viewed increasingly as the property of scholars in the university setting, where such modern historical concerns dominate.[21]

The emergence of religion as a category denoting privatized beliefs occurred between the fifteenth and eighteenth centuries. This creation of religion as many now understand the word coincided with the Bible's transformation from living polymorphic Word to ossified historical text limited to words on paper.[22] La Peyrère's, Hobbes's, and Spinoza's approach to reading the Bible helped to restrict the previously diverse encounters with Scripture. In so doing, especially in the case of Hobbes and Spinoza, they contributed to the redefinition of religion as a modern category. The purpose of this redefinition of religion for Hobbes and Spinoza, and of the Bible's transformation, was primarily political. By regarding the Bible as a historical text accessible to interpretation by natural reason, Hobbes and Spinoza sought to support the state in bringing an end to conflict that they regarded as religiously motivated.

---

21. See Legaspi, *Death of Scripture* for the continuation of that story into the eighteenth century.

22. See Morrow, "Secularization," 14–32.

Conclusion

THE HISTORY OF BIBLICAL scholarship is a relatively recent discipline, with its popularity beginning to rise in the 1970s and 1980s, especially within the history of philosophy. Since then it has continued to grow rapidly each decade.[1] Regrettably, modern biblical scholarship has by and large neglected to examine the history of its discipline. This is especially regrettable given the emphasis on knowing the historical context of the biblical text. Yet biblical scholars have not sought the historical context of the methods they employ.

Hence many of the studies contributing to the history of biblical scholarship have come from ancillary disciplines like intellectual history, the history of philosophy, etc. The examination contained in this book is a contribution to the larger project of detailing the history of modern biblical scholarship. More work remains to be done in this important field of the history of historical biblical scholarship. The intellectual history of such scholarship was shaped by tumultuous political events, including violent warfare, as I hope my initial chapter showed. The long history from antiquity to the seventeenth century, as detailed in chapter one, demonstrates how inextricably bound together were theological, exegetical, philosophical, and political concerns among the various intellectuals who contributed to the rise of modern biblical criticism. It was in the seventeenth century, however, with the new modern turn to history—and in particular the history behind the texts—that figures like La Peyrère, Hobbes, and Spinoza became so central to the later history of what would become recognizable as modern historical biblical scholarship in the eighteenth and nineteenth centuries.

---

1. See the footnotes of Morrow, "Enlightenment University," 899–909, for a partial bibliography containing approximately 130 sources on the history of modern biblical scholarship.

Richard Simon built upon his friend La Peyrère's work, as well as upon Spinoza's work, even as he contested Spinoza's skepticism.[2] Simon's historical criticism was mediated in Germany by Johann Salomo Semler and was later mediated to Germany through English Deism (especially by English thinkers like John Locke).[3] Moreover, as Jonathan Israel and others have shown, there was a broad German reception of Spinoza which played a role in eighteenth century German biblical scholarship.[4] These combined intellectual trends would ensure that the framework erected for biblical criticism in the seventeenth century would survive into the eighteenth and serve as the foundation for what would emerge in the nineteenth century classic works like those of Julius Wellhausen. These trends solidified the continuing influence of La Peyrère, Hobbes, and Spinoza on contemporary historical biblical criticism in the academy.

---

2. Morrow, "Faith, Reason, and History"; Barthélemy, *Studies in the Text*, 58–81; and Mirri, *Richard Simon*.

3. Hahn and Wiker, *Politicizing the Bible*, 396–486; Champion, "Père Richard Simon," 39–61; and Woodbridge, "German Responses," 65–87.

4. Hahn and Wiker, *Politicizing the Bible*, 339–33, 548–52, and 555–62; Israel, "Early Dutch and German Reaction," 72–100; Israel, *Enlightenment Contested*; Israel, *Radical Enlightenment*; and Wollgast, "Spinoza und die deutsche," 163–79.

Bibliography

Aasi, Ghulam Haider. "Muslim Understanding of Other Religions: An Analytical Study of Ibn Ḥazm's *Kitab al-Fasl*." PhD diss., Temple University, 1986.
Abelard, Peter. *Sic et Non: A Critical Edition.* Ed. Blanche B. Boyer and Richard McKeon. Chicago: University of Chicago Press, 1976.
Abu Laila, Muhammad. "Ibn Ḥazm's Influence on Christian Thinking in Research." *Islamic Quarterly* 31 (1987) 103-15.
———. "An Introduction to the Life and Work of Ibn Ḥazm 1." *Islamic Quarterly* 29 (1985) 75-100.
———. "An Introduction to the Life and Work of Ibn Ḥazm 2." *Islamic Quarterly* 29 (1985) 165-71.
Adang, Camilla. "Eléments karaïtes dans la polémique d'Ibn Ḥazm." In *Diálogo filosófico-religioso entre cristianismo, judaísmo e islamismo durante la Edad Media en la Península Ibérica. Actes du Colloque international de San Lorenzo de El Escorial 23-26 juin 1991 organisé par la Société Internationale pour l'Études de la Philosophie Médiévale*, ed. Horacio Santiago-Otero, 419-41. Turnhout: Brepols, 1994.
———. "Ibn Ḥazm de Córdoba sobre los judíos en la sociedad islámica." *Foro Hispánico* (1994) 15-23.
———. "Ibn Ḥazm on Jews and Judaism." Diss., University of Nijmegen, 1985.
———. "Ibn Ḥazm's Critique of Some 'Judaizing' Tendencies Among the Malikites." In *Medieval and Modern Perspectives on Muslim Jewish Relations*, ed. Ronald L. Nettler, 1-15. Oxford: Oxford Center for Postgraduate Hebrew Studies, 1995.
———. *Islam frente a Judaísmo: La polémica de Ibn Ḥazm de Córdoba*. Madrid: Aben Ezra Ediciones, 1994.
———. "Medieval Muslim Polemics Against the Jewish Scriptures." In *Muslim Perceptions of Other Religions: A Historical Survey*, edited by Jacques Waardenburg, 143-59. Oxford: Oxford University Press, 1999.
———. *Muslim writers on Judaism and the Hebrew Bible: from Ibn Rabban to Ibn Ḥazm*. Leiden: Brill, 1996.
———. "Schriftvervalsing als thema in de islamitische polemiek tegen het jodendom." *Ter Herkenning* 16 (1988) 190-202.
———. "Some Hitherto Neglected Biblical Material in the Work of Ibn Ḥazm." *Al-Masaq* 5 (1992) 17-28.

Åkerman, Susanna. "The Answer to the Scepticism of Queen Christina's Academy (1656)." In *Scepticism and Irreligion in the Seventeenth and Eighteenth Centuries*, edited by Richard H. Popkin and Arjo Vanderjagt, 92–101. Leiden: Brill, 1993.

———. *Queen Christina of Sweden and Her Circle: The Transformation of a Seventeenth-Century Philosophical Libertine*. Leiden: Brill, 1991.

———. "Queen Christina of Sweden and Messianic Thought." In *Sceptics, Millenarians and Jews*, edited by David S. Katz and Jonathan I. Israel, 142–60. Leiden: Brill, 1990.

Al-Azmeh, Aziz. *The Times of History: Universal Topics in Islamic Historiography*. Budapest: Central European University Press, 2007.

Albiac, Gabriel. *La sinagoga vacía: un estudio de las fuentes marranas del espinosismo*. Madrid: Hiperión, 1987.

Algermissen, Ernest. "Die Pentateuchzitate Ibn Hazms. Ein beitrag zur Geschichte der arabische Bibelübersetzungen." Thesis, Westfälische Wilhelms-Universität, Münster, 1933.

Almond, Philip C. *Adam & Eve in Seventeenth-Century Thought*. Cambridge: Cambridge University Press, 1999.

———. "Adam, Pre-Adamites, and Extra-Terrestrial Beings in Early Modern Europe." *Journal of Religious History* 30 (2006) 163–74.

Alonso Schökel, L. "Arte narrativa en Josué–Jueces–Samuel-Reyes." *Estudios Bíblicos* 48 (1990) 145–69.

Anderson, Gary A. "Redeem Your Sins by the Giving of Alms: Sin, Debt, and the 'Treasury of Merit' in Early Jewish and Christian Tradition." *Letter & Spirit* 3 (2007) 39–69.

———. *Sin: A History*. New Haven: Yale University Press, 2009.

Antonietta, Eduardo. "Averroes y su influencia en Padua." *Humanitas. Revista de la Facultad de Filosofía y letras. Tucumán* 7 (1959) 151–74.

Aquinas, St. Thomas. *In psalmos Davidis expositio*. Corpus Thomisticum. Online: http://www.corpusthomisticum.org/.

———. *Quaestiones disputatae de potentia*. Corpus Thomisticum. Online: http://www.corpusthomisticum.org/.

———. *Summa Theologiae*. Corpus Thomisticum. Online: http://www.corpusthomisticum.org/.

Aranoff, Deena. "Elijah Levita: A Jewish Hebraist." *Jewish History* 23 (2009) 17–40.

Ardant, Gabriel. "Financial Policy and Economic Infrastructure of Modern States and Nations." In *The Formation of National States in Western Europe*, edited by Charles Tilly, 164–242. Princeton: Princeton University Press, 1975.

Ariew, Roger. *Descartes Among the Scholastics*. Leiden: Brill, 2011.

Arnaldez, Roger. *Grammaire et théologie chez Ibn Ḥazm de Cordoue: Essai sur la structure et les conditions de la pensée musulmane*. Paris: Librairie Philosophique J. Vrin, 1956.

———. "Spinoza et la pensée arabe." *Revue de synthèse Paris* 89–91 (1978) 151–74.

Arnold, Bill T. and David B. Weisberg. "A Centennial Review of Friedrich Delitzsch's 'Babel und Bibel' Lectures." *Journal of Biblical Literature* 121 (2002) 441–57.

Asad, Talal. *Genealogies of Religion: Discipline and Reasons of Power in Christianity and Islam*. Baltimore: Johns Hopkins University Press, 1993.

———. "Where Are the Margins of the State?" In *Anthropology in the Margins of the State*, edited by Veena Das and Deborah Poole, 279–88. Santa Fe: School of American Research, 2004.

Ashcraft, Richard. *Revolutionary Politics & Locke's Two Treatises of Government*. Princeton: Princeton University Press, 1986.

Asín Palacios, Miguel. *Abenházam de Córdoba y su historia crítica de las ideas religiosas Vol. 1*. Madrid: Tipografía de la "Revista de Archivos, Bibliotecas y Museos," 1928.

———. *Abenházam de Córdoba y su historia crítica de las ideas religiosas II*. Madrid: Tipografía de la "Revista de Archivos, Bibliotecas y Museos," 1928.

Augustine. St. *De Civitate Dei*. Accessed from the Patrologia Latina Database.

———. *De Vera Religione*. Accessed from the Patrologia Latina Database.

Auvray, Paul. "Richard Simon et Spinoza." In *Religion, érudition et critique à la fin du XVIIe siècle et au début du XVIIIe*, edited by Baudouin de Gaiffier et al., 201–14. Paris: Presses universitaires de France, 1968.

Averbeck, Richard E. "Pentateuchal Criticism and the Priestly Torah." In *Do Historical Matters Matter to Faith? A Critical Appraisal of Modern and Postmodern Approaches to Scripture*, edited by James K. Hoffmeier and Dennis R. Magary, 151–80. Wheaton, IL: Crossway, 2012.

Bagley, Paul J. *Philosophy, Theology, and Politics: A Reading of Benedict Spinoza's Tractatus Theologico-Politicus*. Leiden: Brill, 2008.

Baglow, Christopher T. *"Modus et Forma": A New Approach to the Exegesis of Saint Thomas Aquinas with an Application to the Lectura super Epistolam ad Ephesios*. Rome: Pontifical Biblical Institute, 2002.

———. "Rediscovering St. Thomas Aquinas as Biblical Theologian." *Letter & Spirit* 1 (2005) 137–46.

———. "Sacred Scripture and Sacred Doctrine in Saint Thomas Aquinas." In *Aquinas on Doctrine: A Critical Introduction*, edited by Thomas Weinandy, Daniel Keating, and John Yocum, 1–25. London: T. & T. Clark, 2004.

Balibar, Étienne. *"Jus-Pactum-Lex*: On the Constitution of the Subject in the *Theologico-Political Treatise*." In *The New Spinoza*, edited by Warren Montag and Ted Stolze, 171–206. Minneapolis: University of Minnesota Press, 1997.

———. "Spinoza: From Individuality to Transindividuality." *Mededelingen vanwege Het Spinozahuis* 71 (1997) 3–36.

Balz, Albert G.A. *Idea and Essence in the Philosophies of Hobbes and Spinoza*. New York: Columbia University Press, 1918.

Barnett, S.J. *The Enlightenment and Religion: The Myths of Modernity*. Manchester: Manchester University Press, 2003.

———. *Idol Temples and Crafty Priests: The Origins of Enlightenment Anticlericalism*. London: Macmillan, 1999.

Barr, James. "Interpretation, History of: Modern Biblical Criticism." In *The Oxford Companion to the Bible*, edited by Bruce M. Metzger and Michael D. Coogan, 305–24. Oxford: Oxford University Press, 1993.

Barron, Robert. "Biblical Interpretation and Theology: Irenaeus, Modernity, and Vatican II." *Letter & Spirit* 5 (2009) 173–91.

Barthélemy, Dominique. *Studies in the Text of the Old Testament: An Introduction to the Hebrew Old Testament Text Project: English Translation of the Introductions to Volumes 1, 2, and 3 Critique textuelle de l'Ancien Testament*. Winona Lake, IN: Eisenbrauns, 2012.

Baskerville, Geoffrey. *English Monks and the Suppression of the Monasteries.* New Haven: Yale University Press, 1937.

Behloul, Samuel-Martin. *Ibn Hazms Evangelienkritik. Eine methodische Utersuchung.* Leiden: Brill, 2002.

Bell, David. *Spinoza in Germany from 1670 to the Age of Goethe.* Leeds: Maney & Sons, 1984.

Benítez, Miguel. "La posterité de La Peyrère: *Dissertation sur l'origine des Négres & des Américains*." In *La geografia dei saperi: Scritti in memoria di Dino Pastine*, edited by Domenico Ferraro and Gianna Gigliotti, 183–202. Florence: La Lettere, 2000.

Bently, Jerry H. "Biblical Philology and Christian Humanism: Lorenzo Valla and Erasmus as Scholars of the Gospels." *Sixteenth Century Journal* 8 (1977) 8-28.

———. *Humanists and Holy Writ: New Testament Scholarship in the Renaissance.* Princeton: Princeton University Press, 1983.

Bernardi, Peter, SJ. "Social Modernism: The Case of the *Semaines sociales*." In *Catholicism Contending with Modernity: Roman Catholic Modernism and Anti-Modernism in Historical Context*, edited by Darrell Jodock, 277–307. Cambridge: Cambridge University Press, 2000.

Bernier, Jean. *La critique du Pentateuque de Hobbes à Calmet.* Paris: Honoré Champion, 2010.

Beyssade, Michelle. "Deux latinistes: Descartes et Spinoza." In *Spinoza to the Letter: Studies in Words, Texts and Books*, edited by Fokke Akkerman and Piet Steenbakkers, 55–68. Leiden: Brill, 2005.

Biale, David. *Not in the Heavens: The Tradition of Jewish Secular Thought.* Princeton: Princeton University Press, 2011.

Blenkinsopp, Joseph. *The Pentateuch: An Introduction to the First Five Books of the Bible.* New Haven: Yale University Press, 2000.

Blockmans, Wim. *Emperor Charles V: 1500–1558.* London: Oxford University Press, 2002.

Borst, Arno. *Der Turmbau von Babel Vol. I.* Stuttgart: A. Miersemann, 1957.

Boss, Gilbert. "L'histoire chez Spinoza et Leibniz." *Studia Spinozana* 6 (1990) 179-200.

———. "Les principles de la philosophie chez Hobbes et Spinoza." *Studia Spinozana* 3 (1987) 87–123.

Bossy, John. *Christianity in the West: 1400–1700.* Oxford: Oxford University Press, 1985.

Bowle, John. *Hobbes and His Critics: A Study in Seventeenth Century Constitutionalism.* London: Jonathan Cape, 1951.

Boyle, John F. "Authorial Intention and the *Divisio textus*." In *Reading John with St. Thomas Aquinas: Theological Exegesis and Speculative Theology*, edited by Michael Dauphinais and Matthew Levering, 3–8. Washington, DC: The Catholic University of America Press, 2005.

Braun, Rudolf. "Taxation, Sociopolitical Structure, and State-Building: Great Britain and Brandenburg-Prussia." In *The Formation of National States in Western Europe*, edited by Charles Tilly, 243–327. Princeton: Princeton University Press, 1975.

Bray, Michael E., Jr. "The Science and Politics of the Efficient Cause in Hobbes and Spinoza." PhD diss., Pennsylvania State University, 2002.

Brecht, Martin. *Martin Luther: Sein Weg zur Reformation 1483–1521.* Stuttgart: Calwer, 1981.

Brewer, John. *The Sinews of Power: War, Money and the English State, 1688–1783.* Cambridge: Harvard University Press, 1990.

Brown, Norman O. "Philosophy and Prophecy: Spinoza's Hermeneutics." *Political Theory* 14 (1986) 195–213.
Büchler, Adolf. "Über die Minim von Sepphoris und Tiberias im zweiten und dritten Jahrhundert." In *Judaica: Festschrift zu Hermann Cohens siebzigstem Geburtstage*, 271–95. Berlin: Cassirer, 1912.
Bucur, Bogdan G. "Exegesis of Biblical Theophanies in Byzantine Hymnography: Rewritten Bible?" *Theological Studies* 68 (2007) 92–112.
———. "Sinai, Zion, and Tabor: An Entry into the Christian Bible." *Journal of Theological Interpretation* 4 (2010) 33–52.
Burke, Peter. *The Renaissance Sense of the Past*. New York: St. Martin's, 1969.
Burke, Victor Lee. *The Clash of Civilizations: War-Making and State Formation in Europe*. Cambridge: Polity, 1997.
Burnett, Stephen G. *From Christian Hebraism to Jewish Studies: Johannes Buxtorf (1564–1629) and Hebrew Learning in the Seventeenth Century*. Leiden: Brill, 1996.
———. "Later Christian Hebraists." In *Hebrew Bible/Old Testament: The History of Its Interpretation Volume II: From the Renaissance to the Enlightenment*, edited by Magne Sæbø, 785–801. Göttingen: Vandenhoeck & Ruprecht, 2008.
Callaghan, G. K. "Nominalism, Abstraction, and Generality in Hobbes." *History of Philosophy Quarterly* 18 (2001) 37–55.
Calvetti, Carla Gallicet. *Spinoza lettore del Machiavelli*. Milan: Università Cattolica del Sacro Cuore, 1972.
Candler, Peter M., Jr. *Theology, Rhetoric, Manuduction, or Reading Scripture Together on the Path to God*. Grand Rapids: Eerdmans, 2006.
Cavanaugh, William T. "The City: Beyond Secular Parodies." In *Radical Orthodoxy*, edited by John Milbank, Catherine Pickstock, and Graham Ward, 182–200. New York: Routledge, 1999.
———. "'A Fire Strong Enough to Consume the House': The Wars of Religion and the Rise of the State." *Modern Theology* 11 (October 1995) 397–420.
———. "Killing for the Telephone Company: Why the Nation-State is Not the Keeper of the Common Good." *Modern Theology* 20 (2004) 243–74.
———. *The Myth of Religious Violence: Secular Ideology and the Roots of Modern Conflict*. Oxford: Oxford University Press, 2009.
———. *Theopolitical Imagination*. New York: T. & T. Clark, 2002.
Chadwick, Owen. *The Secularization of the European Mind in the Nineteenth Century*. Cambridge: Cambridge University Press, 1975.
Chalier, Catherine. *Spinoza Lecteur de Maïmonide: La question théologico-politique*. Paris: Cerf, 2006.
Champion, Justin A. I. "Père Richard Simon and English Biblical Criticism, 1680–1700." In *Everything Connects: In Conference with Richard H. Popkin: Essays in His Honor*, edited by James E. Force and David S. Katz, 39–61. Leiden: Brill, 1999.
———. *The Pillars of Priestcraft Shaken: The Church of England and its Enemies 1660–1730*. Cambridge: Cambridge University Press, 1992.
Ciani, John, SJ. "Cardinal Camillo Mazzella, SJ" In *Varieties of Ultramontanism*, edited by Jeffrey von Arx, SJ, 103–17. Washington, DC: The Catholic University of America Press, 1998.
Clive, Megan. "Hobbes parmi les mouvements religieux de son temps." *Revue des sciences philosophiques et théologiques* 62 (1978) 41–59.

Collins, James B. "State Building in Early-Modern Europe: The Case of France." *Modern Asian Studies* 31 (1997) 603–33.

———. *The State in Early Modern France*. Cambridge: Cambridge University Press, 1995.

Combs, Eugene. "Spinoza's Method of Biblical Interpretation and His Political Philosophy." In *Modernity and Responsibility: Essays for George Grant*, edited by Eugene Combs, 7–28. Toronto: University of Toronto Press, 1983.

Congar, Yves. "Gallicanisme." In *Catholicisme IV*, edited by G. Jacquemet, 1731–1739. Paris: Letouzey et Ané, 1956.

Cooke, Paul D. *Hobbes and Christianity: Reassessing the Bible in Leviathan*. Lanham: Rowman & Littlefield, 1996.

Costigan, Richard F. "Bossuet and the Consensus of the Church." *Theological Studies* 56 (1995) 652–72.

———. "The Consensus of the Church: Differing Classic Views." *Theological Studies* 51 (1990) 25–48.

———. *The Consensus of the Church and Papal Infallibility: A Study in the Background of Vatican I*. Washington, D.C.: The Catholic University of America Press, 2005.

———. "State Appointment of Bishops." *Journal of Church and State* 8 (1966) 82–96.

Curley, Edwin. *Behind the Geometrical Method: A Reading of Spinoza's Ethics*. Princeton: Princeton University Press, 1988.

———. "'I Durst Not Write So Boldly' or How to Read Hobbes' Theologico-Political Treatise." In *Hobbes e Spinoza: Scienza e politica*, ed. Daniela Bostrenghi, 497–593. Naples: Bibliopolis, 1992.

———. "Kissinger, Spinoza, and Genghis Khan." In *The Cambridge Companion to Spinoza*, ed. Don Garrett, 315–42. Cambridge: Cambridge University Press, 1996.

———. "Notes on a Neglected Masterpiece: Spinoza and the Science of Hermeneutics." In *Spinoza: The Enduring Questions*, ed. Graeme Hunter, 64–99. Toronto: University of Toronto Press, 1994.

———. "Spinoza's Exchange with Albert Burgh." In *Spinoza's Theological-Political Treatise: A Critical Guide*, edited by Yitzhak Y. Melamed and Michael A. Rosenthal, 11–28. Cambridge: Cambridge University Press, 2010.

———. "Spinoza's Geometric Method." *Studia Spinozana* 2 (1986) 151–69.

Daly, Gabriel, O.S.A. "Theological and Philosophical Modernism." In *Catholicism Contending with Modernity: Roman Catholic Modernism and Anti-Modernism in Historical Context*, ed. Darrell Jodock, 88–112. Cambridge: Cambridge University Press, 2000.

Davidson, Israel. *Saadia's Polemic Against Ḥiwi al-Balkhi: A Fragment Edited from a Genizah MS*. New York: Jewish Theological Seminary of America, 1915.

D'Costa, Gavin. *Theology in the Public Square: Church, Academy and Nation*. Oxford: Blackwell, 2005.

de Certeau, Michel. *The Practice of Everyday Life*. Berkeley, CA: University of California Press, 1984.

de Mowbray, Malcolm. "Philosophy as Handmaid of Theology: Biblical Exegesis in the Service of Scholarship." *Traditio* 59 (2004) 1–37.

de Mordechai Vaz Dias, Abraham and Willem Gerard van der Tak. "Spinoza Merchant and Autodidact: Charters and Other Authentic Documents Relating to the Philosopher's Youth and His Relations." *Studia Rosenthaliana* 16 (1982) 103–71.

Del Lucchese, Filippo. *Conflict, Power, and Multitude in Machiavelli and Spinoza*. London: Continuum, 2009.
Della Rocca, Michael. "Mental Content and Skepticism in Descartes and Spinoza." *Studia Spinozana* 10 (1994) 19–42.
Delph, Ronald K. "Valla Grammaticus, Agostino Steuco, and the Donation of Constantine." *Journal of the History of Ideas* 57 (1996) 55–77.
Den Uyl, Douglas J. "Power, Politics, and Religion in Spinoza's Political Thought." *Jewish Political Studies Review* 7 (1995) 77–106.
Den Uyl, Douglas J. and Stuart D. Warner. "Liberalism and Hobbes and Spinoza." *Studia Spinozana* 3 (1987) 261–317.
Diamond, James Arthur. "Maimonides, Spinoza, and Buber Read the Hebrew Bible: The Hermeneutical Keys of Divine 'Fire' and 'Spirit' (*Ruach*)." *Journal of Religion* 91 (2011) 320–43.
Djedi, Youcef. "Spinoza et l'islam: un état des lieux." *Philosophiques* 37 (2010) 275–98.
Donagan, Alan. *Spinoza*. Chicago: University of Chicago Press, 1989.
———. "Spinoza's Theology." In *The Cambridge Companion to Spinoza*, edited by Don Garrett, 343–82. Cambridge: Cambridge University Press, 1996.
Droge, Arthur J. *Homer or Moses?: Early Christian Interpretation of the History of Culture*. Tübingen: Mohr, 1989.
Duffy, Eamon. *Saints & Sinners: A History of the Popes*. 3rd ed. New Haven, CT: Yale University Press, 2006 (1997).
———. *The Stripping of the Altars: Traditional Religion in England c. 1400—c. 1580*. New Haven, CT: Yale University Press, 2005.
———. *The Voices of Morebath: Reformation & Rebellion in an English Village*. New Haven: Yale University Press, 2001.
Dungan, David Laird. *A History of the Synoptic Problem: The Canon, the Text, the Composition, and the Interpretation of the Gospels*. New Haven, CT: Yale University Press, 1999.
Dunn, Richard S. *The Age of Religious Wars: 1559–1689*. New York: Norton, 1970.
Eisenach, Eldon J. "Hobbes on Church, State and Religion." *History of Political Thought* 3 (1982) 215–43.
Elazar, Daniel J. "Spinoza and the Bible." *Jewish Political Studies Review* 7 (1995) 5–19.
Epiphanius of Salamis. *The Panarion of Epiphanius of Salamis: Book I (Sects 1–46)*. Translated by Frank Williams. Leiden: Brill, 1987.
Eriksen, Trond Berg. "Some Sociopolitical and Cultural Aspects of the Renaissance." In *Hebrew Bible/Old Testament: The History of Its Interpretation Volume II: From the Renaissance to the Enlightenment*, edited by Magne Sæbø, 94–105. Göttingen: Vandenhoeck & Ruprecht, 2008.
Ertman, Thomas. *Birth of the Leviathan: Building States and Regimes in Medieval and Early Modern Europe*. Cambridge: Cambridge University Press, 1997.
Fasolt, Constantin. "History and Religion in the Modern Age." *History and Theory* 45 (2006) 10–26.
———. *The Limits of History*. Chicago: University of Chicago Press, 2004.
———. "Red Herrings: Relativism, Objectivism, and Other False Dilemmas." *Storia della storiografia* 48 (2005) 17–26.
Faye, Emmanuel. "Dieu trompeur, mauvais génie et origine de l'erreur selon Descartes et Suarez." *Revue philosophique de la France et de l'étranger* 126 (2001) 61–72.
Feuer, Lewis S. *Spinoza and the Rise of Liberalism*. Brunswick: Transaction, 1987.

Fierro, Maribel. "Ibn Hazm et le zindiq juif." *Revue du Monde Musulman et de la Mediterranee* 63–64 (1992) 81–89.

Figgis, John Neville. *From Gerson to Grotius, 1414–1625*. New York: Harper Torchbook, 1960.

Finer, Samuel E. "State- and Nation-Building in Europe: The Role of the Military." In *The Formation of National States in Western Europe*, ed. Charles Tilly, 84–163. Princeton: Princeton University Press, 1975.

Fitzmyer, Joseph A. Review of *Catholic Principles for Interpreting Scripture: A Study of the Pontifical Biblical Commission's The Interpretation of the Bible in the Church*, by Peter S. Williamson. *Biblica* 83 (2002) 439.

Fix, Andrew. "Bekker and Spinoza." In *Disguised and Overt Spinozism Around 1700: Papers Presented at the International Colloquium, Held at Rotterdam, 5–8 October 1994*, edited by Wiep van Bunge and Wim Klever, 23–40. Leiden: Brill, 1996.

Fogarty, Gerald P., SJ. "Cardinal William Henry O'Connell." In *Varieties of Ultramontanism*, ed. Jeffrey von Arx, SJ, 118–46. Washington, DC: The Catholic University of America Press, 1998.

Forteza, Bartomeu. "La influencia de Francisco Suárez sobre Thomas Hobbes." *Convivum* 11 (1998) 40–79.

Fraenkel, Carlos. "Could Spinoza Have Presented the *Ethics* as the True Content of the Bible." *Oxford Studies in Early Modern Philosophy* 4 (2008) 1–50.

———. "Reconsidering the Case of Elijah Delmedigo's Averroism and its Impact on Spinoza." In *Renaissance Averroism and its Aftermath: Arabic Philosophy in Early Modern Europe*, edited by Anna Akasoy and Guido Guiglioni, 213–36. Dordrecht: Springer, 2012.

———. "Spinoza on Philosophy and Religion: The Averroistic Sources." In *The Rationalists: Between Tradition and Innovation*, ed. Carlos Fraenkel, Dario Perinetti and Justin Smith, 58–81. Dordrecht: Springer, 2010.

Frampton, Travis L. *Spinoza and the Rise of Historical Criticism of the Bible*. New York: T. & T. Clark, 2006.

Freedman, R. David. "The Father of Modern Biblical Scholarship." *Journal of the Ancient Near Eastern Society* 19 (1989) 31–38.

Frei, Hans W. *The Eclipse of Biblical Narrative: A Study in Eighteenth and Nineteenth Century Hermeneutics*. New Haven: Yale University Press, 1974.

Freudenthal, J. "Spinoza und die Scholastik." In *Philosophische Aufsätze. Eduard Zeller zu seinem fünfzigjährigen Doctor-Jubiläum gewidmet*, 84–138. Leipzig: Fues's, 1887.

Fried, Johannes. *Donation of Constantine and Constitutum Constantini*. Berlin: Walter de Gruyter, 2007.

Friedlander, Israel. "The Heterodoxies of the Shiites in the Presentation of Ibn Ḥazm." *Journal of the American Oriental Society* 28 (1907) 1–80.

———. "Zur Komposition von Ibn Ḥazm's Milal wa'n-Niḥal." In *Orientalische Studien Theodor Nöldeke zum siebzigsten Geburtstag (2. März 1906) gewidmet von Freunden und Schülern*, I, ed. Carl Bezold, 267–77. Gieszen: Alfred Töpelmann, 1906.

Fubini, Riccardo. "Humanism and Truth: Valla Writes Against the Donation of Constantine." *Journal of the History of Ideas* 57 (1996) 79–86.

Gabbey, Alan. "Spinoza's Natural Science and Methodology." In *The Cambridge Companion to Spinoza*, edited by Don Garrett, 142–91. Cambridge: Cambridge University Press, 1996.

Gabriel, Frédéric. "Periegesis and Skepticism: La Peyrère, Geographer." In *Skepticism in the Modern Age: Building on the Work of Richard Popkin*, edited by José R. Maia Neto et al., 159–70. Leiden: Brill, 2009.

García de Haro, Ramón. *Historia teológica del modernismo*. Pamplona: Ediciones Universidad de Navarra, 1972.

Garrett, Don, ed. *The Cambridge Companion to Spinoza*. Cambridge: Cambridge University Press, 1996.

———. "Spinoza's Ethical Theory." In *The Cambridge Companion to Spinoza*, edited by Don Garrett, 267–314. Cambridge: Cambridge University Press, 1996.

Garrido, Juan José. "El método histórico-crítico de interpretación de la Escritura según Spinoza." In *El método en teología. Actas del primer Simposio de Teología e Historia (29–31 mayo 1980)*, edited by The Faculty of Theology of Saint Vincent Ferrer, 269–81. Valencia: The Faculty of Theology of Saint Vincent Ferrer, 1981.

Garrido Zaragoza, J. "La desmitificación de la Escritura en Spinoza." *Taula* 9 (1988) 3–45.

Gatens, Moira. "Spinoza's Disturbing Thesis: Power, Norms and Fiction in the *Tractatus Theologico-Politicus*." *History of Political Thought* 30 (2009) 455–68.

Gaukroger, Stephen. "The Nature of Abstract Reasoning: Philosophical Aspects of Descartes's Work in Algebra." In *The Cambridge Companion to Descartes*, edited by John Cottingham, 91–114. Cambridge: Cambridge University Press, 1992.

Geerken, John H. "Machiavelli's Moses and Renaissance Politics." *Journal of the History of Ideas* 60 (1999) 579–95.

Gellner, Ernest. *Nations and Nationalism*. Ithaca: Cornell University Press, 1983.

Giancotti, Emilia. "La Teoria dell'Assolutismo in Hobbes e Spinoza." *Studia Spinozana* 1 (1985) 231–58.

Gibert, Pierre. *L'invention critique de la Bible: XVe—XVIIIe siècle*. Paris: Gallimard, 2010.

Giddens, Anthony. *The Nation-State and Violence*. Berkeley: University of California Press, 1987.

Gillespie, Michael Allen. *The Theological Origins of Modernity*. Chicago: University of Chicago Press, 2008.

Gilson, Étienne. *Index scolastico-cartésien*. New York: Burt Franklin, 1912.

Gliozzi, Giuliano. *Adamo e il Nuovo Mondo. La nascita dell'antropologia come ideologia colonial: dalle genealogie bibliche alle teorie razziali (1500–1700)*. Florence: La Nuova Italia, 1977.

Glover, Willis B. "God and Thomas Hobbes." *Church History* 29 (1960) 275–97.

Goldziher, Ignaz. *Die Ẓâhiriten. Ihr Lehrsystem und ihre Geschichte: Beitrag zur Geschichte der muhammedanischen Theologie*. Leipzig: Otto Schulze, 1884.

Goshen-Gottstein, Moshe. "Bible et judaïsm." In *Le Grand Siècle et la Bible*, edited by Jean-Robert Armogathe, 33–38. Paris: Beauchesne, 1989.

———. "Christianity, Judaism and Modern Bible Study." In *Congress Volume: Edinburgh 1974*, 69–88. Leiden: Brill, 1975.

———. "Foundations of Biblical Philology in the Seventeenth Century Christian and Jewish Dimensions." In *Jewish Thought in the Seventeenth Century*, edited by Isadore Twersky and Bernard Septimus, 77–94. Cambridge: Harvard University Press, 1987.

———. "The Textual Criticism of the Old Testament: Rise, Decline, Rebirth." *Journal of Biblical Literature* 102 (1983) 365–99.

Gottheil, Richard J.H. "Some Early Jewish Bible Criticism: Annual Presidential Address to the Society of Biblical Literature and Exegesis." *Journal of Biblical Literature* 23 (1904) 1–12.

Grafton, Anthony T. *Defenders of the Text: The Traditions of Scholarship in an Age of Science, 1450–1800*. Cambridge: Harvard University Press, 1991.

———. "Joseph Scaliger and Historical Chronology: The Rise and Fall of a Discipline." *History and Theory* 14 (1975) 156–85.

———. *Joseph Scaliger: A Study in the History of Classical Scholarship I: Textual Criticism and Exegesis*. Oxford: Oxford University Press, 1983.

———. *Joseph Scaliger: A Study in the History of Classical Scholarship II: Historical Chronology*. Oxford: Oxford University Press, 1993.

Grant, Robert M. "Historical Criticism in the Ancient Church." *Journal of Religion* 25 (1945) 183–96.

Grant, Robert. *A Short History of the Interpretation of the Bible*. 2nd rev. ed. Philadelphia: Fortress, 1984.

Greenblatt, Stephen. *Hamlet in Purgatory*. Princeton: Princeton University Press, 2001.

Gregory, Brad S. *The Unintended Reformation: How a Religious Revolution Secularized Society*. Cambridge: Harvard University Press, 2012.

Greschat, Martin. "Bibelkritik und Politik: Anmerkungen zu Spinozas Theologisch-politischem Traktat." In *Text—Wort—Glaube: Kurt Aland Gewidmet*, edited by Martin Brecht, 324–43. Berlin: Walter de Gruyter, 1980.

Griffiths, Paul J. *Problems of Religious Diversity*. Oxford: Blackwell, 2001.

Gritsch, Eric W. *A History of Lutheranism*. Minneapolis: Fortress, 2002.

Gross, George M. "Reading the Bible with Spinoza." *Jewish Political Studies Review* 7 (1995) 21–38.

Gross, Michael B. *The War Against Catholicism: Liberalism and the Anti-Catholic Imagination in Nineteenth-Century Germany*. Ann Arbor: University of Michigan Press, 2004.

Haarmann, Ulrich. "In Quest of the Spectacular: Noble and Learned Visitors to the Pyramids Around 1200 A.D." In *Islamic Studies Presented to Charles J. Adams*, edited by Wael B. Hallaq and Donald P. Little, 57–68. Leiden: Brill, 1990.

HaCohen, Ran. *Reclaiming the Hebrew Bible: German-Jewish Reception of Biblical Criticism*. Berlin: Walter de Gruyter, 2010.

Hahn, Scott. "Search the Scriptures: Reading the Old Testament with Jesus, John and Thomas Aquinas." *Saint Austin Review* 2 (2002) 12–15.

Hahn, Scott W. and Benjamin Wiker. *Politicizing the Bible: The Roots of Historical Criticism and the Secularization of Scripture 1300–1700*. New York: Herder & Herder, 2013.

Hammill, Graham. *The Mosaic Constitution: Political Theology and Imagination from Machiavelli to Milton*. Chicago: University of Chicago Press, 2012.

Hamilton, James Jay. "The Radical Royalism of Thomas Hobbes: An Historical Interpretation of his Political Theory." PhD diss., Columbia University, 1978.

Haran, Alexandre Y. *Le lys et le globe: Messianisme dynastique et rêve impérial en France aux XVIe et XVIIe siècles*. Seyssel: Champ Vallon, 2000.

Harris, Errol. *Is There an Esoteric Doctrine in the "Tractatus theologico-politicus"?* Leiden: Brill, 1978.

———. *Salvation from Despair: A Reappraisal of Spinoza's Philosophy*. Hague: Martinus Nijhoff, 1973.

Harrison, Peter. *The Bible, Protestantism, and the Rise of Natural Science*. Cambridge: Cambridge University Press, 1998.
———. *'Religion' and the Religions in the English Enlightenment*. Cambridge: Cambridge University Press, 1990.
Harrison, R.K. *Introduction to the Old Testament*. Grand Rapids: Eerdmans, 1969.
Harvey, David Allen. "The Noble Savage and the Savage Noble: Philosophy and Ethnography in the *Voyages* of the Baron de Lahontan." *French Colonial History* 11 (2010) 161–91.
Harvey, Warren Zev. "Spinoza on Ibn Ezra's 'Secret of the Twelve.'" In *Spinoza's Theological-Political Treatise: A Critical Guide*, ed. Yitzhak Y. Melamed and Michael A. Rosenthal, 41–55. Cambridge: Cambridge University Press, 2010.
Hauerwas, Stanley. *The State of the University: Academic Knowledges and the Knowledge of God*. Oxford: Blackwell, 2007.
Hayes, John H. "The History of the Study of Israelite and Judaean History." In *Israelite and Judaean History*, ed. John H. Hayes and J. Maxwell Miller, 1–53. London: SCM, 1977.
Hazard, Paul. *La Crise de la conscience européenne (1680–1715)*. vol. 3. Paris: Boivin, 1935.
Heft, James L. "The Historical Origins of Papal Infallibility." *Catholic Theological Society of America Proceedings* 35 (1980) 208–11.
———. "John XXII and Papal Infallibility: Brian Tierney's Thesis Reconsidered." *Journal of Ecumenical Studies* 19 (1982) 759–80.
———. *John XXII and Papal Teaching Authority*. Lewiston, New York: Edwin Mellen, 1986.
Heller, Henry. *Iron and Blood: Civil Wars in Sixteenth-Century France*. Montreal: McGill-Queen's University Press, 1991.
Hendrix, Scott. *Tradition and Authority in the Reformation*. Brookfield, VT: Variorum, 1996.
Hennesey, James. "Leo XIII's Thomistic Revival: A Political and Philosophical Event." In *Celebrating the Medieval Heritage: A Colloquy on the Thought of Aquinas and Bonaventure*, edited by David Tracy, 185–97. Chicago: University of Chicago Press, 1978.
Herbst, Jeffrey. "States and War in Africa." In *The Nation-State in Question*, edited by T.V. Paul et al., 166–80. Princeton: Princeton University Press, 2003.
Hill, Harvey. "The Politics of Loisy's Modernist Theology." In *Catholicism Contending with Modernity: Roman Catholic Modernism and Anti-Modernism in Historical Context*, edited by Darrell Jodock, 169–90. Cambridge: Cambridge University Press, 2000.
Hippler, Thomas. "Spinoza et l'histoire." *Studia Spinozana* 16 (2008) 155–76.
Hirschfeld, Hartwig. "Mohammedan Criticism of the Bible." *Jewish Quarterly Review* 13 (1901) 222–40.
Hobbes, Thomas. *Leviathan: Volume 2: The English and Latin Texts (i)*. Edited by Noel Malcolm. Oxford: Clarendon, 2012.
———. *Leviathan: Volume 3: The English and Latin Texts (ii)*. Edited by Noel Malcolm. Oxford: Clarendon, 2012.
Hoffmeier, James K. *Ancient Israel in Sinai: The Evidence for the Authenticity of the Wilderness Traditions*. Oxford: Oxford University Press, 2005.

Holt, Mack P. *The French Wars of Religion, 1562–1629*. Cambridge: Cambridge University Press, 1995.

Homan, Michael M. "How Moses Gained and Lost the Reputation of Being the Torah's Author: Higher Criticism prior to Julius Wellhausen." In *Sacred History, Sacred Literature: Essays on Ancient Israel, the Bible, and Religion in Honor of R.E. Friedman on His Sixtieth Birthday*, edited by Shawna Dolansky, 111–32. Winona Lake, IN: Eisenbrauns, 2008.

Horkheimer, Max and Theodor W. Adorno. *Dialektik der Aufklärung*. Frankfurt am Main: Fischer, 1969.

Hornig, Gottfried. *Johann Salomo Semler: Studien zu Leben und Werk des Hallenser Aufklärungstheologen*. Tübingen: Walter de Gruyter, 1996.

Horowitz, Irving I. "Averroism and the Politics of Philosophy." *Journal of Politics* 22 (1960) 698–727.

Howard, Michael. *The Invention of Peace: Reflections on War and International Order*. New Haven, CT: Yale University Press, 2000.

Hsia, R. Po-Chia. *Social Discipline in the Reformation: Central Europe 1550–1750*. London: Routledge, 1989.

Hughes, Ann. *The Causes of the English Civil War*. 2nd ed. London: Macmillan, 1998.

Illich, Ivan. *In the Vineyard of the Text: A Commentary to Hugh's Didascalicon*. Chicago: University of Chicago Press, 1993.

Israel, Jonathan I. "The Changing Role of the Dutch Sephardim in International Trade, 1595–1715." In *Dutch Jewish History Vol. 1*, edited by Jozeph Michman and Tirtsah Levie, 31–51. Jerusalem: Tel-Aviv University 1984.

———. "Dutch Sephardi Jewry, Millenarian Politics, and the Struggle for Brazil." In *Sceptics, Millenarians, and Jews*, edited by David S. Katz and Jonathan I. Israel, 76–97. Leiden: Brill, 1990.

———. "The Dutch-Spanish War and the Holy Roman Empire (1568–1648)." In *1648, War and Peace in Europe Volume 1: Politics, Religion, Law, and Society*, edited by Klaus Bussmann and Heinz Schilling, 111–21. Münster: Westfälisches Landesmuseum, 1998.

———. "The Early Dutch and German Reaction to the *Tractatus Theologico-Politicus*: Foreshadowing the Enlightenment's More General Spinoza Reception?" In *Spinoza's Theological-Political Treatise: A Critical Guide*, edited by Yitzhak Y. Melamed and Michael A. Rosenthal, 72–100. Cambridge: Cambridge University Press, 2010.

———. "The Economic Contribution of Dutch Sephardim in International Trade, 1595–1713." *Tijdschrift voor geschiedenis* 96 (1983) 505–35.

———. *Enlightenment Contested: Philosophy, Modernity, and the Emancipation of Man 1670–1752*. Oxford: Oxford University Press, 2006.

———. *Radical Enlightenment: Philosophy and the Making of Modernity 1650–1750*. Oxford: Oxford University Press, 2001.

———. "Some Further Data on the Amsterdam Sephardim and Their Trade with Spain During the 1650s." *Studia Rosenthaliana* 14 (1980) 7–19.

Jaitner, Klaus. "The Popes and the Struggle for Power during the Sixteenth and Seventeenth Centuries." In *1648, War and Peace in Europe Volume 1: Politics, Religion, Law, and Society*, edited by Klaus Bussmann and Heinz Schilling, 61–67. Münster: Westfälisches Landesmuseum, 1998.

James, Susan. *Spinoza on Philosophy, Religion, and Politics: The Theologico-Political Treatise*. Oxford: Oxford University Press, 2012.

Jansen, Katherine Ludwig. *The Making of the Magdalen: Preaching and Popular Devotion in the Later Middle Ages*. Princeton: Princeton University Press, 2000.

Jodock, Darrell. "Introduction I: The Modernist Crisis." In *Catholicism Contending with Modernity: Roman Catholic Modernism and Anti-Modernism in Historical Context*, edited by Darrell Jodock, 1-19. Cambridge: Cambridge University Press, 2000.

Johnston, David. *The Rhetoric of Leviathan: Thomas Hobbes and the Politics of Cultural Transformation*. Princeton: Princeton University Press, 1986.

Jongeneelen, G. H. "La philosophie politique d'Adrien Koerbagh." *Cahiers Spinoza* 6 (1991) 247-67.

Jorink, Eric. "'Horrible and Blasphemous': Isaac La Peyrère, Isaac Vossius and the Emergence of Radical Biblical Criticism in the Dutch Republic." In *Nature and Scripture in the Abrahamic Religions: Up to 1700: Volume 1*, edited by Jitse M. van der Meer and Scott Mandelbrote, 429-550. Leiden: Brill, 2008.

———. "Reading the Book of Nature in the Seventeenth-Century Dutch Republic." In *The Book of Nature in Early Modern and Modern History*, edited by Klaas van Berkel and Arjo Vanderjagt, 45-68. Leuven: Peeters, 2006.

Jorink, Eric and Dirk van Miert. "Introduction: The Challenger: Isaac Vossius and the European World of Learning." In *Isaac Vossius (1618-1689) Between Science and Scholarship*, edited by Eric Jorink and Dirk van Miert, 1-14. Leiden: Brill, 2012.

Kamen, Henry. *Early Modern European Society*. London: Routledge, 2000.

Kaplan, Yosef. "On the Relation of Spinoza's Contemporaries in the Portuguese Jewish Community of Amsterdam to Spanish Culture and the Marrano Experience." In *Spinoza's Political and Theological Thought*, edited by C. de Deugd, 82-94. Amsterdam: North-Holland, 1984.

———. "The Portuguese Community in the Seventeenth-Century Amsterdam and the Ashkenazi World." In *Dutch Jewish History Vol. 2*, edited by Jozeph Michman, 23-45. Assen: Van Gorcum, 1989.

———. "The Portuguese Jews in Amsterdam: From Forced Conversion to a Return to Judaism." *Studia Rosenthaliana* 15 (1981) 37-51.

———. "The Social Functions of the *Herem* in the Portuguese Jewish Community of Amsterdam in the Seventeenth Century." In *Dutch Jewish History Vol. 1*, edited by Jozeph Michman and Tirtsah Levie, 111-55. Jerusalem: Tel-Aviv University 1984.

Kärkkäinen, Pekka and Henrik Lagerlund. "Philosophical Psychology in 1500: Erfurt, Padua and Bologna." In *Psychology and Philosophy: Inquiries into the Soul from Late Scholasticism to Contemporary Thought*, edited by Sara Heinämaa and Martina Reuter, 27-46. Dordrecht: Springer, 2008.

Katz, David S. "Menasseh ben Israel's Mission to Queen Christina of Sweden, 1651-1655." *Jewish Social Studies* 45 (1983) 57-72.

Kavka, Gregory S. "Hobbes's War of All Against All." *Ethics* 93 (1983) 291-310.

Kennedy, Robert George. "Thomas Aquinas and the Literal Sense of Scripture." PhD diss., University of Notre Dame, 1985.

Kennington, Richard. *On Modern Origins: Essays in Early Modern Philosophy*. Lanham, MD: Lexington, 2004.

Klein, Jacob. *Greek Mathematical Thought and the Origin of Algebra*. New York: Dover, 1992.

Klever, W. N. A. "Spinoza's Life and Works." In *The Cambridge Companion to Spinoza*, edited by Don Garrett, 13-60. Cambridge: Cambridge University Press, 1996.

Knight, Douglas A. *Rediscovering the Traditions of Israel: The Development of the Traditio-Historical Research of the Old Testament, with Special Consideration of Scandinavian Contributions*. Missoula, MT: Society of Biblical Literature, 1973.

Koen, E. M. "The Earliest Sources Relating to the Portuguese Jews in the Municipal Archives of Amsterdam up to 1620." *Studia Rosenthaliana* 4 (1970) 25-42.

Kofsky, Aryeh. *Eusebius of Caesarea Against Paganism*. Leiden: Brill, 2000.

Komonchak, Joseph A. "The Enlightenment and the Construction of Roman Catholicism." *Annual of the Catholic Commission on Intellectual and Cultural Affairs* (1985) 31-59.

Köpf, Ulrich. "The Institutional Framework of Christian Exegesis in the Middle Ages." In *Hebrew Bible/Old Testament Volume I: From the Beginnings to the Middle Ages (Until 1300) Part 2: The Middle Ages*, edited by Magne Sæbø, 148-79. Göttingen: Vandenhoeck & Ruprecht, 2000.

Kraus, Andreas. "Das Bild Ludwigs des Bayern in der bayerischen Geschichtsschreibung der Frühen Neuzeit." *Zeitschrift für Bayerische Landesgeschichte* 60 (1997) 5-70.

Kraus, Hans-Joachim. "Calvins exegetische Prinzipien." *Zeitschrift für Kirchengeschichte* 79 (1968) 329-41.

———. *Geschichte der historisch-kritischen Erforschung des Alten Testaments von der Reformation bis zur gegenwart*. Neukirchen Kreis Moers: Verlag der Buchhandlung des Erziehungsvereins, 1956.

———. *Geschichte der historisch-kritischen Erforschung des Alten Testaments*. 2nd rev. ed. Neukirchen: Vluyn, 1969 (1956).

Krautheimer, Richard. *The Rome of Alexander VII, 1655-1667*. Princeton: Princeton University Press, 1985.

Kreisel, Howard. "Philosophical Interpretations of the Bible." In *The Cambridge History of Jewish Philosophy: From Antiquity Through the Seventeenth Century*, edited by Steven Nadler and T. M. Rudavsky, 88-120. Cambridge: Cambridge University Press, 2009.

Krop, Henri. "Spinoza and the Calvinistic Cartesianism of Lambertus Van Velthuysen." *Studia Spinozana* 15 (1999) 107-36.

Kugel, James L. "The Bible in the University." In *The Hebrew Bible and Its Interpreters*, edited by William Henry Propp et al., 143-65. Winona Lake, IN: Eisenbrauns, 1990.

———. *How to Read the Bible: A Guide to Scripture, Then and Now*. New York: Free Press, 2007.

La Peyrère, Isaac. *La Bataille de Lents*. Paris: Imprimerie du Louvre, 1649.

———. *Men before Adam. Or a Discourse upon the twelfth, thirteenth, and fourteenth Verses of the Fifth Chapter of the Epistle of the Apostle Paul to the Romans. By which are prov'd, That the first Men were created before Adam*. London: n.p., 1656.

———. *Præ-Adamitæ. Sive Exercitatio super Versibus duodecimo, decimotertio, & decimoquarto, capitis quinti Epistolæ D. Pauli ad Romanos. Quibus Inducuntur Primi Homines ante Adamum conditi*. n.p., 1655.

———. *Du Rappel des Juifs*. n.p., 1643.

———. *Systema Theologicum, ex Præ-Adamitarum Hypothesi. Pars Prima*. n.p., 1655.

———. *A Theological Systeme Upon that Presupposition, That Men were before Adam. The first Part*. London: n.p., 1655.

Lachterman, David. *The Ethics of Geometry: A Genealogy of Modernity*. New York: Routledge, 1989.
Lambe, Patrick J. "Critics and Skeptics in the Seventeenth-Century Republic of Letters." *Harvard Theological Review* 81 (1988) 272–92.
Langer, Herbert. "The Royal Swedish War in Germany." In *1648, War and Peace in Europe Volume 1: Politics, Religion, Law, and Society*, edited by Klaus Bussmann and Heinz Schilling, 187–96. Münster: Westfälisches Landesmuseum, 1998.
Lagrée, Jacqueline. "Louis Meyer et la *Philosophia S. Scripturae interpres*. Projet cartésien, horizon spinoziste." *Revue des sciences philosophiques et théologiques* 1 (1987) 31–44.
———. "Sens et vérité: philosophie et théologie chez L. Meyer et Spinoza." *Studia Spinozana* 4 (1988) 75–92.
Lagrée, Jacqueline and Pierre-François Moreau. "La lecture de la Bible dans le cercle de Spinoza." In *Le Grand Siècle et la Bible*, edited by Jean-Robert Armogathe, 97–115. Paris: Beauchesne, 1989.
Larkin, Emmet. "Cardinal Paul Cullen." In *Varieties of Ultramontanism*, edited by Jeffrey von Arx, SJ, 61–84. Washington, DC: The Catholic University of America Press, 1998.
Lasker, Daniel J. "Reflections of the Medieval Jewish-Christian Debate in the *Theological-Political Treatise* and the *Epistles*." In *Spinoza's Theological-Political Treatise: A Critical Guide*, edited by Yitzhak Y. Melamed and Michael A. Rosenthal, 56–71. Cambridge: Cambridge University Press, 2010.
Lawee, Eric. "Isaac Abarbanel: From Medieval to Renaissance Jewish Biblical Scholarship." In *Hebrew Bible/Old Testament: The History of Its Interpretation Vol. II: From the Renaissance to the Enlightenment*, edited by Magne Sæbø, 190–214. Göttingen: Vandenhoeck & Ruprecht, 2008.
Lazarus-Yafeh, Hava. *Intertwined Worlds: Medieval Islam and Bible Criticism*. Princeton: Princeton University Press, 1992.
———. "Some Neglected Aspects of Medieval Polemics against Christianity." *Harvard Theological Review* 89 (1996) 61–84.
———. "Taḥrīf and Thirteen Scrolls of Torah." *Jerusalem Studies in Arabic and Islam* 18 (1992) 81–88.
Lease, Gary. "Vatican Foreign Policy and the Origins of Modernism." In *Catholicism Contending with Modernity: Roman Catholic Modernism and Anti-Modernism in Historical Context*, edited by Darrell Jodock, 31–55. Cambridge: Cambridge University Press, 2000.
Leclercq, Jean. *L'Amour des lettres et le désir de Dieu: Initiation aux auteurs monastiques du moyen age*. 3rd ed. Paris: Cerf, 1990 (1957).
Legaspi, Michael C. *The Death of Scripture and the Rise of Biblical Studies*. Oxford: Oxford University Press, 2010.
———. "What Ever Happened to Historical Criticism?" *Journal of Religion & Society* 9 (2007) 1–21.
Leithart, Peter J. *Deep Exegesis: The Mystery of Reading Scripture*. Waco, TX: Baylor University Press, 2009.
Lemche, Niels Peter. *The Old Testament between Theology and History: A Critical Survey*. Louisville, KY: Westminster John Knox, 2008.

Levene, Nancy. "Ethics and Interpretation, or How to Study Spinoza's *Tractatus Theologico-Politicus* without Strauss." *Journal of Jewish Thought and Philosophy* 10 (2000) 57–110.

Levenson, Jon D. "The Eighth Principle of Judaism and the Literary Simultaneity of Scripture." *Journal of Religion* 68 (1988) 205–25.

———. *The Hebrew Bible, the Old Testament, and Historical Criticism: Jews and Christians in Biblical Studies*. Louisville, KY: Westminster John Knox, 1993.

Levering, Matthew. *Participatory Biblical Exegesis: A Theology of Biblical Interpretation*. Notre Dame, IN: University of Notre Dame Press, 2008.

Lewis, Rhodri. "William Petty's Anthropology: Religion, Colonialism, and the Problem of Human Diversity." *Huntington Library Quarterly* 74 (2011) 261–88.

Linde, J. Cornelia. "Lorenzo Valla and the Authenticity of Sacred Texts." *Humanistica Lovaniensia* 60 (2011) 35–63.

Livingstone, David N. *Adam's Ancestors: Race, Religion, and the Politics of Human Origins*. Baltimore, MD: Johns Hopkins University Press, 2008.

———. "Cultural Politics and the Racial Cartographics of Human Origins." *Transactions of the Institute of British Geographers* 35 (2010) 204–21.

———. "Geographical Inquiry, Rational Religion, and Moral Philosophy: Enlightenment Discourses on the Human Condition." In *Geography and Enlightenment*, edited by David N. Livingstone and Charles W. J. Withers, 93–119. Chicago: University of Chicago Press, 1999.

———. "Geography, Tradition and the Scientific Revolution: An Interpretative Essay." *Transactions of the Institute of British Geographers* 15 (1990) 359–73.

———. "Politics, Culture, and Human Origins: Geographies of Reading and Reputation in Nineteenth-Century Science." In *Geographies of Nineteenth-Century Science*, edited by David N. Livingstone and Charles W. J. Withers, 178–202. Chicago: University of Chicago Press, 2011.

———. "The Preadamite Theory and the Marriage of Science and Religion." *Transactions of the American Philosophical Society* 82 (1992) x–81.

———. "Preadamites: The History of an Idea from Heresy to Orthodoxy." *Scottish Journal of Theology* 40 (1987) 41–66.

Ljamai, Abdelilah. *Ibn Ḥazm et la polémique islamo-chrétienne dans l'histoire de l'islam*. Leiden: Brill, 2003.

Löhr, Winrich. "Did Marcion Distinguish Between a Just God and a Good God?" In *Marcion unde Seine Kirchengeschichtliche Wirkung/Marcion and His Impact on Church History: Vorträge der Internationalen Fachkonferenz zu Marcion, gehalten vom 15.—18. August 2001 in Mainz*, edited by Gerhard May and Katharina Greschat, 131–46. Berlin: Walter de Gruyter, 2002.

Long, V. Philips. "Historiography of the Old Testament." In *The Face of Old Testament Studies: A Survey of Contemporary Approaches*, edited by David W. Baker and Bill T. Arnold, 145–75. Grand Rapids: Baker, 1999.

Lopata, Benjamin B. "Property Theory in Hobbes." *Political Theory* 1 (1973) 203–18.

Lorberbaum, Menachem. "Spinoza's Theological-Political Problem." In *Political Hebraism: Judaic Sources in Early Modern Political Thought*, edited by Gordon Schochet et al., 167–88. Jerusalem: Shalem, 2008.

Lucci, Diego. "Judaism and the Jews in the British Deists' Attacks on Revealed Religion." *Hebrew Political Studies* 3 (2008) 177–214.

———. *Scripture and Deism: The Biblical Criticism of the Eighteenth-Century British Deists*. Bern: Peter Lang, 2008.
Lynch, Christopher. "Machiavelli on Reading the Bible Judiciously." In *Political Hebraism: Judaic Sources in Early Modern Political Thought*, edited by Gordon Schochet et al., 29–55. Jerusalem: Shalem, 2008.
MacCulloch, Diarmaid. *The Reformation*. New York: Penguin, 2003.
Mac Curtain, Benvenuta. "An Irish Agent of the Counter-Reformation, Dominic O'Daly." *Irish Historical Studies* 15 (1967) 391–406.
MacGillivray, Royce. "Thomas Hobbes's History of the English Civil War: A Study of Behemoth." *Journal of the History of Ideas* 31 (1970) 179–98.
Macherey, Pierre. *Avec Spinoza. Études sur la doctrine et l'histoire du spinozisme*. Paris: Presses Universitaires de France, 1992.
MacIntyre, Alasdair. *A Short History of Ethics: A History of Moral Philosophy from the Homeric Age to the Twentieth Century*. 2nd ed. Notre Dame, IN: University of Notre Dame Press, 1998.
Mack, Michael. *Spinoza and the Specters of Modernity: The Hidden Enlightenment of Diversity from Spinoza to Freud*. New York: Continuum, 2010.
Maddox, Graham. "The Secular Reformation and the Influence of Machiavelli." *Journal of Religion* 82 (2002) 539–62.
Maier, Gerhard. "Wahrheit und Wirklichkeit im Geschichtsverständnis des Alten Testaments." In *Israel in Geschichte und Gegenwart*, edited by Gerhard Maier, 9–23. Basel: Brunnen, 1996.
Malcolm, Noel. *Aspects of Hobbes*. Oxford: Oxford University Press, 2002.
———. "Hobbes, Sandys, and the Virginia Company." *Historical Journal* 24 (1981) 297–321.
———. "*Leviathan*, the Pentateuch, and the Origins of Modern Biblical Criticism." In *Leviathan After 350 Years*, edited by Tom Sorell and Luc Foisneau, 241–64. Oxford: Oxford University Press, 2004.
Malet, André. *Le traité théologico-politique de Spinoza et la pensée biblique*. Paris: Sociéte les belles letters, 1966.
Malherbe, Michel. "Hobbes et la Bible." In *Le Grand Siècle et la Bible*, edited by Jean-Robert Armogathe, 691–99. Paris: Beauchesne, 1989.
Mallia-Milanes, Victor. *Louis XIV and France*. London: Macmillan, 1986.
Maltby, William. *The Reign of Charles V*. New York: Palgrave, 2002.
Malter, Henry. *Saadia Gaon: His Life and Works*. Philadelphia: Jewish Publication Society of America, 1921.
Manekin, Charles H. "Hebrew Philosophy in the Fourteenth and Fifteenth Centuries: An Overview." In *History of Jewish Philosophy*, edited by Daniel H. Frank and Oliver Leaman, 292–318. London: Routledge, 2004.
Manrique Charry, Juan Francisco. "La herencia de Bacon en la doctrina spinocista del lenguaje." *Universitas Philosophica* 54 (2010) 121–30.
Marder, Tod A. "Bernini and Alexander VII: Criticism and Praise of the Pantheon in the Seventeenth Century." *The Art Bulletin* 71 (1989) 628–45.
Marenbon, John. *The Philosophy of Peter Abelard*. Cambridge: Cambridge University Press, 1999 (1997).
Marion, J.-L. "A propos de Suarez et Descartes." *Revue internationale de philosophie* 50 (1996) 109–31.

Marius, Richard. *Martin Luther: The Christian between God and Death*. Cambridge: Belknap, 1999.
Markreich, Max. "Notes on Transformation of Place Names by European Jews." *Jewish Social Studies* 23.4 (1961) 265–84.
Marmorstein, Arthur. "The Background of the Haggadah." *Hebrew Union College Annual* 6 (1929) 141–204.
Martin, Craig. "Rethinking Renaissance Averroism." *Intellectual History Review* 17 (2007) 3–28.
Martinez Gros, Gabriel. "Ibn Hazm contre les Juifs: un bouc émissaire jusqu'au jugement dernier." *Atalaya* 5 (1994) 123–34.
Martinich, A. P. *Hobbes: A Biography*. Cambridge: Cambridge University Press, 1999.
———. *The Two Gods of Leviathan: Thomas Hobbes on Religion and Politics*. Cambridge: Cambridge University Press, 1992.
Marx, Anthony W. *Faith in Nation: Exclusionary Origins of Nationalism*. Oxford: Oxford University Press, 2003.
Marx, Steven. "Moses and Machiavellism." *Journal of the American Academy of Religion* 65 (1997) 551–71.
Masuzawa, Tomoko. *The Invention of World Religions: Or, How European Universalism Was Preserved in the Language of Pluralism*. Chicago: University of Chicago Press, 2005.
Matthews, Steven. *Theology and Science in the Thought of Francis Bacon*. Aldershot: Ashgate, 2008.
McDannell, Colleen. *Material Christianity: Religion and Popular Culture in America*. New Haven, CT: Yale University Press, 1995.
McKane, William. *Selected Christian Hebraists*. Cambridge: Cambridge University Press, 1989.
McKee, David Rice. "Isaac de La Peyrère, A Precursor of Eighteenth-Century Critical Deists." *Publications of the Modern Language Association* 59 (1944) 456–85.
McLoughlin, William G., and Walter H. Conser, Jr. "'The First Man Was Red'—Cherokee Responses to the Debate over Indian Origins, 1760–1860." *American Quarterly* 41 (1989) 243–64.
McSorley, Harry J. *Luthers Lehre vom unfreien Willen: Nach seiner Hauptschrift De servo arbitrio im Lichte der biblischen und kirchlichen Tradition*. Munich: Max Hueber, 1967.
Meeks, Wayne A. "A Nazi New Testament Professor Reads the Bible: The Strange Case of Gerhard Kittel." In *The Idea of Biblical Interpretation: Essays in Honor of James L. Kugel*, edited by H. Najman and J. H. Newman, 513–44. Leiden: Brill, 2004.
Metzger, Bruce M., and Michael D. Coogan, ed. *The Oxford Companion to the Bible*. Oxford: Oxford University Press, 1993.
Mews, Constant J., and Micha J. Perry. "Peter Abelard, Heloise and Jewish Biblical Exegesis in the Twelfth Century." *Journal of Ecclesistical History* 62 (2011) 3–19.
Michman, Jozeph. "Historiography of the Jews in the Netherlands." In *Dutch Jewish History Vol. 1*, edited by Jozeph Michman and Tirtsah Levie, 7–29. Jerusalem: Tel-Aviv University 1984.
Miethke, Jürgen. "Der Kampf Ludwigs des Bayern mit Papst und avignonesischer Kurie in seiner Bedeutung für die deutsche Geschichte." In *Kaiser Ludwig der Bayer. Konflikte, Weichenstellungen und Wahrnehmung seiner Herrschaft*, edited by Hermann Nehlsen and Hans-Georg Hermann, 39–74. Paderborn: Schöningh, 2002.

Milbank, John. *Theology and Social Theory: Beyond Secular Reason*. 2nd ed. Oxford: Blackwell, 2006 (1990).

Milner, Benjamin. "Hobbes: On Religion." *Political Theory* 16 (1988) 400–25.

Miner, Robert C. "Suarez as Founder of Modernity: Reflections on a *Topos* in Recent Historiography." *History of Philosophy Quarterly* 18 (2001) 17–36.

Minnis, A. J. "Material Swords and Literal Lights: The Status of Allegory in William of Ockham's *Breviloquium* on Papal Power." In *With Reverence for the Word: Medieval Scriptural Exegesis in Judaism, Christianity, and Islam*, edited by Jane Dammen McAuliffe et al., 292–308. Oxford: Oxford University Press, 2003.

Mintz, Samuel I. *The Hunting of Leviathan: Seventeenth-Century Reactions to the Materialism and Moral Philosophy of Thomas Hobbes*. Bristol: Thoemmes, 1962.

Mirri, F. Saverio. *Richard Simon e il metodo storico-critico di B. Spinoza. Storia di un libro e di una polemica sulla sfondo delle lotte politico-religiose della Francia di Luigi XIV*. Florence: Felice Le Monnier, 1972.

Misner, Paul. "Catholic Anti-Modernism: The Ecclesial Setting." In *Catholicism Contending with Modernity: Roman Catholic Modernism and Anti-Modernism in Historical Context*, edited by Darrell Jodock, 56–87. Cambridge: Cambridge University Press, 2000.

Momigliano, Arnaldo. "Religious History without Frontiers: J. Wellhausen, U. Wilamowitz, and E. Schwartz." *History and Theory* 21 (1982) 49–64.

Moreau, Pierre-François. "Le méthode d'interprétation de l'Écriture Sainte: déterminations et limites." In *Spinoza: science et religion*, edited by Renée Bouveresse, 109–14. Paris: Vrin, 1988.

Morfino, Vittorio. *Il tempo e l'occasione. L'incontro Spinoza Machiavelli*. Milan: LED, 2002.

Morrow, Jeffrey L. "The Bible in Captivity: Hobbes, Spinoza and the Politics of Defining Religion." *Pro Ecclesia* 19 (2010) 285–99.

———. "The Enlightenment University and the Creation of the Academic Bible: Michael Legaspi's *The Death of Scripture and the Rise of Biblical Studies*." *Nova et Vetera* 11 (2013) 899–909.

———. "Faith, Reason, and History in Early Modern Catholic Biblical Interpretation: Fr. Richard Simon and St. Thomas More." *New Blackfriars* 96 (2015) 658–73.

———. "French Apocalyptic Messianism: Isaac La Peyrère and Political Biblical Criticism in the Seventeenth Century." *Toronto Journal of Theology* 27 (2011) 203–13.

———. "The Modernist Crisis and the Shifting of Catholic Views on Biblical Inspiration." *Letter & Spirit* 6 (2010) 265–80.

———. "The Politics of Biblical Interpretation: A 'Criticism of Criticism.'" *New Blackfriars* 91 (2010) 528–45.

———. "Pre-Adamites, Politics and Criticism: Isaac La Peyrère's Contribution to Modern Biblical Studies." *Journal of the Orthodox Center for the Advancement of Biblical Studies* 4 (2011) 1–23.

———. "Revisiting the Seventeenth-Century European 'Wars of Religion.'" *The Ohio Academy of Religion Scholarly Papers* (2005) 66–80.

———. "Secularization, Objectivity, and Enlightenment Scholarship: The Theological and Political Origins of Modern Biblical Studies." *Logos* 18 (2015) 14–32.

Mulier, Eco. *The Myth of Venice and Dutch Republican Thought in the Seventeenth Century*. Assen: Van Gorcum, 1980.

Muller, Richard A. "The Debate Over the Vowel Points and the Crisis in Orthodox Hermeneutics." *Journal of Medieval and Renaissance Studies* 10 (1980) 53–72.

———. "The Hermeneutic of Promise and Fulfillment in Calvin's Exegesis of the Old Testament Prophecies of the Kingdom." In *The Bible in the Sixteenth Century*, edited by David C. Steinmetz, 68–82. Durham: Duke University Press, 1996.

Müller, Sascha. *Kritik und Theologie: christliche Glaubens-und Schrifthermeneutik nach Richard Simon (1638–1712)*. St. Ottilien: EOS, 2004.

———. *Richard Simon (1638–1712) Exeget, Theologe, Philosoph und Historiker*. Bamberg: Echter, 2006.

Muslow, Martin. "Libertinismus in Deutschland? Stile der Subversion in Politik, Religion und Literatur des 17. Jahrhunderts." *Zeitschrift für historische Forschung* 31 (2004) 37–71.

Nadler, Steven. "The Bible Hermeneutics of Baruch de Spinoza." In *Hebrew Bible/Old Testament: The History of Its Interpretation Volume II: From the Renaissance to the Enlightenment*, edited by Magne Sæbø, 827–36. Göttingen: Vandenhoeck & Ruprecht, 2008.

———. *A Book Forged in Hell: Spinoza's Scandalous Treatise and the Birth of the Secular Age*. Princeton: Princeton University Press, 2011.

———. *Spinoza: A Life*. Cambridge: Cambridge University Press, 1999.

Nahkola, Aulikki. *Double Narratives in the Old Testament: The Foundations of Method in Biblical Criticism*. Berlin: Walter de Gruyter, 2001.

Naor, Bezalel. *Ma'amar al Yishma'el/Rabbi Solomon ben Abraham ibn Adret's Mitsvat Hashem Barah/An Elucidation of the Seven Noahide Commandments: With an Introduction and Notes*. Spring Valley, NY: Orot, 2008.

Nativel, Colette. "Isaac Vossius, entre Philologie et Philosophie." In *Isaac Vossius (1618–1689) Between Science and Scholarship*, edited by Eric Jorink and Dirk van Miert, 243–54. Leiden: Brill, 2012.

Nehlsen, Hermann. "Die Rolle Ludwigs des Bayern und seiner Berater Marsilius von Padua und Wilhelm von Ockham im Tiroler Ehekonflikt." In *Kaiser Ludwig der Bayer. Konflikte, Weichenstellungen und Wahrnehmung seiner Herrschaft*, edited by Hermann Nehlsen and Hans-Georg Hermann, 285–328. Paderborn: Schöningh, 2002.

Nellen, H. J. M. "Growing Tension between Church Doctrines and Critical Exegesis of the Old Testament." In *Hebrew Bible/Old Testament: The History of Its Interpretation Vol. II: From the Renaissance to the Enlightenment*, edited by Magne Sæbø, 802–26. Göttingen: Vandenhoeck & Ruprecht, 2008.

Nelson, Eric. *The Hebrew Republic: Jewish Sources and the Transformation of European Political Thought*. Cambridge: Harvard University Press, 2010.

Newman, Zelda Kahan. "Elye Levita: A Man and His Book on the Cusp of Modernity." *Shofar* 24 (2006) 90–109.

Nichols, Francis W. "Richard Simon: Faith and Modernity." In *Christianity and the Stranger: Historical Essays*, edited by Francis W. Nichols, 115–68. Atlanta: Scholars, 1995.

Nongbri, Brent. *Before Religion: A History of a Modern Concept*. New Haven: Yale University Press, 2013.

Novick, Peter. *That Noble Dream: The "Objectivity Question" and the American Historical Profession*. Cambridge: Cambridge University Press, 1988.

Oddos, Jean-Pierre. "Recherches sur la vie et l'oeuvre d'Isaac de La Peyrère (1596?–1676)." PhD diss., Grenoble University, 1974.
Offler, H. S. "Empire and Papacy: The Last Struggle." *Transactions of the Royal Historical Society* 6 (1956) 21–47.
O'Loughlin, Thomas. "Biblical Contradictions in the *Periphyseon* and the Development of Eriugena's Method." In *Iohannes Scottus Eriugena and the Scriptures*, edited by Carlos Steel et al., 103–26. Leuven: Leuven University Press, 1996.
———. "The Controversy over Methuselah's Death: Proto-Chronology and the Origins of the Western Concept of Inerrancy." *Recherches de théologie ancienne et médiévale* 62 (1995) 182–225.
———. "Inventing the Apocrypha: The Role of Early Latin Canon Lists." *Iristh Theological Quarterly* 74 (2009) 53–74.
———. "Julian of Toledo's *Antikeimenon* and the Development of Latin Exegesis." *Proceedings of the Irish Biblical Association* 16 (1993) 80–98.
———. "*Res, Tempus, Locus, Persona*: Adomnán's Exegetical Method." *Innes Review* 48 (1997) 95–111.
O'Neill, J.C. "Adolf von Harnack and the Entry of the German State into War, July–August 1914." *Scottish Journal of Theology* 55 (2002) 1–18.
Ong, Walter J., SJ. *The Presence of the Word: Some Prolegomena for Cultural and Religious History*. New Haven, CT: Yale University Press, 1967.
Oresko, Robert. "The House of Savoy and the Thirty Years' War." In *1648, War and Peace in Europe Volume 1: Politics, Religion, Law, and Society*, edited by Klaus Bussmann and Heinz Schilling, 142–53. Münster: Westfälisches Landesmuseum, 1998.
Osier, Jean Pierre. "L'herméneutique de Hobbes et de Spinoza." *Studia Spinozana* 3 (1987) 319–47.
Overhoff, Jürgen. "The Theology of Thomas Hobbes's *Leviathan*." *JEH* 51 (2000) 527–55.
The Oxford English Dictionary Vol. XIV: Rob–Sequyle. 2nd ed. Edited by J. A. Simpson and E. S. C. Weiner. Oxford: Clarendon, 1989.
Pacchi, Arrigo. *Filosofia e Teologia in Hobbes: Dispense de Corso di Storia della Filosofia per l'A.A. 1984–'85*. Milan: UNICOPLI, 1985.
———. "Hobbes and Biblical Philology in the Service of the State." *Topoi* 7 (1988) 231–39.
———. "Hobbes e l'epicureismo." *Rivista critica di storia dell filosofia* 33 (1975) 54–71.
Pacheco, Juan Antonio. "El 'Mahâsim al-mayâlis' de Ibn al-Arif y la Etica de Spinoza." *La Ciudad de Dios* 203 (1990) 671–87.
Padberg, John W., SJ. "Cardinal Louis-Edouard-Désiré Pie." In *Varieties of Ultramontanism*, edited by Jeffrey von Arx, SJ, 39–60. Washington, DC: The Catholic University of America Press, 1998.
Palm, Franklin C. *Calvinism and the Religious Wars*. New York: Henry Holt, 1932.
Parente, Fausto. "Isaac de la Peyrère interprète de Paul: Pourquoi le *Rappel des Juifs* a-t-il été presque entièrement détruit au moment de sa publication?" *Revue des études juives* 167 (2008) 169–86.
———. "Isaac de La Peyrère e Richard Simon. Osservazioni preliminari ad uno studio del ms. Chantilly, Musée de Consé, n. 191 (698)." In *La Geografia dei saperi. Scritti in memoria di Dino Pastine*, edited by D. Ferraro and G. Gigliotti, 161–82. Florence: Casa editrice Le Lettere, 2000.

Parker, David. *Class and State in Ancien Régime France: The Road to Modernity?* London: Routledge: 1996.
Parker, Geoffrey, ed. *The Thirty Years' War.* London: Routledge, 1984.
Parkin, Jon. "The Reception of Hobbes's *Leviathan.*" In *The Cambridge Companion to Hobbes's Leviathan*, edited by Patricia Springborg, 441–59. Cambridge: Cambridge University Press, 2007.
Payne, Alina A. "Architectural Criticism, Science, and Visual Eloquence: Teofilo Gallaccini in Seventeenth-Century Siena." *Journal of the Society of Architectural Historians* 58 (1999) 146–69.
Pelikan, Jaroslav. *The Christian Tradition: A History of the Development of Doctrine Volume 3: The Growth of Medieval Theology (600–1300).* Chicago: University of Chicago Press, 1978.
———. *The Christian Tradition: A History of the Development of Doctrine Volume 4: Reformation of Church and Dogma (1300–1700).* Chicago: University of Chicago Press, 1984.
Pernoud, Régine. *Héloïse et Abélard.* Paris: Le Livre de Poche, 1970.
Pesic, Peter. "Wrestling with Proteus: Francis Bacon and the 'Torture' of Nature." *Isis* 90 (1999) 81–94.
Philpott, Daniel. *Revolutions in Sovereignty: How Ideas Shaped Modern International Relations.* Princeton: Princeton University Press, 2001.
Pickstock, Catherine. *After Writing: On the Liturgical Consummation of Philosophy.* Oxford: Blackwell, 1998.
Pietsch, Andreas Nikolaus. *Isaac La Peyrère: Bibelkritik, Philosemitismus und Patronage in der Gelehrtenrepublik des 17. Jahrhunderts.* Berlin: Walter de Gruyter, 2012.
Pines, Shlomo. "Spinoza's *Tractatus theologico-politicus,* Maimonides and Kant." *Scripta Hierosolymitana* 20 (1968) 3–54.
Polka, Brayton. *Between Philosophy and Religion: Spinoza, the Bible, and Modernity Volume I: Hermeneutics and Ontology.* Lanham, MD: Lexington, 2007.
———. *Between Philosophy and Religion: Spinoza, the Bible, and Modernity Volume II: Politics and Ethics.* Lanham, MD: Lexington, 2007.
Poole, William. "Francis Lodwick's Creation: Theology and Natural Philosophy in the Early Royal Society." *Journal of the History of Ideas* 66.2 (2005) 245–63.
———. *The World Makers: Scientists of the Restoration and the Search for the Origins of the Earth.* Whitney: Peter Lang, 2010.
Popkin, Richard H. "Afterward—Discovering the Abbé Grégoire." In *The Abbé Grégoire and His World*, edited by Jeremy D. Popkin and Richard H. Popkin, 183–86. Dordrecht: Kluwer Academic, 2000.
———. "Bible Criticism and Social Science." In *Methodological and Historical Essays in the Natural and Social Sciences*, edited by Robert S. Cohen and Marx W. Wartofsky, 339–60. Dordrecht: Reidel, 1974.
———. "Cartesianism and Biblical Criticism." In *Problems of Cartesianism*, edited by Thomas M. Lennon et al., 61–81. Kingston: McGill-Queen's University Press, 1982.
———. "The Development of Religious Scepticism and the Influence of Isaac La Peyrère's Pre-Adamism and Bible Criticism." In *Classical Influences on European Culture, AD 1500–1700*, edited by Robert Ralf Bolgar, 271–80. Cambridge: Cambridge University Press, 1976.

―――. "The First Published Reaction to Spinoza's *Tractatus*: Col. J. B. Stouppe, the Condé Circle, and the Rev. Jean Lebrun." In *The Spinozistic Heresy: The Debate on the Tractatus Theologico-Politicus, 1670-1677*, edited by Paolo Christofolini, 6-12. Amsterdam and Maarssen: APA-Holland University Press, 1995.

―――. "Grégoire's American Involvements." In *The Abbé Grégoire and His World*, edited by Jeremy D. Popkin and Richard H. Popkin, 157-66. Dordrecht: Kluwer Academic, 2000.

―――. *The History of Scepticism: From Savonarola to Bayle*. Oxford: Oxford University Press, 2003.

―――. "Hume and Spinoza." *Hume Studies* 5 (1979) 65-93.

―――. "Introduction: Warts and All, Part 2." In *Everything Connects: In Conference with Richard H. Popkin: Essays in His Honor*, edited by James E. Force and David S. Katz, xi-lxxvi. Leiden: Brill, 1999.

―――. *Isaac La Peyrère (1596-1676) His Life, Work and Influence*. Leiden: Brill, 1987.

―――. "Jewish-Christian Relations in the Sixteenth and Seventeenth Centuries: The Conception of the Messiah." *Jewish History* 6 (1992) 163-77.

―――. "The Marrano Theology of Isaac La Peyrère." *Studi Internaxionali di Filosofia* 5 (1973) 97-126.

―――. "Menasseh ben Israel and Isaac La Peyrère." *Studia Rosenthaliana* 8 (1974) 59-63.

―――. "Menasseh ben Israel and Isaac La Peyrère, II." *Studia Rosenthaliana* 18 (1984) 12-20.

―――. "Millenarianism and Nationalism—A Case Study: Isaac La Peyrère." In *Millenarianism and Messianism in Early Modern European Culture: Continental Millenarians: Protestants, Catholics, Heretics*, edited by John Christian Laursen and Richard H. Popkin, 78-82. Dordrecht: Kluwer Academic, 2001.

―――. "Philosophy and the History of Philosophy." *Journal of Philosophy* 82 (1985) 625-32.

―――. "The Pre-Adamite Theory in the Renaissance." In *Philosophy and Humanism: Renaissance Essays in Honor of Paul Oskar Kristeller*, edited by Edward P. Mahoney, 50-69. Leiden: Brill, 1976.

―――. "The Religious Background of Seventeenth-Century Philosophy." In *The Cambridge History of Seventeenth-Century Philosophy Volume I*, edited by Daniel Garber and Michael Ayers, 393-422. Cambridge: Cambridge University Press, 1998.

―――. "Some New Light on the Roots of Spinoza's Science of Bible Study." In *Spinoza and the Sciences*, edited by Marjorie Grene and Debra Nails, 171-88. Dordrecht: Kluwer Academic, 1986.

―――. *Spinoza*. Oxford: Oneworld, 2004.

―――. "Spinoza and Bible Scholarship." In *The Cambridge Companion to Spinoza*, edited by Don Garrett, 383-407. Cambridge: Cambridge University Press, 1996.

―――. "Spinoza and La Peyrère." *Southwestern Journal of Philosophy* 8 (1977) 172-95.

―――. "Spinoza, the Quakers and the Millenarians, 1656-1658." *Manuscrito* 6 (1982) 113-33.

―――. "Spinoza and Samuel Fisher." *Philosophia* 15 (1985) 219-36.

―――. "Spinoza's Earliest Philosophical Years, 1655-61." *Studia Spinozana* 4 (1988) 37-54.

———. "Spinoza's Relations with the Quakers in Amsterdam." *Quaker History* 73 (1984) 14–28.
———. *The Third Force in Seventeenth-Century Thought*. Leiden: Brill, 1992.
Porter, Bruce D. *War and the Rise of the State: The Military Foundations of Modern Politics*. New York: Free Press, 1994.
Portier, William L. "Church Unity and National Traditions: The Challenge to the Modern Papacy, 1682–1870." In *The Papacy and the Church in the United States*, edited by Bernard Cooke, 25–54. New York: Paulist, 1989.
———. *Divided Friends: Portraits of the Roman Catholic Modernist Crisis in the United States*. Washington, DC: The Catholic University of America Press, 2013.
Powers, David S. "Reading/Misreading One Another's Scriptures: Ibn Ḥazm's Refutation of Ibn Nagrella al-Yahū d ī." In *Studies in Islamic and Judaic Traditions: Papers Presented at the Institute for Islamic-Judaic Studies*, edited by William M. Brinner and Stephen D. Ricks, 109–21. Atlanta: Scholars, 1986.
Preus, J. Samuel. "The Bible and Religion in the Century of Genius: Part II: The Rise and Fall of the Bible." *Religion* 28 (1998) 15–27.
———. "A Hidden Opponent in Spinoza's *Tractatus*." *Harvard Theological Review* 88 (1995) 361–88.
———. *Spinoza and the Irrelevance of Biblical Authority*. Cambridge: Cambridge University Press, 2001.
———. "Spinoza, Vico, and the Imagination of Religion." *Journal of the History of Ideas* 50 (1989) 71–93.
Pulcini, Theodore. *Exegesis as Polemical Discourse: Ibn Ḥazm on Jewish and Christian Scriptures*. Atlanta: Scholars, 1998.
Quennehen, Élisabeth. "L'auteur des *Préadamites*», Isaac Lapeyrère. Essai biographique." In *Dissidents, excentriques et marginaux de l'Âge classique: Autour de Cyrano de Bergerac: Bouquet offert à Madeleine Alcover*, edited by Patricia Harry et al., 349–73. Paris: Honoré Champion, 2006.
———. "Lapeyrère, la Chine et la chronologie biblique." *La Lettre clandestine* 9 (2000) 243–55.
Raeder, Siegfried. "The Exegetical and Hermeneutical Work of Martin Luther." In *Hebrew Bible/Old Testament: The History of Its Interpretation Volume II: From the Renaissance to the Enlightenment*, edited by Magne Sæbø, 363–406. Göttingen: Vandenhoeck & Ruprecht, 2008.
Rahe, Paul A. *Against Throne and Altar: Machiavelli and Political Theory Under the English Republic*. Cambridge: Cambridge University Press, 2008.
Räisänen, Heikki. *Marcion, Muhammad and the Mahatma: Exegetical Perspectives on the Encounter of Cultures and Faith*. London: SCM, 1997.
Ramón Guerrero, Rafael. "Filósofos hispano-musulmanes y Spinoza: Avempace y Abentofail." In *Spinoza y España: Actas del Congreso Internacional sobre «Relaciones entre Spinoza y España (Almagro, 5–7 noviembre 1992)*, edited by Atilano Domínguez, 125–32. Almagro: Ediciones de la Universidad de Castilla-La Mancha, 1994.
Ratzinger, Joseph. "Der Einfluss des Bettelordensstreites auf die Entwicklung der Lehre vom päpstlichen Universalprimat, unter besonderer Berücksichtigung des heiligen Bonaventura." In *Theologie in Geschichte und Gegenwart. Festgabe für f. Michael Schmaus zum 60. Geburstag*, edited by Johann Auer and Hermann Volk, 697–724. Munich: Zink, 1957.

Repgen, Konrad. "Negotiating the Peace of Westphalia: A Survey with an Examination of the Major Problems." In *1648, War and Peace in Europe Volume 1: Politics, Religion, Law, and Society*, edited by Klaus Bussmann and Heinz Schilling, 355–72. Münster: Westfälisches Landesmuseum, 1998.

Reventlow, Henning Graf. *Bibelautorität und Geist der Moderne, Die bedeutung des Bibelverständnisses für die geistesgeschichtliche und politische Entwicklung in England von der Reformation bis zur Aufklärung*. Göttingen: Vandenhoeck & Ruprecht, 1980.

———. *Epochen der Bibelauslegung II: Von der Spätantike bis zum Ausgang des Mittelalters*. Munich: Beck, 1994.

———. *Epochen der Bibelauslegung IV: Von der Aufklärung bis zum 20. Jahrhundert*. Munich: Beck, 2001.

Rif'at, Nurshif. "Ibn Ḥazm on Jews and Judaism." Diss., Exeter University, 1988.

Robinson, Ira. "Isaac de la Peyrère and the Recall of the Jews." *Jewish Social Studies* 40 (1978) 117–30.

Rosenthal, Frank. "Heinrich von Oyta and Biblical Criticism in the Fourteenth Century." *Speculum* 25 (1950) 178–83.

Rosenthal, Judah. *Ḥiwi al-Balkhi*. Philadelphia: Dropsie College, 1949.

———. "Ḥiwi al-Balkhi: A Comparative Study." *Jewish Quarterly Review* 38 (1948) 317–42.

———. "Ḥiwi al-Balkhi: A Comparative Study (Continued)." *Jewish Quarterly Review* 38 (1948) 419–30.

———. "Ḥiwi al-Balkhi: A Comparative Study (Continued)." *Jewish Quarterly Review* 39 (1948) 79–94.

Rosenthal, Michael A. "Miracles, Wonder, and the State." In *Spinoza's Theological-Political Treatise: A Critical Guide*, edited by Yitzhak Y. Melamed and Michael A. Rosenthal, 231–49. Cambridge: Cambridge University Press, 2010.

Roth, Norman. "Forgery and Abrogation of the Torah: A Theme in Muslim and Christian Polemic in Spain." *Proceedings of the American Academy for Jewish Research* 54 (1987) 203–36.

Rowland, Ingrid D. "Etruscan Inscriptions from a 1637 Autograph of Fabio Chigi." *American Journal of Archaeology* 93 (1989) 423–8.

Rudolph, Ross Avron. "Thomas Hobbes and the Political Philosophy of Skepticism." PhD diss., Columbia University, 1975.

Rummel, Erika. "The Textual and Hermeneutic Work of Desiderius Erasmus of Rotterdam." In *Hebrew Bible/Old Testament: The History of Its Interpretation Volume II: From the Renaissance to the Enlightenment*, edited by Magne Sæbø, 215–30. Göttingen: Vandenhoeck & Ruprecht, 2008.

Russell, G. A. "Introduction: The Seventeenth Century: The Age of 'Arabick.'" In *The 'Arabick' Interest of the Natural Philosophers in Seventeenth-Century England*, edited by G. A. Russell, 1–19. Leiden: Brill, 1994.

Ryan, John J. "Evasion and Ambiguity: Ockham and Tierney's Ockham." *Franciscan Studies* 46 (1986) 285–94.

———. "Ockham's Dilemma: Tierney's Ambiguous Infallibility and Ockham's Ambiguous Church." *Journal of Ecumenical Studies* 13 (1976) 37–50.

Sabra, Adam. "Ibn Ḥazm's Literalism: A Critique of Islamic Legal Theory (I)." *Al-Qanṭara* 28 (2007) 7–40.

Sacchi, Paolo. "Le pentateuque, le deutéronomiste et Spinoza." In *Congress Volume: Paris 1992*, edited by J. A. Emerton, 275–88. Leiden: Brill, 1995.

Sacksteder, William. "How Much of Hobbes Might Spinoza Have Read?" *Southwestern Journal of Philosophy* 11 (1980) 25–39.

Sæbø, Magne. "From the Renaissance to the Enlightenment—Aspects of the Cultural and Ideological Framework of Scriptural Interpretation." In *Hebrew Bible/Old Testament: The History of Its Interpretation Volume II: From the Renaissance to the Enlightenment*, edited by Magne Sæbø, 21–45. Göttingen: Vandenhoeck & Ruprecht, 2008.

Sáenz-Badillos, Angel. "Abraham ibn Ezra: Between Tradition and Philology." *Zutot* 2 (2003) 85–94.

Salmon, J. H. M. *Society in Crisis: France in the Sixteenth Century.* New York: St. Martin's, 1975.

Sandmel, Samuel. *The Hebrew Scriptures: An Introduction to their Literature and Religious Ideas.* New York: Alfred A. Knopf, 1963.

Schatz, Klaus. *Der päpstliche Primat: seine Geschichte von den Ursprüngen bis zur Gegenwart.* Würzburg: Echter, 1990.

Schechter, S. "Geniza Specimens. The Oldest Collection of Bible Difficulties, by a Jew." *Jewish Quarterly Review* 13 (1901) 345–74.

Schnapp, Alain. "The Pre-adamites: An Abortive Attempt to Invent Pre-history in the Seventeenth Century?" In *History of Scholarship: A Selection of Papers from the Seminar on the History of Scholarship Held Annually at the Warburg Institute*, edited by Christopher Ligota and Jean-Louis Quantin, 399–412. Oxford: Oxford University Press, 2006.

Schochet, Gordon, Fania Oz-Salzberger, and Meirav Jones, ed. *Political Hebraism: Judaic Sources in Early Modern Political Thought.* Jerusalem: Shalem, 2008.

Schoeps, Hans-Joachim. "Philosemitism in the Baroque Period." *Jewish Quarterly Review* 47 (1956) 139–44.

Schumann, Karl. "Methodenfragen bei Spinoza und Hobbes: Zum Problem des Einflusses." *Studia Spinozana* 3 (1987) 47–86.

Schweitzer, Albert. *Von Reimarus zu Wrede. Eine Geschichte der Leben Jesu forschung.* Tübingen: J. C. B. Mohr (Paul Siebeck), 1906.

Scribner, R. W. and C. Scott Dixon. *The German Reformation.* 2d ed. New York: Palgrave Macmillan, 2003.

Sela, Shlomo. *Abraham Ibn Ezra and the Rise of Medieval Hebrew Science.* Leiden: Brill, 2003.

Septimus, Bernard. "Biblical Religion and Political Rationality in Simone Luzzato, Maimonides and Spinoza." In *Jewish Thought in the Seventeenth Century*, edited by Isadore Twersky and Bernard Septimus, 399–433. Cambridge: Harvard University Press, 1987.

Sermoneta, Joseph B. "Biblical Anthropology in 'The Guide of the Perplexed' by Moses Maimonides, and its Reversal in the 'Tractatus Theologico-Politicus' by Baruch Spinoza." *Topoi* 7 (1988) 241–7.

Shadle, Matthew A. "Cavanaugh on the Church and the Modern State: An Appraisal." *Horizons* 37 (2010) 246–70.

Shalev, Zur. "Measurer of All Things: John Greaves (1602–1652), the Great Pyramid, and Early Modern Metrology." *Journal of the History of Ideas* 63 (2002) 555–75.

Sheehan, Jonathan. *The Enlightenment Bible: Translation, Scholarship, Culture*. Princeton: Princeton University Press, 2005.

———. "Sacred and Profane: Idolatry, Antiquarianism and the Polemics of Distinction in the Seventeenth Century." *Past and Present* 192 (2006) 35–66.

Shogimen, Takashi. "The Relationship Between Theology and Canon Law: Another Context of Political Thought in the Early Fourteenth Century." *Journal of the History of Ideas* 60 (1999) 417–31.

Shuger, Debora Kuller. *The Renaissance Bible: Scholarship, Sacrifice, and Subjectivity*. Berkeley, CA: University of California Press, 1994.

Shulman, Harvey. "The Use and Abuse of the Bible in Spinoza's *Tractatus Theologico-Politicus*." *Jewish Political Studies Review* 7 (1995) 39–55.

Siegfried, C. *Spinoza: als Kritiker und Ausleger des Alten Testaments*. Naumburg: Druck von Heinrich Sieling, 1867.

Simon, Uriel. "Abraham ibn Ezra." In *Hebrew Bible/Old Testament Volume I: From the Beginnings to the Middle Ages (Until 1300) Part 2: The Middle Ages*, edited by Magne Sæbø, 377–87. Göttingen: Vandenhoeck & Ruprecht, 2000.

Sinai, Nicolai. "Spinoza and Beyond: Some Reflections on Historical–Critical Method." In *Kritische Religionsphilosophie: Eine Gedenkschrift für Friedrich Niewöhner*, edited by Wilhelm Schmidt-Biggemann and Georges Tamer, 193–213. Berlin: Walter de Gruyter, 2010.

Ska, Jean-Louis. *The Exegesis of the Pentateuch: Exegetical Studies and Basic Questions*. Tübingen: Mohr Siebeck, 2009.

Skinner, Quentin. *The Foundations of Modern Political Thought*. Vol. 2. Cambridge: Cambridge University Press, 1978.

———. "The Ideological Context of Hobbes's Political Thought." *Historical Journal* 9 (1966) 286–317.

———. "Thomas Hobbes and His Disciples in France and England." *Comparative Studies in Society and History* 8 (1966) 153–67.

Smend, Rudolf. *From Astruc to Zimmerli*. Tübingen: Mohr Siebeck, 2007.

———. "Wellhausen und das Judentum." *Zeitschrift für Theologie und Kirche* 79 (1982) 249–82.

Smith, Steven B. *Spinoza, Liberalism, and the Question of Jewish Identity*. New Haven: Yale University Press, 1997.

Smith, Wilfred Cantwell. *The Meaning and End of Religion*. New York: Macmillan, 1962.

Snobelen, Stephen D. "'To Us There Is But One God, the Father': Antitrinitarian Textual Criticism in Seventeenth- and Early Eighteenth-Century England." In *Scripture and Scholarship in Early Modern England*, edited by Ariel Hessayon and Nicholas Keene, 116–36. Aldershot: Ashgate, 2006.

Southern, R. W. *Western Society and the Church in the Middle Ages*. Harmondsworth: Penguin, 1970.

Spinoza, Baruch. *Œuvres III: Tractatus Theologico-Politicus/Traité théologico-politique*. 2nd ed. Edited by Pierre-François Moreau. Text established by Fokke Akkerman. Translated by Jacqueline Lagrée and Pierre-François Moreau. Paris: Presses Universitaires de France, 2012.

———. *Spinoza Opera*. Edited by Carl Gebhardt. Heidelberg: C. Winters, 1925.

———. *Theological-Political Treatise*. Edited by Jonathan Israel. Translated by Michael Silverthorne and Jonathan Israel. Cambridge: Cambridge University Press, 2007.

Springborg, Patricia. "Hobbes and Epicurean Religion." In *Der Garten und die Moderne: Epikureische Moral und Politik vom Humanismus bis zur Aufklärung*, edited by Gianni Paganini and Edoardo Tortarolo, 161-214. Stuttgart: Rommann-holzboog, 2004.

———. "Hobbes's Biblical Beasts: *Leviathan* and *Behemoth*." *Political Theory* 23 (1995) 353-75.

———. "Hobbes's Theory of Civil Religion." In *Pluralismo e religione civile*, edited by Gianni Paganini and Edoardo Tortarolo, 61-98. Milan: Bruno Mondatori, 2003.

———. "Leviathan and the Problem of Ecclesiastical Authority." *Political Theory* 3 (1975) 289-303.

Spruyt, Hendrik. *The Sovereign State and Its Competitors*. Princeton: Princeton University Press, 1994.

Starobinski-Safran, Esther. "Raison et conflits de traditions." In *L'Europe et les Juifs*, edited by Esther Benbassa and Pierre Gisel, 95-128. Geneva: Labor et Fides, 2002.

Stein, Edmund. *Alttestamentliche Bibelkritik in der späthellenistischen Literatur*. Lwów: Zwiazkowe Zaklady, 1935.

Steinberg, Justin. "Spinoza's Curious Defense of Toleration." In *Spinoza's Theological-Political Treatise: A Critical Guide*, edited by Yitzhak Y. Melamed and Michael A. Rosenthal, 210-30. Cambridge: Cambridge University Press, 2010.

Steinmetz, David C. "John Calvin as an Interpreter of the Bible." In *Calvin and the Bible*, edited by Donald K. McKim, 282-91. Cambridge: Cambridge University Press, 2006.

Strauss, Leo. "On a Forgotten Kind of Writing." *Independent Journal of Philosophy* 2 (1978) 27-31.

———. *Persecution and the Art of Writing*. Chicago: University of Chicago Press, 1988.

———. *Spinoza's Critique of Religion*. Translated by E. M. Sinclair. Chicago: University of Chicago Press, 1997.

Strayer, Joseph R. *On the Medieval Origins of the Modern State*. Princeton: Princeton University Press, 1970.

Stroumsa, Guy G. "Richard Simon: From Philology to Comparatism." *Archiv für Religionsgeschichte* 3 (2001) 89-107.

Subrahmanyam, Sanjay. "Intertwined Histories: *Crónica* and *Tārīkh* in the Sixteenth-Century Indian Ocean World." *History & Theory* 49.4 (2010) 118-45.

Sutherland, Stewart R. "God and Religion in *Leviathan*." *Journal of Theological Studies* 25 (1974) 373-80.

Swetschinski, Daniel M. "Kinship and Commerce: The Foundations of Portuguese Jewish Life in Seventeenth-Century Holland." *Studia Rosenthaliana* 15 (1981) 52-74.

Tabet Balady, Miguel Angel. "La hermenéutica bíblica de san Agustín en la carta 82 a san Jerónimo." In *San Agustín: Meditación de un Centenario*, edited by José Oroz Reta, 181-93. Salamanca: Universidad Pontificia de Salamanca, 1987.

Talar, C. J. T. "Innovation and Biblical Interpretation." In *Catholicism Contending with Modernity: Roman Catholic Modernism and Anti-Modernism in Historical Context*, edited by Darrell Jodock, 191-211. Cambridge: Cambridge University Press, 2000.

Tavard, George H. "Blondel's *Action* and the Problem of the University." In *Catholicism Contending with Modernity: Roman Catholic Modernism and Anti-Modernism*

in Historical Context, edited by Darrell Jodock, 142–68. Cambridge: Cambridge University Press, 2000.
Thomas, Heinz. *Ludwig der Bayer: Kaiser und Ketzer*. Regensburg: Pustet, 1993.
Tierney, Brian. "John Peter Olivi and Papal Inerrancy: On a Recent Interpretation of Olivi's Ecclesiology." *Theological Studies* 46 (1985) 315–28.
———. "Ockham's Ambiguous Infallibility." *Journal of Ecumenical Studies* 14 (1977) 102–5.
———. "Ockham's Infallibility and Ryan's Infallibility." *Franciscan Studies* 46 (1986) 295–300.
———. "Origins of Papal Infallibility." *Journal of Ecumenical Studies* 8 (1971) 841–64.
———. *Origins of Papal Infallibility 1150–1350: A Study on the Concepts of Infallibility, Sovereignty and Tradition in the Middle Ages*. Leiden: Brill, 1972.
———. "Papal Infallibility: A Response to Dr. D'Avray." *Catholic Historical Review* 67 (1981) 275–77.
———. "Sovereignty and Infallibility: A Response to James Heft." *Journal of Ecumenical Studies* 19 (1982) 787–93.
Tilly, Charles, ed. *The Formation of National States in Western Europe*. Princeton: Princeton University Press, 1975.
———. "Reflections on the History of European State-Making." In *The Formation of National States in Western Europe*, ed. Charles Tilly, 3–83. Princeton: Princeton University Press, 1975.
———. "War Making and State Making as Organized Crime." In *Bringing the State Back In*, edited by Peter B. Evans et al., 169–91. Cambridge: Cambridge University Press, 1985.
Tinland, F. "Droit a la vie, fondement contractuel de la paix civile et nécessités de l'ordre public selon Th. Hobbes et J.-J. Rousseau." *Revue d'histoire et de philosophie religieuses* 65 (1985) 153–68.
Titzmann, Michael. "Herausforderungen der biblischen Hermeneutik in der Frühen Neuzeit: Die neuen Diskurse der Wissenschaft und der Philosophie." In *Geschichte der Hermeneutik und die Methodik der textinterpretierenden Disziplinen*, edited by Jörg Schönert and Friedrich Vollhardt, 119–56. Berlin: Walter de Gruyter, 2005.
Tornay, Stephen Chak. "Averroes' Doctrine of the Mind." *Philosophical Review* 52 (1943) 270–88.
Torrell, Jean-Pierre, OP. *Initiation à saint Thomas d'Aquin: Sa personne et son oeuvre*, 2nd ed. Fribourg: Editions Universitaires Fribourg, 2002 (1993).
———. "Quand Saint Thomas méditait sur le Prophète Isaïe." *Revue thomiste* 96 (1996) 179–208.
Toulmin, Stephen. *Cosmopolis: The Hidden Agenda of Modernity*. Chicago: The University of Chicago Press, 1992.
Tracy, James D. *Emperor Charles V, Impresario of War: Campaign Strategy, International Finance, and Domestic Politics*. Cambridge: Cambridge University Press, 2002.
Troilo, Erminio. *Averroismo e aristotelismo padovano*. Padua: Antonio Milani, 1939.
———. "L'averroismo di Marsilio da Padova." In *Marsilio da Padova. Studi raccolti nel VI centenario della morte*, edited by Aldo Checchini and Norberto Bobbio, 44–77. Padua: Cedam, 1942.
Tumbleson, Raymond D. *Catholicism in the English Protestant Imagination: Nationalism, Religion, and Literature, 1660–1745*. Cambridge: Cambridge University Press, 1998.

Turley, Thomas. "John Baconthorpe on Papal Infallibility." *Journal of Ecumenical Studies* 19.4 (1982) 744–58.
Turner, Denys. *Eros and Allegory: Medieval Exegesis of the Song of Songs*. Kalamazoo, MI: Cistercian, 1995.
Tyson, Joseph B. "Anti-Judaism in Marcion and His Opponents." *Studies in Christian-Jewish Relations* 1 (2005–6) 196–208.
van Asselt, Willem. "Adam en Eva als Laatkomers. De pre-adamitische speculaties van Isaac La Peyrère (1596–1676)." In *Adam en Eva in het paradijs. Actuele visies op man en vrouw uit 2000 jaar christelijke theologie*, edited by Harm Goris and Susanne Hennecke, 99–115. Zoetermeer: Meinema, 2005.
van Bunge, Wiep. *From Stevin to Spinoza: An Essay on Philosophy in the Seventeenth-Century Dutch Republic*. Leiden: Brill, 2001.
———. "Spinoza and the Idea of Religious Imposture." In *On the Edge of Truth and Honesty: Principles and Strategies of Fraud and Deceit in the Early Modern Period*, edited by Toon van Houdt et al., 105–26. Leiden: Brill, 2002.
———. *Spinoza Past and Present: Essays on Spinoza, Spinozism, and Spinoza Scholarship*. Leiden: Brill, 2012.
———. "Spinoza's Jewish Identity and the Use of Context." *Studia Spinozana* 13 (1997) 100–18.
van der Coelen, Peter. "Pictures for the People? Bible Illustrations and their Audience." In *Lay Bibles in Europe 1450–1800*, edited by M. Lamberigts and A. A. den Hollander, 185–205. Leuven: Leuven University Press and Peeters, 2006.
Van der Wall, Ernestine. "The *Tractatus Theologico-politicus* and Dutch Calvinism, 1670–1700." *Studia Spinozana* 11 (1995) 201–26.
Vaysse, Jean-Marie. "Spinoza dans la problématique de l'idéalisme allemande: Historicité et manifestation." In *Spinoza au XIXe siècle*, edited by André Tosel et al., 65–74. Paris: Sorbonne, 2007.
Verbeek, Theo. "Spinoza on Theocracy and Democracy." In *Everything Connects: In Conference with Richard H. Popkin: Essays in His Honor*, edited by James E. Force and David S. Katz, 326–38. Leiden: Brill, 1999.
———. *Spinoza's Theologico-Political Treatise: Exploring the "Will of God."* Hampshire: Ashgate, 2003.
Vick, Brian. "Greek Origins and Organic Metaphors: Ideals of Cultural Autonomy in Neo-Humanist Germany from Winckelmann to Curtius." *Journal of the History of Ideas* 63 (2002) 483–500.
Viroli, Maurizio. *Machiavelli's God*. Princeton: Princeton University Press, 2010.
Visser, Arnoud. "Thirtieth Annual Erasmus Birthday Lecture: Erasmus, the Church Fathers and the Ideological Implications of Philology." *Erasmus of Rotterdam Society Yearbook* 31 (2011) 7–31.
Vlessing, Odette. "The Excommunication of Baruch Spinoza: A Conflict Between Jewish and Dutch Law." *Studia Spinozana* 13 (1997) 15–47.
———. "The Jewish Community in Transition: From Acceptance to Emancipation." *Studia Rosenthaliana* 30 (1996) 195–211.
———. "New Light on the Earliest History of the Amsterdam Portuguese Jews." In *Dutch Jewish History Vol. 3*, edited by Jozeph Michman, 43–75. Assen: Van Gorcum, 1993.

von Arx, Jeffrey, SJ. "Cardinal Henry Edward Manning." In *Varieties of Ultramontanism*, edited by Jeffrey von Arx, SJ, 85-102. Washington, DC: The Catholic University of America Press, 1998.

———. "Introduction." In *Varieties of Ultramontanism*, edited by Jeffrey von Arx, SJ, 1-11. Washington, DC: The Catholic University of America Press, 1998.

von Greyerz, Kaspar. "Switzerland during the Thirty Years' War." In *1648, War and Peace in Europe Volume 1: Politics, Religion, Law, and Society*, ed. Klaus Bussmann and Heinz Schilling, 133-9. Münster: Westfälisches Landesmuseum, 1998.

Wachtel, Nathan. "Théologies marranes: Une configuration millénariste." *Annales. Histoire, Science sociales* 62 (2007) 69-100.

Waldstein, Michael Maria. "*Analogia Verbi*: The Truth of Scripture in Rudolf Bultmann and Raymond Brown." *Letter & Spirit* 6 (2010) 93-140.

———. "On Scripture in the *Summa Theologiae*." *Aquinas Review* 1 (1994) 73-94.

Walther, Manfred. "Biblische Hermeneutik und historische Erklärung: Lodewijk Meyer und Benedikt de Spinoza." *Studia Spinozana* 11 (1995) 227-300.

———. "Biblische Hermeneutik und/oder theologische Politik bei Hobbes und Spinoza: Historische Studie zur Theorie der Ausdifferenzierung von Religion und Politik in der Neuzeit." In *Hobbes e Spinoza: Scienza e politica*, edited by Daniela Bostrenghi, 623-69. Naples: Bibliopolis, 1992.

Wawrykow, Joseph. "Aquinas on Isaiah." In *Aquinas on Scripture: An Introduction to his Biblical Commentaries*, edited by Thomas G. Weinandy, OFM et al., 43-71. London: T. & T. Clark, 2005.

Weinfeld, Moshe. *Normative and Sectarian Judaism in the Second Temple Period*. London: T. & T. Clark, 2005.

Wellhausen, J. *Prolegomena zur Geschichte Israels*. 5th ed. Berlin: Georg Reimer, 1899 (1882).

Wells, Norman J. "Objective Reality of Ideas in Descartes, Caterus, and Suárez." *Journal of the History of Philosophy* 28 (1990) 33-61.

Weststeijn, Thijs. "Spinoza Sinicus: An Asian Paragraph in the History of the Radical Enlightenment." *Journal of the History of Ideas* 68, (2007) 537-61.

Wetsel, David. "Biblicism and Historicity: The *Pensées* of Pascal and Christian Humanism." *South Central Review* 2 (1985) 9-16.

———. "'Histoire de la Chine': Pascal and the Challenge to Biblical Time." *Journal of Religion* 69 (1989) 199-219.

———. "Isaac de La Peyrère and His *Pre-Adamites*." In *Dissidents, excentriques et marginaux de l'Âge classique: Autour de Cyrano de Bergerac: Bouquet offert à Madeleine Alcover*, edited by Patricia Harry et al., 375-82. Paris: Honoré Champion, 2006.

Wielema, Michiel. "Adriaan Koerbagh: Biblical Criticism and Enlightenment." In *The Early Enlightenment in the Dutch Republic, 1650-1750: Selected Papers of a Conference held at the Herzog August Bibliothek, Wolfenbüttel 22-23 March 2001*, edited by Wiep van Bunge, 61-80. Leiden: Brill, 2003.

Wilken, Robert L. *The Christians as the Romans Saw Them*. New Haven, CT: Yale University Press, 1984.

Williamson, George S. *The Longing for Myth in Germany: Religion and Aesthetic Culture from Romanticism to Nietzsche*. Chicago: University of Chicago Press, 2004.

Wilson, Margaret D. "Spinoza's Theory of Knowledge." In *The Cambridge Companion to Spinoza*, edited by Don Garrett, 89–141. Cambridge: Cambridge University Press, 1996.

Wolf, Abraham, ed. *The Oldest Biography of Spinoza*. Port Washington, NY: Kennikat, 1927.

Wolfson, Harry Austryn. *The Philosophy of Spinoza: Unfolding the Latent Processes of His Reasoning: Volume I*. Cambridge: Harvard University Press, 1934.

Wollgast, Siegfried. "Spinoza und die deutsche Frühaufklärung." *Studia Spinozana* 9 (1992) 163–79.

Woodbridge, John D. "German Responses to the Biblical Critic Richard Simon: From Leibniz to J. S. Semler." In *Historische Kritik und biblischer Kanon in der deutschen Aufklärung*, edited by Henning Graf Reventlow et al., 65–87. Wiesbaden: Harrossowtiz, 1988.

———. "Richard Simon le «père de la critique biblique»." In *Le Grand Siècle et la Bible*, edited by Jean-Robert Armogathe, 193–206. Paris: Beauchesne, 1989.

Yaffe, Martin D. "'The Histories and Successes of the Hebrews': The Demise of the Biblical Polity in Spinoza's *Theologico-Political Treatise*." *Jewish Political Studies Review* 7 (1995) 57–75.

Yamauchi, Edwin M. *Gnostic Ethics and Mandaean Origins*. Cambridge: Harvard University Press, 1970.

Yardeni, Miriam. "La religion de La Peyrère et 'Le Rappel des Juifs.'" *Review d'histoire et de philosophie religieuses* 51 (1971) 245–59.

Yocum, John. "Aquinas' Literal Exposition on Job." In *Aquinas on Scripture: An Introduction to his Biblical Commentaries*, edited by Thomas G. Weinandy, OFM et al., 21–42. London: T. & T. Clark, 2005.

Yonke, Eric. "Cardinal Johannes von Geissel." In *Varieties of Ultramontanism*, edited by Jeffrey von Arx, SJ, 12–38. Washington, D.C.: The Catholic University of America Press, 1998.

Young, Edward J. "Celsus and the Old Testament." *Westminster Theological Journal* 6 (1944) 166–97.

———. *An Introduction to the Old Testament*. Grand Rapids: Eerdmans, 1989 (1949).

———. *The Prophecy of Daniel: A Commentary*. Grand Rapids: Eerdmans, 1949.

Yovel, Yirmiyahu. "Marrano Patterns in Spinoza." In *Proceedings of the First Italian International Congress on Spinoza*, edited by Emilia Giancotti, 461–85. Naples: Bibliopolis, 1985.

———. *The Other Within: The Marranos: Split Identity and Emerging Modernity*. Princeton: Princeton University Press, 2009.

———. *Spinoza and Other Heretics Vol. 1: The Marrano of Reason*. Princeton: Princeton University Press, 1989.

———. *Spinoza and Other Heretics Vol. II: The Adventures of Immanence*. Princeton: Princeton University Press, 1989.

———. "Spinoza: The Psychology of the Multitude and the Uses of Language." *Studia Spinozana* 1 (1985) 305–33.

Zac, Sylvain. "Le chapitre XVI du *Traité théologico-politique*." *Tijdschrift voor de studie van de Verlichting* 6 (1978) 137–50.

———. "Durée et histoire chez Spinoza." *La nouvelle critique* 113 (1978) 29–36.

———. "Philosophie et théologie chez Spinoza." *Revue de synthèse* 89–91 (1978) 81–95.

———. "Spinoza et l'état des Hébreux." *Revue philosophique* 80 (1977) 201–32.
———. *Spinoza et l'interprétation de l'Écriture*. Paris: Presses universitaires de France, 1965.
———. "Spinoza et le langage." *Giornale critic della filosofia italiana* 8 (1977) 612–33.
Zachman, Randall C. "Gathering Meaning from the Context: Calvin's Exegetical Method." *Journal of Religion* 82 (2002) 1–26.

www.ingramcontent.com/pod-product-compliance
Lightning Source LLC
Chambersburg PA
CBHW051743230426
43670CB00012B/2140